UNIVERSITY OF NORTH CAROLINA AT CHAPEL HILL
DEPARTMENT OF ROMANCE LANGUAGES

NORTH CAROLINA STUDIES
IN THE ROMANCE LANGUAGES AND LITERATURES

*Founder:* URBAN TIGNER HOLMES
*Editors:* MARÍA A. SALGADO
CAROL L. SHERMAN

*Distributed by:*

UNIVERSITY OF NORTH CAROLINA PRESS

CHAPEL HILL
North Carolina 27515-2288
U.S.A.

NORTH CAROLINA STUDIES IN THE
ROMANCE LANGUAGES AND LITERATURES
Number 251

VOID AND VOICE: QUESTIONING NARRATIVE
CONVENTIONS IN ANDRÉ GIDE'S MAJOR
FIRST-PERSON NARRATIVES

# VOID AND VOICE:
## QUESTIONING NARRATIVE CONVENTIONS IN
# ANDRÉ GIDE'S MAJOR
## FIRST-PERSON NARRATIVES

BY
CHARLES O'KEEFE

CHAPEL HILL

NORTH CAROLINA STUDIES IN THE ROMANCE
LANGUAGES AND LITERATURES
U.N.C. DEPARTMENT OF ROMANCE LANGUAGES

1996

**Library of Congress Cataloging-in-Publication Data**

O'Keefe, Charles, 1942-
 Void and voice: questioning narrative conventions in André Gide's major first-person narratives / by Charles O'Keefe.
 257 p. – cm. – (North Carolina Studies in the Romance Languages and Literatures: no. 251)

 Includes bibliographical references.
 ISBN 0-8078-9255-6 (alk. paper)

 1. Gide, André, 1869-1951 – Criticism and interpretation. 2. Gide, André, 1869-1951. Immoraliste. 3. Gide, André, 1869-1951. Porte étroite. 4. Gide, André, 1869-1951. Symphonie pastorale. 5. First person narrative. I. Title. II. Series
 PQ2613.I2Z65685   1996
 848'.91209 – dc20

                                                                      95-21311
                                                                          CIP

© 1996. Department of Romance Languages. The University of North Carolina at Chapel Hill.

ISBN 0-8078-9255-6

DEPÓSITO LEGAL: V. 1.202 - 1996     I.S.B.N. 84-599-3447-0

ARTES GRÁFICAS SOLER, S. A. - LA OLIVERETA, 28 - 46018 VALENCIA - 1996

AMGD

This book is dedicated to my teachers. While they really are too numerous for me to be able to name them all here, I must single out the ones who taught me the most: my family, those students at Denison University who insist on asking troublesome questions, and my Denison colleagues whose work in and out of the classroom I have tried to imitate in this book.

I would like to offer a word of special thanks to Dr. François Rigolot whose NEH seminar on narrative theory helped me articulate my main arguments, to the National Endowment for the Humanities for making that seminar possible, and to Denison University and its many, many generous supporters, whose funding for summer research, for leaves, and for a sabbatical encouraged me ever so concretely.

Last but not least, I want to express my gratitude to the librarians at Denison University, and to those librarians around the country whom I have never met but who deal with interlibrary loans: if this book is found worthy of professional dialogue, other scholars will, I hope, reveal its strengths and weaknesses; but like me, they will not be able to do their work without the able help of librarians.

# TABLE OF CONTENTS

|  | Page |
|---|---|
| INTRODUCTION | 11 |
| **CHAPTER ONE:** *L'Immoraliste* | 28 |
|    I. Narrative Form Touched by Excess | 28 |
|    II. Questioning the Conventional Interpretation of the Framed Narrative in *L'Immoraliste* | 29 |
|       A) Who Speaks? | 29 |
|       B) Historical Context of Framed Narrative | 39 |
|       C) New Critical Space | 50 |
|       D) Paradigmatic Value of the Frame in *L'Immoraliste* | 55 |
|    III. Contradictions Inherent in the Accessible Voice | 67 |
|       A) Michel, An Echo of Ménalque | 67 |
|       B) Michel, An Intertext of Rousseau | 70 |
|       C) The Palimpsest | 80 |
| **CHAPTER TWO:** *La Porte étroite* | 96 |
|    I. Jérôme as Editor | 96 |
|       A) Jérôme the Misquoting "Author" | 96 |
|       B) Narrator vs. Editor | 102 |
|          i) Narrative Unreliability | 103 |
|          ii) The "Main" Text | 112 |
|       C) Critical Yield | 124 |
|          i) Editing and Jérôme's Personality | 126 |
|          ii) Editorial Unreliability | 139 |
|       D) *Forme et Fond* | 144 |
|    II. Onomastics | 152 |
|       A) Names of Secondary Characters | 153 |
|       B) "Alissa" and "Jérôme" | 157 |

| | Page |
|---|---|
| **CHAPTER THREE:** *La Symphonie pastorale* ............................... | 162 |
|    I. How Do We Read a Lying Narrator? ........................... | 162 |
|       A) The Critical Dawning ................................................ | 163 |
|       B) Accusing the Pastor ................................................. | 168 |
|       C) Justifying a Consideration of Narrative Lying .......... | 173 |
|          i) External Justifications .......................................... | 173 |
|          ii) Internal Justifications .......................................... | 176 |
|       D) Reading the Lie ........................................................ | 181 |
|       E) Lying or Evangelizing? ............................................. | 185 |
|       F) The Hidden Agendas ............................................... | 190 |
|       G) Verbal and Erotic Anarchy ...................................... | 194 |
|          i) Narrative Disorder ............................................... | 195 |
|          ii) Limping Comparisons: *Parabole>Parole>Parler* ... | 199 |
|          iii) The Erotic *Parole* ............................................... | 204 |
|          iv) The Destructive *Parole* ....................................... | 208 |
|       H) Semiosis and the Drama of Substitution ................. | 209 |
|    II. Onomastics ............................................................... | 211 |
|       A) Onomastics in Gide's Text ....................................... | 211 |
|          i) Names and the *Fatum* of Writing ..................... | 211 |
|          ii) Names and Subversion ....................................... | 213 |
|       B) Onomastics in the Pastor's Text ................................ | 216 |
|          i) Naming and Point of View ................................. | 216 |
|          ii) Naming as Assault .............................................. | 220 |
| **CONCLUSION** ............................................................................. | 226 |
| **WORKS CITED** ........................................................................... | 250 |

# INTRODUCTION

> "Jusqu'à présent je n'ai vu clairement qu'une chose: c'est que je n'étais ni ceci ni cela. Et pourtant *je suis*, malgré que le monde m'affirme que je ne puis être que l'un ou l'autre. Et je suis en dépit de l'un et de l'autre, et de tout . . . et du moi-même qui, hier encore, souriait. Voilà pourquoi mon lot est, d'abord, d'être suspect à tous."
>
> André Gide, *Correspondance*, lettre de Gide à F-P. Ali-bert, 17 jan. 1914.

Among literary critics, André Gide has long enjoyed considerable and justified renown – the term "notoriety" would not be inappropriate – for unsettling but cogent works that challenge both traditional morality and traditional forms: *Les Nourritures terrestres* (1897), a rapturously lyric narrative of the problems of liberation no less sensual than textual; *Les Caves du Vatican* (1914), a rollicking *sotie* that, using for instance Lafcadio's homicidal *acte gratuit*, comically assaulted traditional novelistic techniques and values, to the applause of restless and rebellious intellectuals reacting to war-spawning "rationality" at the beginning of the century; and *Les Faux-Monnayeurs* (1925), Gide's most complex subversion of the traditional novel and of traditional mores that, among other provocations, pushes the conceit of the *mise en abyme* to the point where the book becomes a "diary within a novel within a diary within a novel within a diary" (Guérard 164).

Even Gide's heretofore less read and much dismissed *oeuvres de jeunesse* have been recognized of late for their revolutionary qualities. Consider for instance *Paludes* (published in 1895), which "swamps" the reader in a self-reflective send-up of a book about a book representing the tedious Symbolist *vie de salon*. Emily Apter has written:

[*Paludes'*] exposure of fictive illusions; its ambiguous first-person pronoun (confusing narrator, author, character and reader); its multiple framing of events and non-events; its mechanical repetitions of phrases and narrative fragments; its dialogue punctuated by *non-sequiturs* and its typographical and stylistic likeness to a sketch or tentative plan of a narrative (close to what Marguerite Duras, in reference to her own work, dubbed "blueprints of novels"), all these features, as many critics have noted, announce "l'ère du soupçon" – the era in which the presumed innocence of fiction is severely and irrevocably called into question. Similar in its narrative experimentation to the works of Robbe-Grillet, Sarraute, Butor, Simon and Duras among others, *Paludes* offers an early paradigm of the twentieth-century "oeuvre-critique," or genre of theoretical fiction. (Apter 72)

And yet his most famous first-person narratives, *L'Immoraliste* (1902), *La Porte étroite*, (1909) and *La Symphonie pastorale* (1919), have had an entirely different critical history. On the one hand, these works – eventually called *récits* by Gide[1] – have subject matter truly no less provocative than that of anything he wrote: (respectively) repressed pederasty, suicidal religiosity, and clerical hypocrisy, with lethal misogyny at work in each. To heighten the provocation, each of the main characters views his/her deadly conduct as ennobling moral exploration: Michel sees himself embarked on a renegade hunt for his "authentic being," Alissa feels that she is striving for spiritual perfection via *la porte étroite* advocated in the Gospels, and the Pastor claims to be rejecting hidebound Pauline limits on Christ's teaching on love. Understandably, a great deal has been written about what happens in these truly striking stories. On the other hand, not nearly as much has been done to determine if the aesthetically scrupulous Gide used his great sense of literary form to create in these three *récits* basic narrative structures provocative enough to suit the subject matter. This lacuna exists even though the *récits* were written during roughly the same time span as the more "notorious" works that have gotten a more balanced critical reception.

Not that in any number of critical studies ample insightful scrutiny has been spared on certain aspects of their form, for in-

---

[1] See Maisani-Léonard, 21-30, for Gide's use of the term and for an attempt to identify the characteristics of a Gidean *récit*.

stance, on the gradual change in rhythm and tone of Michel's words, on the impact of Jérôme's progressively incorporating Alissa's direct words into his own narrative, and on the consequences of the Pastor's time of narration slowly coinciding with the time of the story. Moreover and quite naturally, given recent critical tendencies, increasing attention has been brought to bear on narrational reflexivity in Gide's *récits*, on the fact that, as David H. Walker has succinctly put it: "The 'story' is used as a pretext for examining 'storytelling'" (Walker, *'Les Nourritures terrestres' et 'la Symphonie pastorale,'* 189. See also Helbo, Sonnenfeld ["On Readers and Reading"], Ireland ["Le Jeu des 'je' "], Babcock [*Portraits of Artists*], Kapetanoviç). But there still remains to be pursued the formal provocation worked by the fundamental narrative stratagems of each of those three *récits*, widely recognized as Gide's best. What follows will be an attempt to bring out those formal provocations by taking the analysis of each work's basic narrative convention beyond its current limits. Thus, a new reading of *L'Immoraliste* will be offered, by insisting extensively on the consequences of its frame: since the voice of the main character, Michel, comes to us through his anonymous friend, we have no direct access to his account. This uncertain status will be shown to connect tightly to several of the book's key themes, such as individualism. Then, pressing the main narrative ploy used in *La Porte étroite* – "Jérôme" wrote the text – and heuristically considering him (instead of Gide) as exclusively responsible for every feature of what we read, we will be able not only to consolidate a number of contemporary critical insights into this book (essentially involving its semantic openness), but also to elucidate aspects of Jérôme's personality, especially his narcissistic response to the text that he endeavors to put together. Finally, by using as a point of departure inconsistencies in the Pastor's account in *La Symphonie pastorale*, we will see how recent criticism has enlarged his chief narrative shortcomings from long-recognized hypocrisy and insincerity, to allow the possibility of lying itself. But we will then pursue aggressively the obvious question: how does one read a text by a fictional liar? Addressing that question will take us at several levels into a reconsideration of reasons why the Pastor offers his text in the first place.

For each of the three *récits*, the elemental narrative modes of presentation will be shown to subvert variously the foundations of first-person narration, traditionally understood. The very stories that the *récits* purport to convey are, each in its own way, thereby rendered inaccessible, leaving us only with the story-teller and his story-telling. But if there is no knowable story, how does one gauge the teller as such and his telling? That troublesome question notwithstanding, I will argue that diegetic inaccessibility in Gide's *récits* paradoxically plays off against the slippery but insistent presence of the narrator's voice, such that the texts fix the reader at the unstable juncture of textual absence and the illusion of mimetic presence, consequently forcing – and pondering – the complicity of the reader in the arbitrariness of reading these (and all) fictions.

Diegetic inaccessibility and the illusion of mimetic presence, however trendy their formulation might currently appear to some, can nonetheless ring quite true for both traditional and contemporary *gidiens*. Confronted as they have been by the inextricability of Gide's life and work, and by the way in which, throughout his life, Gide's very sense of ego and of the world shimmered for him in irreality (Brosman), critics have had little cause to dispute the conclusion that:

> L'absence de contours précis dans son caractère et son sentiment de la non-existence tantôt du monde, tantôt de lui-même, sont ainsi liés à son impulsion créatrice et constituent le fond même de son esthétique. (Brosman 43-44)

In his benchmark psychobiography of the young Gide, Jean Delay anchored that condition in narcissism, one of the leitmotifs to be found weaving its way through so much of what Gide wrote:[2]

> Le Narcisse romantique est souvent un Narcisse névrotique. Son exaltation de l'imaginaire recouvre une peur de vivre, son mépris de l'action une impuissance à décider et à agir, sa psychologie de

---

[2] Alain Goulet too demonstrates the centrality of Narcissus in Gide's oeuvre. Among his conclusions: "En identifiant un thème obsédant de sa conscience psychique, il le convertissait en un principe de création littéraire, et ce faisant, réorientait sa recherche pour se dégager de son emprise mortifère . . ." (Goulet, "Narcisse" 194); "Dans toutes les oeuvres suivantes [after his first published work, *Les Cahiers d'André Walter*)], Narcisse ne cesse en effet de se réincarner, mais Gide saura désormais ménager une distance de plus en plus grande d'avec lui, et la référence implicite ou explicite à Narcisse prendra chaque fois une dimension ironique plus accusée. C'est donc en rusant avec son propre narcissisme que Gide parviendra peu à peu à le conjurer" (Goulet, "Narcisse" 197-98).

> rêveur une psychologie de douteur, sa poursuite du moi une maladie du moi. S'il se mire constamment dans sa glace ou le journal intime, c'est moins pour s'admirer que pour comprendre son mal. Son attitude penchée est moins une inclination amoureuse qu'une préoccupation anxieuse. Il s'inquiète de se sentir étrange et comme étranger non pas seulement aux autres mais à lui-même; un mystère indéfinissable le trouble, l'enveloppe et jette un voile sur la réalité. . . . (Delay, vol. 1, 556-57)

The chapters that follow will argue that the elemental narrative gambits of the major *récits* lead to a similar anxiety about the nonexistence of the text as mimetic world. The diagesis of the *récits* will come to appear as an artistic analogue for reality as Gide personally experienced it, leading him to compensate with the affirming presence of the creative voice.

We will necessarily read the *récits* à la Jauss, that is, against the generic conventions continually shared and yet revised by the community of readers. Still, while making sense of Gide's *récits* does indeed require and even foster our engagement in the common, ongoing staking out of narrative horizons, I will try to show that *L'Immoraliste*, *La Porte étroite*, and *La Symphonie pastorale* allow – even solicit – readings that frustrate the application of narrative conventions. We expect as much from texts commonly recognized to hinge on irony.

There is as well a less direct but not less vital reason for maintaining that the *récits* create tension between the implementation and frustration of narrative conventions, viz., Gide's principle of *disponibilité*. While this principle evolved throughout his career in regard to, e.g., his sense of the future or his relationship with others (see Freyburger), we can be certain that ". . . la disponibilité constitue bien l'astre autour duquel tourne la pensée gidienne" (Freyburger 201), and that it always implied a simultaneous "availability" to contraries.

As one might expect, in order to articulate the frustration of conventions and the ensuing textual irreality or absence, the following pages will use a loosely deconstructive approach. (Should deconstruction be anything other than "loose"? – by its very nature, one is almost tempted to say.) But the point will not be what some might abusively call "fashionable criticism," but rather to advance the dialogue on Gide's works, in a way that gives credit to, while playing off against, earlier (logocentric) studies. Furthermore, a deconstructive stance has a lot in common with Gide's *disponibilité*. As Jonathan Culler observes (Culler 132), it is essential to remember that Derrida, for instance, far from insisting only on attention to absence and to the free play of meaning, abjures the either/or choice between semantic presence and absence:

> Il y a donc deux interprétations de l'interprétation, de la structure, du signe et du jeu. L'une cherche à déchiffrer, rêve de déchiffrer une vérité ou une origine échappant au jeu et à l'ordre du signe, et vit comme un exil la nécessité de l'interprétation. L'autre, qui n'est plus tournée vers l'origine, affirme le jeu et tente de passer au-delà de l'homme et de l'humanisme .................
>
> On pourrait percevoir à plus d'un signe aujourd'hui que ces deux interprétations de l'interprétation – qui sont absolument inconciliables même si nous les vivons simultanément et les concilions dans une obscure économie – se partagent le champ de ce qu'on appelle, de manière si problématique, les sciences humaines.
>
> Je ne crois pas pour ma part, bien que ces deux interprétations doivent accuser leur différence et aiguiser leur irréductibilité, qu'il y ait aujourd'hui à *choisir*. D'abord parce que nous sommes là dans une région – disons encore, provisoirement, de l'historicité – où la catégorie de choix paraît bien légère. Ensuite parce qu'il faut essayer d'abord de penser le sol commun, et la *différance* de cette différence irréductible. (Derrida, *L'Ecriture et la Différence* 427-28)

Or in Richard Rorty's plain language:

> Literature which does not connect with anything, which has no subject and no theme, which does not have a moral tucked up its sleeve, which lacks a dialectical context, is just babble. You can't have a ground without a figure, a margin without a page of text. (Rorty 94)

Just as the emptiness of Gide's margins is a function of his present texts, so too the fullness of what will be found in his margins is a function of his texts that, under scrutiny, empty themselves. A properly deconstructive attitude, an openness to the *différance* of the irreconcilably different, is quite compatible with Gide's eager "availability" to opposites. The affinity is quite suggestive about

Gide's place in contemporary thought, for his *disponibilité* comes closer than most characteristics to defining this deliberately indefinable author.

Styling himself as coming from "deux systèmes de vie très différents" (*Journal*, vol. 1, août 24, 1905), one Normand protestant and the other Provençal catholic – neither one of which he would allow any ascendancy – Gide said of himself:

> Rien ne se tient, rien n'est constant ni sûr, dans ma vie. Tour à tour je ressemble et diffère; il n'y a pas de créature si étrangère que je ne puisse jurer d'approcher. Je ne sais encore, à 36 ans, si je suis avare ou prodigue, sobre ou glouton . . . ou plutôt, me sentant porté soudain de l'un à l'autre extrême, dans ce balancement même je sens que ma fatalité s'accomplit. Pourquoi formerai-je, en m'imitant facticement moi-même, la factice unité de ma vie. C'est dans le mouvement que je peux trouver l'équilibre. (*Journal*, vol. 1, 24 août, 1905)

So important was "availability" to Gide that he felt repeatedly the need to express it variously, resorting on occasion to the strength of grotesque images:

> Je n'ai jamais rien su renoncer; et protégeant en moi, à la fois le meilleur et le pire, c'est en écartelé que j'ai vécu. Mais comment expliquer que cette cohabitation en moi des extrêmes n'amenât point tant d'inquiétude et de souffrance, qu'une intensification pathétique du sentiment de l'existence, de la vie. Les tendances les plus opposées n'ont jamais réussi à faire de moi un être tourmenté; mais perplexe – car le tourment accompagne un état dont on souhaite de sortir, et je ne souhaitais point d'échapper à ce qui mettait en vigueur toutes les virtualités de mon être; cet *état de dialogue* qui, pour tant d'autres, est à peu près intolérable, devenait pour moi nécessaire. (*Journal*, "Feuillets," vol. 1, 777; emphasis Gide's)

Not surprisingly, more than one critic – and of the most diverse persuasions – have found in his *balancement* or *écartèlement* a generative principle of much of Gide's work and so a key to an understanding of his work:

> "Il y a chez lui de l'inexpliqué, je ne crois pas qu'il y ait beaucoup d'inexplicable, si l'on admet chez l'homme . . . la cohabita-

> tion des sentiments contradictoires." Dans cette phrase de son *Dostoïevsky*, Gide a livré la clef de son propre caractère qui était essentiellement ambigu. Nous avons déjà précisé [vol. 1, 211-286] les origines de cette ambiguïté qui tenait à la diversité de ses hérédités, à son tempérament de douteur, à des complexes névrotiques [narcissism], à une éducation protestante et à une réaction contre le protestantisme; mais, après l'avoir subie, il l'a entretenue à des fins littéraires. Homme divisé, il a entendu devenir un artiste unique en faisant de son oeuvre l'expérience de ses contradictions. (Delay, vol. 2, 636)

(Not so incidentally, Delay, in appealing to Gide's struggle against narcissism as a partial explanation of his *disponibilité*, helps argue for the profound integrity of this oeuvre that is so distinctively marked by both qualities.) G. W. Ireland for his part asserts that "... the plenitude of life which is our knowledge of God on earth is experienced by Gide as the state of impassioned deadlock in which powerful conflicting impulses are held in check, the one by the other" (Ireland, *Gide* 217). Doris Kadish, in an article about the heuristic value of viewing Gide's *récits* as "self-consciously oppositional, [and] proto-structuralist" (Kadish, "Meaning" 391), grounds her quite different argument in this same tendency, which she calls "binary opposition," and which she finds in his fictional, nonfictional, and autobiographical work (Kadish, "Meaning" 383-84), to such a degree that:

> Gide resembles Michel in *L'Immoraliste*, who is genuinely puzzled when Charles admonishes him for wanting both to improve and destroy the farm in Normandy: in response to Charles's remark, "Vous ne pouvez protéger à la fois le garde et le braconnier," Michel asks, "Pourquoi?"......................................................
> [Gide] clearly has a natural affinity with a method based on binary opposition. (Kadish, "Meaning" 384)

As a consequence, then, of Gide's widely recognized if variously defined insistence on sustaining the tension of opposites, while we can expect a deconstructive stance to be indispensable in revealing the slippery status of the *récits*' texts, we should expect as well – if we are to avoid a *factice unité critique* – that the three *oeuvres disponibles* generate no less a sense of presence, and so incidentally challenge a reductive appreciation of the dynamics of deconstruction.

This suggest that Sartre's characterization of Gide's ideological evolution can be applied to the use of form in the *récits*, that formally too Gide is a "mélange de cautèle et d'audace" (Sartre 1538).

It makes sense that a writer so unrelentingly torn between hostility and fascination for church, home, and family would be inclined to what could be called subversive traditionalism in narrative structures. A dialectic compatible with such traditionalism has already been noted by Robert W. Greene, who argues that in Gide's *récits* a tension exists between their reflexive and realist narrative modes. Even though textual reflexivity and textual absence are far from identical (often appearing together, however, as topics of contemporary critical inquiry), Greene's persuasive point on polar reflexivity-realism reinforces the conviction that even contemporary analysis is most faithful to Gide's work when polar tensions can be felt.

On that note of polarity, a more general point can be made. Within the context of deconstructive criticism, some might be tempted to dismiss the sense of presence in Gide's *récits* as logocentric illusion. We can dismiss the dismissal, however, by pointing to its reductive approach to the problem of textual absence/presence, but more importantly by opposing to it a willful refusal *à la Gide* to choose between contraries, for no other reason than, for example, the intellectual pleasures to be gotten from working within both the vast corpus of traditional, presence-oriented criticism, and the newer, growing corpus that challenges it. The refusal to chose, moreover, does not stem from an airy irrationalist rejection of the principle of contradiction, but rather from the sense that in the realm of literature contraries can find in each other, to use Gide's expression, "une permission secrète" (see below, the first paragraph of the chapter on *L'Immoraliste*). Or one could argue that while the Copernican-like revolution brought about by the contributions of thinkers like Saussure, Freud, Lacan, and Derrida may undermine the bases for traditional notions of how language and literature work, they do not necessarily invalidate all the uses of those notions, most usually consistent among themselves in practice if not in principle. Not any more, for example, than Copernicus totally invalidated all conducts and conclusions deriving from the erroneous impression that the sun moves in relation to the "stable" earth: I can still find east by noting where the sun "rises," the weather gets cooler in the winter because the sun "moves north" in the winter

horizon, etc. So too, there are readerly pleasures and insights to be had by dealing with the "presence" of narrators.

Or one can take something of a long-term philosophical view (in two senses of that latter adjective). Because of the postmodernist revolution, the liveliest arena of the terms of the debate between philosophical realism and idealism has been moved from the mind to language. (Not entirely for the first time though, witness the arguments, e.g., of the Sophists and of Duns Scotus over the relationship between world and word.) Instead of arguing among ourselves whether the mind is in essential contact with reality or only with itself, we now ponder what is viewed as language's relationship to reality and to itself. While we wait to identify a thinker who will arc the poles created by the force field of language-reality opposition as Kant did for the mind-reality opposition, we can follow the prescient example of Gide, at once one of the great practitioners as well as observers of language, by refusing to reject either of the incompatible extremes of the current debate over the status of language/literature. If we take his word for it, we will remain closer to the literary life-spark:

> Certains de ces jeunes gens font de grands efforts un peu ridicules pour réduire les contradictions qu'ils ont senti se dresser en eux ou devant eux, sans comprendre que l'étincelle de vie ne saurait jaillir qu'entre deux pôles contraires, et d'autant plus belle et grande qu'il est entre eux plus de distance et que chacun de ces pôles reste chargé d'une plus riche opposition. (*Journal*, I 801)

It may even be that cultivation of the unresolved conflict of opposites has considerable merit for thinkers in *all* fields. In 1955 the Nobel Prize winning physicist Wolfgang Pauli, called "the conscience of physics" in his day (Feyerabend 30), dared speak of it as a means to salvation for scientists:

> Today, rationalism has passed its peak. One definitely feels that it is too narrow.... It seems plausible to abandon the merely rational in whose background the Will to Power always had played an important role and to adopt its opposite, for example a Christian or Buddhist mysticism. However I believe that for those who are no longer convinced by a narrow rationalism and whom the spell of a mystical outlook, an outlook that views the external

world with its oppressive multitude of events as a mere illusion fails to affect with sufficient strength, I feel that for such people there remains only one choice: to expose themselves to these . . . opposites and to their conflict. This is how a scientist . . . can find an inner path towards salvation. (Pauli, as quoted by Feyerabend 30)

So Gide's proclivity toward *disponibilité* would seem to mark him less as an idiosyncratic, or dated, or fashionable thinker, and more as a universal one.

Another, related point needs to be made. To repeat, the narrative subversion of the three frameworks will be brought out by pushing their ramifications beyond conventional limits. But the discussion of each *récit* could have begun with an immediate plunge into an arbitrary extension of reading conventions. That would have been warranted, because all reading conventions are by nature and definition deeply arbitrary. (Deeply, but not completely.)[3] Tra-

---

[3] Literary conventions are not completely arbitrary either in essence or in use. In many of its undefined references to convention, recent literary theory has whistled past a logical graveyard wherein lies many a philosophical effort to delineate the concept of convention adequately. My goal not being a theoretical exercise but rather a pragmatic reading of Gide's *récits*, I will place my bet on the (only seemingly) pedestrian definition of "convention" offered by Paul Dumouchel: "the regularities of behavior that emerge in various circumstances as a result of abiding by . . . more stable rules" (Dumouchel, "Hobbes on Rules and Conventions," in Hjort, *Rules and Conventions*, 109). The problems remain numerous (and not the least of them for me is that Dumouchel does not define "rule"). For instance, if as Alain Boyer finds, "[c]onvention is rooted in the insufficiency of nature" (Boyer, "Conventions and Arbitrariness," in Hjort, *Rules and Conventions* 127), the paradox follows that it may be in human nature to be conventional. Or, how did literature get started, if one maintains that it is essentially conventional?: since such a position usually assumes that language, the matrix of literature, is conventional, how could (literary) convention be initiated or even considered outside of (linguistic) convention, that is, where are we to locate the non-conventional ground on which to start the process of convention? Failing to find that ground, do we assume that people agreed to agree without first having agreed on "agreed"? If we do so assume, we would seem to be approaching an acceptance of a natural, perhaps originary sign. (For an interesting compendium of current philosophical efforts to pin down "convention," see *Rules and Conventions*, Hjort.)

In a similar vein, I should acknowledge here that while I, like so many of my colleagues, am persuaded, à la Saussure, of the differential, arbitrary nature of the sign, I have not yet, in my limited experience as a non-philosopher dealing with such issues, seen it proved that, as a necessary consequence, discourse is equally arbitrary. I *do* find it profoundly, exhilaratingly arbitrary, but pragmatically, in a limited but coherent and satisfactory way, discourse can work by my lights, whence this book.

dition chooses, for instance, to start suspending disbelief at the beginning of the story of *L'Immoraliste*, at the epistolary salutation "A Monsieur D. R., Président du Conseil," not at the epigraph, and not at the title. But is there any reason why Michel could not have recommended both to his amanuensis? So, in an abrupt, seemingly arbitary break with tradition, I could have insisted at the start of my first chapter that, since the anonymous friend relays Michel's account, his voice should be considered the only one to which the reader has direct access, and that in consequence we never hear Michel. Instead, I chose to show how such a critical move, *before* being arbitrary, is an historically logical extension of reading conventions. When we look at it in the long term – as I will at the beginning of each chapter – the traditional scholarship on these *récits* leads up to and virtually elicits the questions that I raise. Those questions and/or their consequences have, nonetheless and in general, been studiously avoided, I propose, because of a logocentric, essentialist reluctance to apply the conclusion to which they must lead, a conclusion widely accepted, but only in the abstract, namely, that literature, literary conventions, and the very stuff that constitutes them, language itself, are, when all is (never) said and done, profoundly arbitrary. My point, however, is not to fault in any way traditional approaches to the *récits*, on the contrary. Traditional scholarship has produced far too many enjoyable, satisfying studies of Gide to be dismissed out of hand, and much of what follows will relay, it is hoped, the pleasures to be had from engaging those informed, agile readings (although the aim will be a representative, *not* exhaustive, review of the scholarship on the points in question). I want to suggest that traditional and contemporary approaches, while incompatible in their basic assumptions, imply and need and can work off the other, for a fuller apprehension of Gide's work.

Nonetheless, it could legitimately be protested that a pushing of reading conventions can be seen under scrutiny to approach logical circularity: if we move beyond conventional readings, we discover unconventional – i.e., subversive – readings. But the protest not only fails to take adequate account of the arbitrary in literature, it also amounts to a rejection of Gide's rejection of limits, of convention, of conformity. Or, to look at the matter in slightly different terms, these *récits*, like the rest of Gide's *oeuvre*, have at their centers a subversive dynamic (not unrelated to what is often called Gide's pervasive irony – see e.g. Maisani-Léonard, Yaari). There is no reason not to try to consider all aspects of them in a way consistent with that dynamic. In so regarding the basic forms of the *récits*, we will rectify an oversight on the part of critics: the main narrative stratagems of *L'Immoraliste*, *La Porte étroite*, and *La Symphonie pastorale* are as subversive as any other aspect of them. To couch the point in a Gidean image, one can say that the textual inaccessibility that results from the *récits*' framework is the formal equivalent of the charge by the narrator of *Les Nourritures terrestres*: "Nathanaël, à présent, jette mon livre" (Gide, *Romans* 248). The effect of a systematic questioning of the means whereby the texts are conveyed will be finally to deprive readers, like Nathanaël, of those texts that they erroneously assumed they possessed and needed to possess. Should one expect less from a writer "passionné, amoureux de l'ouverture de l'oeuvre" (Kapetanoviç, m3)?

To say, then, that one will read Gide's first-person narratives while pushing the limits of their narrative conventions is to say that one will read them in a Gidean spirit. Regarding Gide's much quoted diary entry of 13 October 1918 about the need for an esthetic point of view in order to understand his work ("C'est du point de vue de l'art qu'il sied de juger ce que j'écris . . . [etc.]," see below, 24), Michel Décaudin strikes a salutory note appropriate here: ". . . on dénature la citation en l'amputant, comme on le fait souvent, de sa dernière phrase: 'C'est du reste le seul point de vue qui ne soit exclusif d'aucun des autres'" (Décaudin 132). In that spirit of critical non-exclusiveness, the following chapters will play at testing the limits of the narrative conventions used in the *récits*.

It is assumed, furthermore, that Gidean *disponibilité* authorizes the proposed free approach to reading the *récits*, especially since the eminent Jean Hytier has pointed out that they deal with and repudiate conventions and choices that imprison:

> Tous ces récits [*L'Immoraliste*, *La Porte étroite*, *Isabelle*, *La Symphonie pastorale*] sont des *déceptions*. Tous nous touchent, nous navrent et nous irritent; mais, intellectuellement, ils nous montrent des personnages enfermés dans une formule, prisonniers d'une règle, d'une loi, d'une convention ou d'une habitude, et par leur faute. Ils ont tous *choisi* et se sont trouvés prisonniers d'un choix. D'un choix dont l'âpreté [IM], l'étroitesse [PE], la facilité [ISABELLE] ou le mensonge [SP] sont tour à tour la marque. Vous reconnaissez encore l'horreur du choix, signe chez

> Gide d'ossification, de raidissement dans une attitude, de manque de liberté, d'appauvrissement, et sans doute, pour aller jusqu'au bout, d'imbécillité, de faiblesse, de déficience, que celle-ci vienne de l'absolutisme du désir, de l'exaltation de la vertu, de la séduction de l'imagination, de la complaisance de la conscience. (Hytier 169-70)

So, for a while, we will rephrase – but only slightly – the famous *cri du coeur* from *Les Nourritures terrestres*, "Familles, je vous hais!" to read, "Conventions, je vous hais!"

Another justification for the emphasis on form is in order. The formal preoccupation to be found in the following pages is, we can be sure, representative of a pronounced Gidean trait:

> For an artist, one obsessed with perfection of form, as was Gide, the *raison suffisante*, the symbol, of the work, was its structure and composition: "Une oeuvre bien composée est nécessairement symbolique. Autour de quoi viendrait se grouper les parties? qui guiderait leur ordonnance? sinon l'idée de l'oeuvre, qui fait cette ordonnance symbolique." (Journal, 1896, *Littérature et morale*, 94, in Davies, *Gide: 'L'Immoraliste' and 'La Porte Etroite'* 54)

Twenty-two years after that diary entry, in 1918, the year before the publication of *La Symphonie pastorale*, Gide found himself still having to underscore much the same point. As just mentioned above, in two of his characteristically quotable but tantalizing observations about his own work, he expressed the need for his readers to appreciate the "point de vue esthétique" and "l'art" of his creations:

> Je relis ce matin l'étude de [André] Ruyters sur moi (manuscrit encore) reprise de sa conférence. Elle ne me satisfait pas plus que celle de [Jacques] Rivière. Le point de vue esthétique est le seul où il faille se placer pour parler de mon oeuvre sainement. (Gide, *Journal*, 25 avril, 1918)

> C'est du point de vue de l'art qu'il sied de juger ce que j'écris, point de vue où ne se place jamais, ou presque jamais, le critique – et que celui qui, par miracle, s'y place, éprouve le plus grand mal à faire admettre par ses lecteurs. (*Journal*, 13 octobre, 1918)

Although what precisely Gide understood by "esthétique" and "art" is more vital and nuanced (see Lachasse, and Holdheim) than many seem to have assumed, virtually unanimous understanding has it that Gide was reacting to the tiresome, nearly exclusive emphasis by earlier critics on just the subjects raised in his *récits* (see for example Trahard, 93, 96), and that he deemed the form/subject bond (identity) in his work to be worthy of more attention. Regardless of the exact sense of "art" and "esthétique," knowledge of Gide's oeuvre leads rounded critics to accept that "les problèmes de structure et de techniques sont toujours au premier plan chez lui" (Brée 26). So detailed, methodic consideration of the form of the *récits* will not, we can be reassured, take us away from what is vital in Gide's art.

(A slight disclaimer is called for. While there exists no essential difference between *forme* and *fond*, we should accept that the same text can be approached in profoundly different ways. For reasons of heuristic convenience and logical analysis, therefore, in the following pages I will discuss narrative form – by which I understand, "elemental mode of narrative presentation" – as if it were independent of subject matter, assuming [and striving to show] that if the discussion remains accurate, the two will appear as ultimately reducible to each other.)

As if to illustrate visually the importance of form in his work, in 1899, just two years before he finished writing *L'Immoraliste*, Gide had published *Le Prométhée mal enchaîné*, where an aspect of structure literally and continually gets in the way of the story. Here was a work 1) that made it impossible for the reader not to wrestle explicitly with the question of form, and 2) that created a formal dualism which prefigured what would follow in the three *récits*. An audacious puzzle formally, *Le Prométhée* uses, within its own pages, two autonomous systems of organization for sections of its four chapters, the one a series of numbers (I, II, III, etc.), the other titles ("Histoire du garçon et du miglionnaire," "Histoire de Damoclès," etc.). The two systems – intersecting, overlapping, and working seemingly at cross purposes on the same paragraphs – forbid reading the book without dealing with the role of form. W. Wolfgang Holdheim, in his authoritative *Theory and Practice of the Novel: A Study on André Gide*, characteristically offers a carefully marshalled, persuasive argument (Holdheim 192-212) that results in an excellent schema for explaining the systems. For him they incarnate two phenomena often in tension in the novel, and always at issue in Gide's works. Nuancing his argument as he advances, Holdheim characterizes those phenomena differently at various points, calling them the horizontal and the vertical, the objective and the subjective, the rhetorical and the logical, plot and character, the refusal of the problematical and the self-conscious. The first two sets of characterizations doubtless appear idiosyncratic to those unfamiliar with his book; their rigorous, careful definition by Holdheim turns them into specialized terms. But the last three anticipate well enough the narrative oppositions to be explored in the following pages, oppositions that, in my telling, will be characterized as, for example, story and story-telling, textual absence and textual presence, the subversion of mimesis and the illusion of mimesis. So for this study, *Le Prométhée mal enchaîné* will be a graphic authorization from Gide for focussing on the interplay between the how and the what of narration in the *récits*. Holdheim's findings declare as well the portent of such a focus:

> And the two principles of organization are at odds with one another, they interest without coinciding. An impression of disturbing irony emanates from this structural ambiguity. It seems to imply that traditional certainties have disintegrated, that the relationship between the self and "objective reality" has become questionable. (Holdheim 194)

My first chapter will show how *L'Immoraliste* brings that philosophical and existential portent to ample realization.

Another measure of the faithfulness of the following pages to the spirit of Gide's oeuvre is that, in addressing textual inaccessibility, they will suggest indirectly the bedrock affinity between the three works in question and *Le Traité du Narcisse*, Gide's *ars poetica*. The central event in the first work published under his name was the loss of *the* text, "le livre du Mystère – où se lisait la vérité qu'il faut connaître" (*TN* 5). Because of the convulsive storm brought on by Adam's fault of self-affirmation against his submissive role of perfect observer sustaining reality, *the* text is whisked away from his contemplation, lost forever: "vers l'inconnu d'un ciel nocturne et vers de hasardeux parages, . . . fuit l'éparpillement . . . des pages arrachées au grand livre sacré qui s'effeuille" (*TN* 6). Thereafter, "des poètes . . . recueilleront pieusement les feuillets déchirés du Livre immémorial où se lisait la vérité qu'il faut connaître" (*TN* 7). The three *récits* too will be seen to be marked by the post-lapsarian experience, "l'inquiet désir" (*TN* 6), offering only a text of scattered "feuillets déchirés," "incomplet encore et qui ne suffira pas" (*TN* 6).

In addition, the fact of the story's inaccessibility will tie the three *récits* with *all* of Gide's early works, for Emily Apter has observed that the strategy of the absent text marked his initial Symbolist productions:

> [Litotes'] reliance on grammatical forms that endow subdued, self-effacing language with an unsettling affective charge was the ideal instrument for a writer who sought to discredit the hyperbolic affectations of Symbolism without relinquishing Symbolism's sophistication of formal invention. Its kinship with irony, or with a family of tropes (such as preterition, periphrasis, ellipsis, zeugma, asteism, anacoluthon, etc.) all of which deliver their message by evoking an absent text that must be inferred from context and tone, provided a perfect means of satirizing the dagger-sharp innuendos and precious circumlocutions of Symbolist dialogue. (Apter 11)

We may then embark on this demonstration, sure that the absent story of the *récits* has deep roots in Gide's literary genesis. We may even come to suspect that the absent story *is* the root of that genesis.

Chapter One

*L'IMMORALISTE*[1]

I. Narrative Form Touched by Excess

Gide himself recognized that *L'Immoraliste* and *La Porte étroite*, intimately tied together in his mind (as they would be in the minds of many critics), are disturbing books on the level of subject matter, dealing as they do with polar but complementary examples of excess:

> Qui donc persuaderai-je que ce livre [*La Porte étroite*] est jumeau de *L'Immoraliste* et que les deux sujets ont grandi concurremment dans mon esprit, l'excès de l'un trouvant dans l'excès de l'autre une permission secrète et tous deux se maintenant en équilibre? (Gide, *Journal*, vol. 1, mercredi 7 février, 1912)

*L'Immoraliste* takes us into a personality that opens itself up to intemperate affirmation of the self, whereas *La Porte étroite* exposes us to a denial of the self no less immoderate. In both instances, moreover, sexuality is repressed to the point of devastation. The disturbing nature of these contents and of their consequences – the death-murder of Marceline, the virtual suicide of Alissa – understandably rivet the attention of the reader.

---

[1] The ideas for this chapter were first sketched out in the Spring of 1986 as part of a successful application for an NEH Summer Seminar offered by Professor François Rigolot of Princeton University. Dr. Rigolot was characteristically insightful, persuasive, and generous in helping me articulate my ideas. The following Fall a Robert E. Good Fellowship from Denison University allowed me to finish the first version of this chapter, and to extract from it the section on Rousseau for publication as an article in *The Comparatist* (vol. 13, May 1989). I thank *The Comparatist* for permission to include here that article.

Perhaps too much so, as explained in the "Introduction," above. Some recent criticism (Babcock, Helbo, Kapetanoviç) has been progressively building a strong case for the radical implications of various narrative elements of both *récits* but without addressing directly the fundamental one: appearances notwithstanding, readers are denied direct access to the main narrative voices. As we shall see, what has been taken to be Michel's voice is – at a questionable best – his anonymous friend's transmitted version of what was said, and Alissa's words come to us only through the selective, tendentious editing performed by the less than reliable Jérôme. But it may be that because of the great quantity of penetrating criticism regularly done on both works for some time, those who work with *L'Immoraliste* and *La Porte étroite* have grown familiar with them, to the point of comfort, a point not easily reconciled with Gide's inspiration: "C'est peut-être ce que j'ai de plus protestant en moi: l'horreur du confort" (*Journal*, vol. 1, 14 juillet, 1914). We need to make the effort to recall that their initial, deep-reaching impact is to unsettle. Consequently, in the following pages an attempt will be made to arrive at conclusions about the correspondence between the structures of the two works and what Gide characterized as their "excessive" contents. The point, though, will not just be to address the intriguing question of the correspondence itself, but also to consider the heuristic value of the attendant rethinking of details of both books.

## II. Questioning the Conventional Interpretation of the Framed Narrative in *L'Immoraliste*

### A) *Who Speaks?*

From the start, *L'Immoraliste* has been plagued by readers' improper answer to a key if deceptively simple question that Roland Barthes has posed variously about any narrative: "Qui est le donateur du récit?" or more simply, "Qui parle?" (Barthes, "Introduction à l'analyse structurale du récit," 19).[2] After Gide's book ap-

---

[2] Barthes's general and famous answer to his question can be found in S/Z: "Plus l'origine de l'énonciation est irréparable, plus le texte est pluriel. Dans le texte moderne, les voix sont traitées jusqu'au déni de tout repère: le discours, ou mieux encore, le langage parle, c'est tout" (48).

peared in 1902, he was upbraided for personally advancing the doctrines and ideas to be found in its pages – doctrines and ideas that should have been more accurately described as those of his main character.³ Fault was found, for instance, with the text's portrayal of an uncritical pursuit of individualism. (The latter, it should be noted, is on its very face not indifferent to the nature of first-person narration and is an issue to which we will be returning.)

Although expecting for other reasons a less than favorable reception for his book,⁴ Gide was nonetheless upset when even highly literate friends like the poet Francis Jammes, out of insensitivity to the book's ironic artistry, confused the voice of Michel with that of the author himself.⁵ Gide showed in a personal letter how stung he had been by the widespread failure to appreciate his technique: he called "*imbéciles*" readers who made a simple identification of him with the *je* of the narrative (Gide, *Romans* 1514). While Gide's irritation may seem readily understandable to readers today, we should recognize that at the beginning of this century there was little appreciation of the distinction between author and fictional narrator. Frank Stanzel's encompassing study of narration makes a point of this slow progress in critical understanding of first-person novels:

> For a long time older views of first-person narration stood in the way of an accurate understanding of the peculiarity of this type

---

³ For a highly useful overview of critical reception of *L'Immoraliste*, see Fortier, 2-12.

⁴ That Gide expected at a minimum an unenthusiastic reception for *L'Immoraliste* is made clear in the entry dated January 8, 1902 of his *Journal*, where his expectations are adduced to explain why the initial printing counted only three hundred copies: "Pourquoi je tire *L'Immoraliste* à trois cents exemplaires?. . . Pour me dissimuler un tout petit peu ma mévente. Tirant à douze cents, elle le paraîtrait quatre fois pire; j'en souffrirais quatre fois plus" (*Journal*, vol. 1, 111).

⁵ Evidencing perhaps the impact of Hippolyte Taine's prevailing critical determinism, the poet, in a letter to Gide, viewed the book and the author in these terms: "[*L'Immoraliste*] est l'expression d'une douleur épouvantable à laquelle tu n'as pu échapper, un soulèvement d'âme et d'estomac correspondant sans doute à des événements que le choc a transposés............................................

Tu n'es sûrement pas un arbre de souche française, ni un ormeau, ni un hêtre, ni un chêne, ni un frêne de la prairie qui dévale jusqu'au torrent. Chaque année, tu pousses de singulières feuilles chinées, de sombres fleurs qui déroutent ma mince science, des cornets d'apparence vénéneuse, malsains mais superbes" (Gide, *Romans* 1515-16).

Similar reactions prompted from the maligned author the preface appearing in the second printing and all subsequent editions, a preface in which Gide tried to redirect such misguided readings. See Gide, *Romans* 367.

of narration in contrast to third-person narration. One of these views, for example, asserted that the "I" of a first-person narrator was largely identical with the author. This view evolved especially in conjunction with the interpretation of the great *Bildungsromane* in the first person, such as *David Copperfield* and Gottfried Keller's *Green Henry*, which actually suggested an identification of this kind. (Stanzel 80-81)

Stanzel can go back only as far as 1924 to find a clearly articulated theoretical appreciation of the distinction between author and first-person narrator. He cites "the first German theorist of the first-person novel [Kurt Forstreuter].... For Forstreuter, the first-person narrator is no longer mainly a mouth-piece for the author, but rather an independent fictional character" (Stanzel 81). An additional measure, moreover, of how long it took for critical sophistication to be brought to bear generally on *any* narrative is that even as late as 1948 – Robert Murray Davis reminds us – "René Wellek and Austin Warren wrote that the criticism of fiction was inferior both in quantity and quality to the criticism of poetry...." (Davis v).[6]

So time has only slowly allowed the view to prevail that Michel, not Gide, speaks in the pages of *L'Immoraliste*. But the very slowness of the dawning of an understanding that seems patently obvious to us today suggests that first-person narration poses unusual problems for readers. Current critical circumstances, however, permit us to press the matter further, to maintain in fact that it is not Michel either who speaks directly to the reader. In confronting, moreover, historic details behind confusion over narrative voices, not just regarding *L'Immoraliste* but other first-person fictional texts as well, a larger point can be made. I will try to lay the groundwork for viewing this work by Gide, master artist of the narrating self, as a paradigm useful in addressing critical issues raised most readily by first-person narratives, but of relevance for any narrative whatsoever.

Whereas almost all critics of *L'Immoraliste* have continually assumed immediate access to a "primary" narrative voice, Michel's, in fact we have at best direct contact only with the "secondary" voice of his anonymous friend, for the entire text is merely a long letter by the friend who attempts to write down Michel's oral account.

---

[6] See also Wellek and Warren 201.

That point was, to my knowledge, first stressed in 1967 by Catharine H. Savage:

> A first glance at the composition [of *L'Immoraliste*] reveals a central feature which is integral to the meaning. The novel is begun by a *je* writing in the first person to his brother, to whom he is going to report a long confession made to him. Immediately we are introduced to a second *je*, the protagonist, who narrates his own story in the rest of the book. This device, while affording certain fictional advantages not usually found in first-person narration, creates at the same time difficulties of interpretation. (Savage, *L'Immoraliste* 43)

In 1979 G. W. Ireland observed like Savage that this narrative is quite literally just a single letter that puts Michel's spoken words into writing in another's hand. But Ireland highlighted wittily the physical limitations faced by Michel's amanuensis and demonstrates convincingly how large a leap of faith is called for if one is to assume direct access to Michel's voice:

> Rappelons-nous que formellement *L'Immoraliste* TOUT ENTIER a la forme d'une lettre, est une lettre (de deux cent cinquante pages imprimées, ce qui fait combien de feuilles manuscrites?). [The first narrator] doit voyager, à tout hasard, avec une provision impressionnante de papier, d'encre, de plumes, etc. Pour rapporter mot à mot tout ce que Michel est censé avoir dit (durant combien d'heures?) il doit posséder une mémoire sans défaillance; et pour fournir cet effort, à peine débarqué après un voyage qui était alors difficile et fatigant, il doit être un ami à toute épreuve. (Ireland, "Le Jeu des 'je'" 78)

Even if one opts to maintain that Michel's account was recorded at the time that he spoke, there remains a daunting difficulty: "Michel . . . fit [his account] sur sa terrasse où près de lui nous étions étendus dans l'ombre et dans la clarté des étoiles" (*L'Immoraliste*, in *Romans* 370). Even a prodigious amanuensis would have had to admit defeat when faced with the position required (stretched out) and the amount of light available in which to write (starlight).

Ireland views any such difficulties, however, as just a blunder in narrative technique on Gide's part, not acknowledging in them a contribution to a pattern of elements raising the problem of direct access to an individual narrative voice. Furthermore, Ireland took care to make explicit his refusal to accept some of the implications of his own observation, asserting circularly that readers simply *must* presume they hear Michel's narration directly, because otherwise the narrative would not be Gidean, insofar as a Gidean self cannot, it is alleged, manifest itself through the voice of another.[7]

Paul Fortier too, in his superbly detailed 1988 study of *L'Immoraliste*, trips on a similar assumption of access to Michel's voice. As my preceding pages have, his *Décor et Dualisme* uses the question, *qui parle?*,[8] to bring out the implications of the frame. Reading the anonymous friend's introduction closely and well, Fortier insists at one point (31-34) that, within the fiction, the amanuensis could even have, and may well have, deliberately modified what he heard: for reasons of friendship, he may have wanted to keep from shocking his powerful brother (from whom he wants a position for Michel). But after acknowledging succinctly that the faithful transmission of Michel's account is humanly impossible (Fortier 32), his argument drifts ever so slightly toward a presupposition that what was modified by the friend had indeed been a faithful rendition of Michel's every word. For instance: "On peut se demander si un individu qui tient tellement à la réussite de sa demande n'aurait pas usé d'autres moyens pour encourager son frère à trouver un poste qui occuperait Michel, s'il n'aurait pas, par exemple, modifié *le récit de Michel* afin de noircir un peu moins ce dernier" (*ibid.*, 32; my emphasis). Strictly speaking, should Fortier not have written something like "*ce qu'il se rappelait du récit de Michel*"? Is textual presence worming its way back into Fortier's working assumptions, in the notion "*le récit de Michel*," which allows for the confusion of production and product, ambiguously covering both Michel's act

---

[7] "... [C]e qui est avant tout important ici, ce qui est *capital*, c'est que le lecteur du livre entende le récit de Michel, tel qu'il l'a fait, que le Je du lecteur entre directement en contact avec le Je de Michel. Le premier élément constitutif d'un Je gidien, c'est qu'il ne *peut pas* se manifester par la bouche d'un autre." Ireland, 74. The assertion – unconvincing to this reader – does, however, allow Ireland to make an excellent, subtle analysis of how Gide allegedly develops a state of intersubjectivity between his narrator and his reader.

[8] In one of her studies of *L'Immoraliste*, Vicki Mistacco too raises the question, "qui parle?," but at a higher level of subtlety than Fortier or I, posing it for an implied author (and not an explicit conventional voice within the fiction as Fortier and I do). As I will in the pages to come, she finds that this *récit* works systematically to deny any conclusive reading.

(only initially available to his friend) and his exact account (not completely available to him in recollection)? The fussy questions are justified, when we see that the assumption of textual presence has indeed penetrated the very thesis of this informative book: "dans L'Immoraliste les descriptions, y compris celles de la nature, révèlent l'état d'âme *du protagoniste*" (*ibid.* 44; my emphasis). The Talmudic detail with which Fortier reads his computer-aided breakdown of descriptive vocabulary, finding in the process a pervasive health-illness dualism at work *in Michel*, make no sense whatsoever, unless one assumes that Michel controlled the inclusion of each and every word of this account.[9]

The logic of the form of the text, however, necessarily suggests a conclusion different from Ireland's and Fortier's. Unless we are prepared to acknowledge and accept the unreasonable leap of faith that the first narrator must have some how managed to write down every exact word uttered during Michel's lengthy monologue, both faith in Gide's not insignificant artistic skills and consistent application of the verisimilitude operative in this text dictate a troubling observation: those reading the first narrator's text at no time can be assured of anything resembling either direct or undistorted contact with the main character's voice. After all, there remains in the text evidence that it was actually following Michel's account, over a period of twelve days, that the friend composed his document (and hastily at that), a fact that surely entails the filtering mechanisms of recollection and re-creation. Having written on his opening page that he had listened to Michel twelve days ago ("depuis les douze jours que Denis, Daniel et moi sommes ici..." *I*, 369), the narrator alludes to prior arrangements with his powerful brother in a way that conveys the impression that he had spent the twelve days in hurried writing in order to satisfy the *Président du Conseil* as quickly as possible:

> Oui, tu le pensais bien: Michel nous a parlé, mon cher frère. Le récit qu'il nous fit, le voici. Tu l'avais demandé; je te l'avais promis; mais à l'instant de l'envoyer, j'hésite encore... (*I* 369)

---

[9] The latest overview of Gide's fiction, David Walker's *André Gide* (1990), refers in passing to the problem of the frame (Walker 27), but still assumes complete and direct access to Michel's words. Walker's arguments and conclusions are, however, compatible with mine: "The meaning of the text is, precisely, the reader's inability to sum up or definitively assess Michel's project" (Walker, *Gide* 35).

Subsequently, the friend periodically reannounces his presence by including headings that divide Michel's account into three parts, and the first two parts into chapters. Who speaks then in *L'Immoraliste*? At this point, the logic of the frame would incline us to conclude that the voice with which we have contact is neither Gide's *nor* Michel's, but rather only that of the epistolary relayer of Michel's story, his anonymous friend. (I take the term "relayer" from Jean Rousset, who calls the technique "le relais des narrateurs," that is, a text by a fictional character that is relayed to the reader by still another fictional character, Rousset 22.)

But logic usually has to strain mightily when trying to control the literariness of a text. It could, for example, be argued in a psychological sense that the reader cannot be sure which voice of the friend it is that speaks in *L'Immoraliste*. As can be asked of any written presentation, real or fictional, does a letter such as the one written by the narrator to his brother not spring from a persona, that is, from one of many possible reflective, constructed, and so artificial voices that correspondents can and do assume? With that question, the very notion of "the" main voice loses just a little bit more of its simplicity. Furthermore, among the epistolary personae that the first narrator could have assumed, there is one, a very likely one, that raises even more troublesome problems of narrative authority. The narrating friend has been profoundly moved and influenced by the most recent words of *his* friend Michel. To such an extent in fact, that at the end of the book he admits that he feels a malaise, sensing that he has somehow become what he calls a virtual accomplice of Michel, experiencing, he tells us, almost an involvement in Michel's actions:

> Michel resta longtemps silencieux. Nous nous taisions aussi, pris chacun d'un étrange malaise. Il nous semblait hélas! qu'à nous la raconter, Michel avait rendu son action plus légitime. De ne savoir où la désapprouver, dans la lente explication qu'il en donna, nous en faisait presque complices. Nous y étions comme engagés. (*I* 470)

We have to recognize, therefore, that Michel, after telling his story and *before* his friend has started writing, had already partially appropriated the narrator's own feelings, his point of view, and so to a certain degree his very voice. So in trying to answer the question of whose voice it is that we hear in *L'Immoraliste*, we have moved from Gide's to Michel's, then to the friend's, and now to a voice that is not quite the friend's, but rather one that M. M. Bakhtin would call "unfinalizable," one in which there is a dynamic "in-living" of both Michel's and the friend's voices.[10] But . . ., since the friend wrote this letter to his brother, one could maintain well within the limits of plausibility that the brother, having received and read it, is responsible for then having taken the trouble to have the text published: did he do so with or without having "prepared" it for printing? Did *he* introduce the division into parts and chapters? Did he then, as others will in the *L'École des femmes* trilogy, pass it on to "M. A. Gide," who then . . . ?

In short, *L'Immoraliste* has no discernable voice in the traditional sense of the term. Ultimately, readers of *L'Immoraliste* have to accept Barthes's general conclusion in the matter of literary voice: "l'être de l'écriture (le sens du travail qui la constitue) est d'empêcher de jamais répondre à cette question: *Qui parle?*" (Barthes, *S/Z* 146).

So the individual voice of the main character gets absorbed and inextricably lost in that of another, thereby showing how a strict reappraisal of the narrative form of this book casts doubt on the very possibility of Michel's (?) doctrine of authentic individualism

---

[10] One of the problems with Bakhtin is that, not at all surprisingly, his thought and terminology evolved over the course of his long and productive career. Consequently, his key terms are not subject to concise, static definitions. Nonetheless, the Bakhtin scholars Gary Saul Morson and Caryl Emerson offer a serviceable sketch of the qualities that characterize Bakhtin's view of the novel: "Bakhtin's various descriptions of the novel do have a number of important features in common. Whatever the principle governing his generic classification, Bakhtin always treats the novel as the form best satisfying his favorite values and expressing his global concepts. The novel is sure to be the genre that is most dialogic. More than any competitor, it treats character, society, and knowledge as unfinalizable; it is closest to prosaic values, an appreciation of centrifugal forces, and a sense of the world's essential messiness. In any given classificatory scheme, genres antithetical to the novel are given to claims of certainty, expressions of absolute truth, and assertions of timeless wisdom; by contrast, the novel is ever skeptical, experimental, and open to the unpredictable experience of every present moment. Rivals are set at a reverential distance from their readers; the novel partakes of everyday life. Other genres claim to know, the novel asks how we know; novels are most aware of the multiplicity of languages, conceptual schemes, and social experiences; where others might prophesy, the novel merely conjectures" (Morson and Emerson, 303). It is easy to recognize in this sketch of Bakhtin's understanding of the novel values close to Gide's *disponibilité*, and so values at work in my proposed reading of his *récits*.

articulating itself appropriately. That outcome, of course, anchors *L'Immoraliste* in Gide's patently ironic oeuvre, a quality Gide himself was the first to acknowledge: "A la seule exception de mes *Nourritures*, tous mes livres sont des livres ironiques; ce sont des livres de critique. . . . *L'Immoraliste* d'une forme de l'individualisme" (*Oeuvres complètes d'André Gide* vol. XIII, 439-40). Which is another way of saying that his work is inclined to self-refutation: "J'aime que chaque livre porte en lui, mais cachée, sa propre réfutation" (*Romans* 1479). Through the framed narrative structure, then, individualism becomes dependent and thus denied in its very attempt at independent self-communication. Not at all *in – dividuus*, as it would have itself be, it is instead *dividuus* and inherently contradictory. Indeed, in considering Michel's relayed voice, one comes up against an obvious question: how can *anyone* express individuality outside and independently of the vast, complex play of a language already used by others, a language each word of which has the potential for pulling in directions unknown and unintended by the would-be independent individual?[11] This suggests that a vigorous expression of individualism such as Michel may have envisaged is inconceivable in its form, and so, to the extent that all concepts and most experiences are language-bound, that his putative individualism itself is inconceivable in its essence. (It also corroborates Martine Maisani-Léonard's conclusion, arrived at through a study of Gide's narrative "shifters" integrating *discours* into *histoire* [verb tenses, adverbs of time and place, and personal, possessive, and demonstrative pronouns], that in his first-person narratives: "le préambule est le lieu destiné à soulever les problèmes spécifiques du récit," Maisani-Léonard 62.)

Such a form-based position is not, moreover, without solid grounds in Gide's work. In mythical and literary terms there is no better archetype of the would-be individual than Narcissus (and no

---

[11] As Gide himself was aware: "Avant d'expliquer aux autres mon livre, j'attends que d'autres me l'expliquent. Vouloir l'expliquer d'abord c'est en restreindre aussitôt le sens; car si nous savons ce que nous voulions dire, nous ne savons pas si nous ne disions que cela. – Et ce qui surtout m'y intéresse, c'est ce que j'y ai mis sans le savoir, – cette part d'inconscient, que je voudrais appeler la part de Dieu. – Un livre est toujours une collaboration, et tant plus le livre vaut-il, que plus la part du scribe y est petite, que plus l'accueil de Dieu sera grand. – Attendons de partout la révélation des choses; du public, la révélation de nos oeuvres" ("Prologue" to *Paludes*, in *Romans* 89).

figure more central to Gide). Significantly, in his very first signed work, *Le Traité du Narcisse,* Gide used a very subtle frame, but one nonetheless similar to that of *L'Immoraliste,* in that it puts into explicit question the status of the text it encompasses and so of the vision that it relays, Narcissus's:

> A metacritical gloss that challenges the value of the interior text opens and closes the *Traité*. The prologue begins: "Les livres ne sont peut-être pas une chose bien nécessaire; quelques mythes d'abord suffisaient" and the epilogue echoes with: "Ce traité n'est peut-être pas quelque chose de bien nécessaire. Quelques mythes d'abord suffisaient." (Apter 14)

Furthermore, viewed from the vantage point of the phenomenon of quotation – and, as already noted, almost all of *L'Immoraliste* is one long quotation – the relayed form of this narrative intimates an insight explored at length in Antoine Compagnon's *La Seconde Main* (an insight quite compatible with Bakhtin's earlier, wider ranging, but – until recently – unpublicized "dialogism"). Considering the nature of quotation, Compagnon ultimately finds in it the reflection of a quality characteristic of literary expression itself. The basis for his argument is what he considers the confusion that a quotation generates between borrowed words and what he calls grafted words:

> Bienheureuse citation! Elle a ce privilège parmi tous les mots du lexique de désigner tout à la fois deux opérations, l'une de prélèvement, l'autre de greffe, et encore l'objet de ces deux opérations, l'objet prélevé et l'objet greffé, comme s'il demeurait le même dans différents états. Connaît-on ailleurs, dans quelque autre champ de l'activité humaine, une semblable réconciliation, dans un seul et même mot, des incompatibles fondamentaux que sont la disjonction et la conjonction, la mutilation et l'ente, le moins et le plus, l'export et l'import, le découpage et le collage? Il y a une dialectique toute-puissante de la citation, l'une des vigoureuses mécaniques du déplacement, plus forte encore que la chirurgie. (Compagnon 29)

That insight leads to his principal conclusion:

> Écrire, car c'est toujours récrire, ne diffère pas de citer. La citation, grâce à la confusion métonymique à laquelle elle préside,

est lecture et écriture: elle conjoint l'acte de lecture et celui d'écriture. Lire ou écrire, c'est faire acte de citation. (Compagnon 34)

This means that *L'Immoraliste*, like every framed (quoting) narrative, not only justifies but also illustrates simply and directly Compagnon's argument, a provocative one for the understanding of the functioning of any would-be individual literary voice.

On a different register but one no less important for our purposes, because of the relayed status of Michel's words the foundation for virtually all the criticism done heretofore on *L'Immoraliste* gets called into serious theoretical question: since previous studies have assumed direct access to Michel's voice, what is left of them if that access is in serious doubt? The stakes – intrinsic for the text and extrinsic for the criticism applied to it – seem large indeed, large enough to warrant a cautious attempt to sketch an historical explanation of some of the issues behind readers' difficulties with framed narrative.

B) *Historical Context of Framed Narrative*

In dealing with any relayed text, not just *L'Immoraliste* but also for example Prévost's *Manon Lescaut* or Conrad's *The Heart of Darkness*, critics have apparently been unanimously prepared to violate the principles of consistency and verisimilitude and have made whatever illogical acts of faith are necessary to assure direct access to the words of main characters, of a Michel, a Des Grieux, or a Marlow. The illogicality of that procedure has rarely been an issue, in part because we are dealing in these cases far less with logic than with reading conventions heretofore found indispensable for relayed texts, and of course *all* reading conventions can be seen, upon reflection, to be ultimately arbitrary; and illogical in a very profound way. The convention in this case, no more or less illogical than most, has been called "the convention of perfect or faithful memory" (Showalter 81-82). Wayne Booth, moreover, in a section of *The Rhetoric of Fiction* entitled "The 'Impurity' of Great Literature," articulates the values behind such conventions, arguing against logic alone in dealing with literature, and for what he calls the "rhetorical dimension": "the very concept of writing a story seems to have implicit within it the notion of finding techniques of expression that will make the work accessible in the highest possible degree" (Booth 105).

Aside from the fact that Booth does not answer here why an accessible text would be superior to other possible kinds, the word "accessible" itself is naturally synonymous with the word "present." Readers of Jacques Derrida could then readily wonder if Booth's pragmatic but peremptory "rhetorical dimension" is not simply another logocentric assertion. It seems less an argument than a begging of the question of the accessibility of a literary work, a more abstract and sweeping version of Ireland's circular assertion above that one must have direct access to a Gidean narrative voice because otherwise . . . it would not be a Gidean voice. In brief, one can maintain that critical conventions, claims, and assumptions about access to relayed narrative voices are grounded in what Derrida characterizes as the notion of the sign revealed in the metaphysics of presence [12] ubiquitous in the West, and so are marred by the flaws that the French philosopher finds in that notion. [13]

But to explain why readers have insisted on having direct and reliable access to relayed texts, one need not depend solely on appeals to the metaphysics of presence. One can turn as well to more traditional literary history which offers a variety of contributing insights. We will now give brief consideration to facets of that history. What follows should not, however, be construed as an attempt to lay bare the historical explanation behind the critical reception of

---

[12] "Derrida shows with exhaustive ingenuity that the fate of Western metaphysics is inextricably involved with the notion of the sign, and that the representation of the sign paradoxically requires a transcendental signified to be 'present' to consciousness, even as that signified is always absent, always already displaced by another signifier." (Adams and Searle 80). See also Culler 92-96.

[13] We should note, moreover, that in dealing with fictional relayed narrative voices, which are usually described as oral, we are dealing ultimately with fictional examples of what Derrida calls phonocentrism. "Le privilège de la *phonè* ne dépend pas d'un choix qu'on aurait pu éviter. Il répond à un moment de l'*économie* (disons de la 'vie' de l' 'histoire' ou de l' 'être comme rapport à soi'). Le système du 's'entendre-parler' à travers la substance phonique – qui *se donne* comme signifiant non-extérieur, non-mondain, donc non empirique ou non-contingent – a dû dominer pendant toute une époque l'histoire du monde, a même produit l'idée de monde, l'idée d'origine du monde à partir de la différence entre le mondain et le non-mondain, le dehors et le dedans, l'idéalité et la non-idéalité, l'universel et le non-universel, le transcendantal et l'empirique, etc." (Derrida, *De la grammatologie* 17).

relayed texts, a vast enterprise far, far beyond the scope of this study.[14] Rather, the next few pages offer only reflections on elements underscored by scholars of the history of the novel. Those elements are, however, important, not only because they help to contribute to a working sense of the background of a framed structure such as *L'Immoraliste*'s, but also because they can be linked closely to its themes.

We do well to begin with one of the more striking features of earlier reception of Western prose fiction, the notable disrepute in which it labored in the seventeenth and eighteenth centuries (disrepute that Georges May, in his *Le Dilemme du roman au XVIIIe siècle* for example, finds indispensable to explaining the very nature of the novel in eighteenth-century France), and indeed in which it continued to labor, perceptibly if less notably, on into our own times.[15] If we accept, as Ian Watt for example has argued, that prose fiction was part of the vast cultural evolution marked by the rise of capitalism and bourgeois individualism and by the decline of authority and illiteracy, then we are positioned to take more seriously what might otherwise appear to our eyes to have been silly retrograde ideological attacks on the novel as a corruptor of taste and morals.[16] By not anachronistically dismissing the threat implied

---

[14] See instead Bertil Romberg, *Studies in the Narrative Technique of the First-Person Novel*.

[15] "The reasons [for the inferiority in quantity and quality of criticism of the novel vis-à-vis poetry] are . . ., one thinks, the widespread association of the novel with entertainment, amusement, and escape rather than serious art – the confounding of tha great novels, that is, with manufactures made with a narrow aim at the market. The lingering American popular view, disseminated by pedagogues, that the reading of nonfiction was instructive and meritorious, that of fiction, harmful or at best self-indulgent, was not without implicit backing in the attitude toward the novel of representative critics like Lowell and Arnold" (Wellek and Warren, 201).

[16] "[Le roman] est accusé indistinctement de tous les crimes et de tous les maux, tant et si bien qu'au premier coup d'oeil, on se perd un peu dans ces vitupérations et on a tendance à les mettre simplement au compte de la mauvaise humeur de leurs auteurs" (May, 8). ". . . [E]n 1761, l'abbé Irailh demande, sans soupçonner qu'on puisse donner à ses interrogations oratoires une réponse autre qu'affirmative à la première et négative à la seconde: 'Le genre romanesque n'est-il pas un genre pernicieux de sa nature? Peut-il s'allier avec le bon sens, les bonnes moeurs, le bon goût, et le progrès des lettres?' [Abbé Augustin-Simon Irailh, *Querelles littéraires* (Paris: Durand, 1761), t. II, p. 338.] Et, la même année, Diderot, rappelant à deux reprises dans la même phrase les deux grands chefs d'accusation contre le roman, observe: 'Par un roman, on a entendu jusqu'à ce jour un tissu d'événements chimériques et frivoles, dont la lecture était dangereuse pour le goût et pour les moeurs' [Diderot, *Eloge de Richardson*, éd. Assézat-Tourneaux, t. V, pp. 212-13]" (May, *Dilemme* 10).

by those attacks, we better appreciate how high the ideological stakes were.

It was precisely in prefaces that authors concerned with censorship and similar unpleasantries often refined the wily art of using juridical, orthodox, and of course ineffectual language to seem to repudiate the messages of their more subversive[17] texts:

> . . . le fait frappant que les romans se publient volontiers en ces années à l'abri d'une préface doctrinale, et le fait surtout que la doctrine exprimée dans la préface paraît souvent incompatible avec celle qui se dégage de la lecture du roman qu'elle précède et auquel elle est censée s'appliquer, ces faits sont significatifs et révélateurs. En même temps qu'ils rappellent que bien des pièces illustres de l'époque classique – *Tartuffe* ou *Phèdre*, par exemple – furent aussi précédées de préfaces peu en harmonie avec leur portée idéologique ou affective, en même temps ils sont révélateurs de la situation inconfortable, voire intenable faite aux romanciers par une atmosphère littéraire hostile. (May, 15-16)

The point is an especially important one for our purposes, because one has to consider the strong possibility that the frequent trivialization of prefaces in the seventeenth and eighteenth centuries exactly during the rise and maturation of European first-person fiction allowed and indeed trained readers virtually to dismiss all literary prefaces. *A fortiori*, given prose fiction's officially low status, such trivialization in all likelihood dimmed awareness of ideological or aesthetic implications carried by fictional relaying prefaces.

The history of Western fictional autobiography offers further illustrations of how readers adopted conventions that ignored issues related to narrative reliability. In his book *Pícaros, Madmen, Naïfs, and Clowns: The Unreliable First-Person Narrator*, William Riggan,

---

[17] Summarizing and personalizing some of Bakhtin's ideas about the novel, Kristeva has written: "The novel, and especially the modern, polyphonic novel, incorporating Menippean elements, embodies the effort of European thought to break out of the framework of causally determined identical substances and head toward another modality of thought that proceeds through dialogue (a logic of distance, relativity, analogy, nonexclusive and transfinite opposition). It is therefore not surprising that the novel has been considered as an inferior genre (by neoclassicism and other similar regimes) or as subversive (I have in mind the major writers of polyphonic novels over many centuries – Rabelais, Swift, Sade, Lautréamont, Kafka, and Bataille – to mention only those who have always been and still remain on the fringe of official culture)" (Kristeva 85-86).

qualifying appropriately and noting exceptions as he goes, establishes "fictional first-person narrative [as] a relatively modern phenomenon, dating back to the Spanish picaresque tales of the sixteenth and seventeenth centuries" (Riggan 27). Given the suspect nature of picaresque narrators, one might expect readers to have had from the start serious reservations about the reliability of any such voice and of any voice patterned after them. But it was only slowly that "the fictional first-person form [began] to be used with any frequency and literary skill in fully and distinctly characterizing the individual performing the narrative function" (Riggan 27). It was, in other words, only slowly that the duplicitous nature of a fictional voice addressing the reader could come into conscious aesthetic play for the reader. Of doubtless relevance here is that sixteenth- and seventeenth-century (and of course later) Europe hardly considered prose fiction to deserve the levels of artistic craft and of reader attention that we today assume as a matter of course. Subversion survives only inconspicuously.

In addition, French literary taste even in presumedly frivolous prose fiction seems to have conspired to marginalize even further the fictional first-person. As Jean Rousset in *Narcisse Romancier* reminds us, seventeenth-century prose fiction in which one would expect to encounter first-person intrusions studiously avoided them at first (but not for long):

> On connaît le système qui domine la plus grande partie du XVIIe siècle, de l'*Astrée* à *Clélie* et à *Zaïde*: une structure rayonnante produite par l'insertion, sur l'axe central, d'une série d'épisodes intercalés racontant le passé d'un héros survenant. Si le récit premier reste constamment fidèle à la forme externe (3e personne), il devrait en être autrement de ces récits latéraux et rétrospectifs qui ont pour fonction de rendre compte des événements antérieurs tels qu'ils ont été vécus par les divers protagonistes, au fur et à mesure de leur apparition; on s'attend à un foisonnement autobiographique. La réalité est assez différente; la plupart des romanciers s'ingénient à éluder le *je* que le système d'insertions qu'ils pratiquent semble pourtant leur prescrire. (Rousset 49-50) [18]

---

[18] The problem did not go unnoticed at the time, as Rousset's quotation from Boileau proves: "Vous voyez bien que vous ne saviez pas son histoire [Cyrus's]. Mais faites approcher son écuyer Feraulas. Il ne demande pas mieux que de vous la con-

It was precisely this reluctance to speak of the self on the part of *personnages bien élevés* that contributed to entrenching the convention of perfect memory, whereby a story about a third person is relayed with unquestionable accuracy, as for example in the voices of dutiful servants endowed with prodigious memory and unfailing appreciation of the innermost thoughts of their more refined and delicate masters.

But even when French *bienséances* came to tolerate and then cultivate use of the first-person, the impressive examples of Boccaccio and his imitators Chaucer and Marguerite de Navarre served to limit its impact even when it did appear, for they had created authoritative precedents, that is, successful conventions, whereby framed autobiographical narrative does not raise issues of narrative reliability. As Showalter claims in his study of the evolution of the French novel from 1641-1782:

> The device of frame narration had a strong tradition leading up to 1713: *The Decameron, The Canterbury Tales, The Heptameron,* are well-known frame narratives while . . . Segrais's *Nouvelles Françoises* and Subligny's *La Fausse Clélie* had adopted the technique. In most of these works, the tales are completely independent of the frame situation, which serves as a pretext, but little more. The personalities of the narrators may be reflected in the tales they tell, and the frame situation may bear a thematic relationship to the stories, but these links had always been subtle and generally inessential. (Showalter 213-14).

Such examples provided reassuring frames for relayed stories in which, Riggan (like Stanzel above) finds, "the narrator was closely and often even expressly identified with the author" (Riggan 27), identified that is with a voice of absolute authority and reliability, one not to be questioned.

A similar historical impediment to the realization of the fictional first-person's potential for raising issues of reliability lies in appeals that were made to the prestige of writers such as Homer and Virgil. Because novelists were, as we have seen, under attack in a world

---

ter. Il sait par coeur tout ce qui s'est passé dans l'esprit de son maître et a tenu un registre exact de toutes les paroles que ce maître a dites en lui-même depuis qu'il est au monde . . ." (Boileau, *Dialogue des héros de romans* [éd. Pléiade des *Oeuvres complètes*, Paris, 1966], 456, in Rousset 51).

where a classic antecedent could be a weighty matter indeed, they claimed as their authorizing model the respected epic poem (May, 33), a genre that allows an absolutely reliable authorial voice to relay a story by a fictional character, such as Odysseus's own account of his adventures to the Phaeacians in Book VII of the *Odyssey*, and Aeneas's own narrative in books II and III of Virgil's masterpiece.

The foregoing aspects of a key part of the history of the texts loosely called "novels" are, moreover, compatible with the battle over the metaphysics of presence. It now seems apparent that this genre of newness has always been open to infinite innovation, infinite reworking of past materials to new purposes.[19] Or as Boileau put it in *L'Art poétique*, comprehensively and even more rightly than he supposed, "Dans un roman frivole aisément tout s'excuse" (Chant III, 119). Does that excused *tout* not open the novel ultimately to a freely fluid, endlessly evanescent, ever challenged and challenging present, that is, to a "novel," anti-canonical present? In short, does not "newness" as practiced in the novel and conceived of in modern culture have affinities with Derridian *différance*, is the novel not the genre par excellence of *différance*?[20] No wonder then that earlier thinkers representative of, and secure in, their times attacked novels as being a threat to their aesthetic and moral values.[21]

---

[19] "The house of fiction has in short not one window, but a million – a number of possible windows not to be reckoned, rather; every one of which has been pierced, or is still pierceable, in its vast front, by the need of the individual vision and by the pressure of the individual will" (Henry James, "Preface" to *The Portrait of a Lady*, in Davis 4).

[20] "The term *différance* . . . alludes to [the] undecidable, nonsynthetic alternation between the perspectives of structure and event. The verb *différer* means to differ and to defer. *Différance* sounds exactly the same as *différence*, but the ending *ance*, which is used to produce verbal nouns, makes it a new form meaning 'difference-differing-deferring.' *Différance* thus designates both a 'passive' difference already in place as the condition of signification and an act of differing which produces differences. An analogous English term is *spacing*, which designates both an arrangement and an act of distribution or arranging. Derrida occasionally uses the corresponding French term *espacement*, but *différance* is more powerful and apposite because *différence* has been a crucial term in the writings of Nietzsche, Saussure, Freud, Husserl, and Heidegger. Investigating systems of signification, they have been led to emphasize difference and differentiation, and Derrida's silent deformation of the term, as well as showing that writing cannot be seen as simply the representation of speech, makes apparent the problem that both determines and subverts every theory of meaning" (Culler 97). See also Derrida, "la Différance" 43-68, in *Théorie d'ensemble*.

[21] Bakhtin had stimulating insights in this area. While his definition of 'novel' is an idiosyncratic, elusive one that evolved over the course of his long life of schol-

No wonder pioneer novelists sought protection in duplicitous prefaces and exaggerated, ill-founded appeals to classical antecedents: their anarchic genre could not help but be an assault on past-oriented certitudes and fixities that were geared to the continuity of stable being, not to the fits and starts of evolutionary becoming, either on an artistic or philosophic level.

In addition, to put the focus back on the first-person sub-genre within the amorphous genre of the threatening novel, is it mere coincidence that our uncertain contemporary culture, continuing the post-Renaissance penchant for individualism and for preoccupation with the complex, shifting self, shares with the late seventeenth century a preference for novels uttered by an "I," a period that prominently both defended and questioned individualism and the period that saw the rise of first-person narrative? ("Notre roman moderne, comme celui du XVIIe siècle, est dans une très large mesure un roman de la première personne," Rousset 9). Our own involvement and preoccupation with the "I" needs no elaboration, but regarding the seventeenth century's, let us recall that this period saw, to list just a few examples, the popularity of fictional and then factual autobiography, that it saw the "I" sundered for some time to come from the material world in the Cartesian *cogito* (a rift sustained in the philosophic subjectivism of the rationalists Spinoza, Leibnitz, Wolff, of the empiricists Locke, Berkeley, Hume, and only warily reconciled on up to our own time through the still influential Kant). The seventeenth century saw as well Pascal try to reflect the fractious, fractured, impermanent workings of the "I" in the studied disorder and fragmentation of *Pensées*.

---

arship, it is safe to say that he too understood the novel, the "developing genre," the "genre of becoming" (Bakhtin, *Dialogic Imagination* 7, 22). So he too saw it as a serious threat to neo-classical attempts to affirm timeless values based on authority, and indeed subversive of all historical attempts to impose centering ideology: "The novel is the expression of a Galilean perception of language, one that denies the absolutism of a single and unitary language – that is, that refuses to acknowledge its own language as the sole verbal and semantic center of the ideological world. . . . The novel begins by presuming a verbal and semantic decentering of the ideological world, a certain linguistic homelessness of literary consciousness, which no longer possesses a sacrosanct and unitary linguistic medium for containing ideological thought; it is a consciousness manifesting itself in the midst of social languages that are surrounded by a single [national] language, and in the midst of [other] national languages that are surrounded by a single culture (Hellenistic, Christian, Protestant), or by a single cultural-political world (the Hellenistic kingdoms, the Roman Empire and so forth)" (Bakhtin, *Dialogic Imagination* 366-67).

Some have even argued that the rise of both fictional and autobiographical first-person narrative was in response to the very anxieties about the status of the self:

> First-person novels and autobiographies are, among other things, an answer to the doubts raised by empiricists about the very existence of the self. Tying up in a causal plot – that is, in a possible "story" – multiple moments of his past, the author unites the unrelated dots of his former existence into a continuous line that reaches the present. While writing a past for himself, he recovers consciousness of his self. Thus, after receiving from the author (*je*) the gift of existence, the autobiographical character or hero (*moi*) repays the author by returning to him the gift with good interest, enabling him to say: "I remember, therefore I am."[22] (Fido 178)

Whatever the deepest causes, we can be sure from contemporary observations that the favorable reception of first-person narratives lay in what was perceived at the time to be a heightened sense of reality: "... le transfert de l'instance narrative aux acteurs eux-mêmes favorise, grâce à la proximité accrue du lecteur et des événements racontés, l'illusion de réalité ..." (Rousset 113).

The ideological implications of first-person narration are rich and widely recognized indeed. Stanzel so reminds us (125-26) in referring first to the arguments of Robert Weimann,[23] then to Sartre's attacks on François Mauriac in *Qu'est-ce que la littérature?*, and finally to David Lodge's essay on Muriel Spark. Stanzel quotes Lodge, who puts it broadly:

> ... it is no coincidence that the convention of the omniscient and intrusive narrator in fiction (of which Fielding [1707-1754]

---

[22] This could apply to Gide, who suffers from classic causes of narcissism, anxieties about the existence of self. It could also help explain Michel's need to narrate. Having engaged in the search for his 'self' precisely because he was troubled by a sense of its absence, at the tragic conclusion of the events (before narration) he was still confused and empty. Narration of events from his recent past could have lured him on, in the hope that there was a retrospective self to have experienced those events, or at the very least that to narrate is to be. The section below on the palimpsest will have more to say about the role of absence in Michel's personality.

[23] "Erzählerstandpunkt und 'Point of View.' Zur Geschichte und Ästhetik der Perspektive im englischen Roman," in *Zeitschrift für Anglistik und Amerikanistik* 10 (1962): 369-416.

was a supreme exponent) began to lose favor at about the time that Nietzsche announced the death of God, or that most of the significant modern novelists who have persevered with this convention have been professed Christians. (Lodge 119)

Furthermore, to the extent that the framed first-person narrative functions as a long quotation, it ceases being a fixed, serene product, becoming instead an uncertain, uneasy process, i.e., disturbing to received attitudes:

> La citation est un fait de langage: la forme simple d'une relation interdiscursive de répétition. Une telle description, obtenue au terme d'une brève exploration des cas de répétition dans le langage, est en contradiction avec la définition courante des dictionnaires: "passage rapporté d'un auteur ou d'un personnage célèbre". C'est là un effet de la canonisation métonymique, qui confond dans la citation la production et le produit. Le produit (un passage rapporté, un énoncé répété) est tenu pour immédiatement donné, l'acte de production (le rapportage) est passé sous silence, comme s'il était idéalement transparent et idéologiquement neutre. (Compagnon 55)

Enormously provocative epistemological and metaphysical possibilities, then, that are threatening to the traditional ideological fabric of both the seventeenth and twentieth centuries, are raised by the novel in general:

> The one general statement that can be made about the novel is that it is always in some ways vitally associated with the problem of reality. Historically, it is an extremely sensitive barometer reflecting every concern with the nature of the 'real,' every question or doubt as to its authenticity. (Holdheim 88)

Those threatening possibilities are easily exacerbated in the subcategory that constitutes relayed first-person novels. One can easily sense in them for instance that the "I" is caught up in an elusive verbal chain, that our access to ourselves, and perhaps to being itself is somehow inherently indirect. In this, such narrative may have been guided ever so subtly by intellectual currents first channelled by pioneering philosophers. For instance, notwithstanding Descartes's basing certitude on the intuition of the thinking self, the resulting mind-body dualism implied by his popular and influential philosophy removed the self from easy contact with more concrete-seeming corporeality. It is in a relayed voice that the self can find and express that distant, more tentative status vis-à-vis the object of thought and language. Writing in France about a century after the publication of the *Discours de la méthode*, Hume pressed suppositions of his Empiricist predecessors, presumably at a far cry from Idealist positions. Nonetheless, he used his ideas on constant conjunction and imagination to much the same effect, undermining received ideas on the very idea of identity itself:

> The whole of this doctrine leads us to a conclusion, which is of great importance in the present affair, viz. that all the nice and subtle questions concerning personal identity can never possibly be decided, and are to be regarded rather as grammatical than as philosophical difficulties. Identity depends on the relations of ideas; and these relations produce identity, by means of that easy transition they occasion. But as the relations, and the easiness of the transition may diminish by insensible degrees, we have no just standard by which we can decide any dispute concerning the time when they acquire or lose a title to the name of identity. All the disputes concerning the identity of connected objects are merely verbal, except so far as the relation of parts gives rise to some fiction or imaginary principle of union, as we have already observed. (Hume, vol. 1, Part IV, Section VI, 248)

His attack stands comparison to the radical implications of relayed narrative. So at key moments of its formation, the modern received notion of the individual was accompanied prominently and dialectically by an artistic form that, in keeping with philosophical developments, implicitly challenged the self both as working reality and concept. Possibilities such as these are unbearable in a popular genre – unless readers can ignore them thanks to reassuring conventions such as that of "faithful memory" which offers certainty, stability, and direct contact with a would-be unitary, uncomplicated self.

Or, to consider an entirely different tack, it does not seem inconsequential that the tone and some of the themes of many early attacks on the novel find an echo in critiques of, for example, Derrida and Lacan.

To return now to the main subject, how then does this bear on *L'Immoraliste* (and *mutatis mutandis*, and subsequently, on *La Porte étroite* and *La Symphonie pastorale*)? Even a brief consideration of factors behind historical responses to the novel and to the relayed version of first-person narratives intimates that ideological issues involving change, self, and individualism – issues that preoccupied Gide, and no where more than in *L'Immoraliste* – are tightly bound up with the genesis and functioning of relayed narrative. In other words, the narrative structure of this book is neither a flaw (as Ireland and Pierre Lafille, for example, have maintained) nor a storytelling convenience of incidental importance. It is instead an historically resonant embodiment of central problems represented by the book, or to put it even more accurately and "aesthetically," it is the producer of the book's issues, indeed, of the book itself as we experience it.

> Genres (of literature and speech) throughout the centuries of their life accumulate forms of seeing and interpreting particular aspects of the world. For the writer-craftsman the genre serves as an external template, but the great artist awakens the semantic possibilities that lie within it. (Bakhtin, *Speech Genres and Other Late Essays* 5)

In *L'Immoraliste*, then, Gide awakened the semantic possibilities that had been lying suppressed within framed narrative since its rise.

### C) *New Critical Space*

Another benefit of not dismissing the value and impact of the framing text is to open up new critical space, for the frame contains precious hints about the first narrator's personality, that is, about the filter through which Michel's story has passed. Significantly and, in the end not surprisingly, one can discern important parallels between the personalities of the two men. These parallels, to be developed below, have the important effect of undoing to a significant degree our earlier *mise en question* of previous readings of *L'Immoraliste*. Instead of being left theoretically suspect, they will be seen simply to acquire a necessary caveat. On the one hand, if the two men are similar and if one sensibly assumes good faith on the part of the devoted friend-amanuensis, it becomes easy to accept the friend's version as a heart-felt reflection of Michel's words that is accurate in spirit at least. On the other hand, similarity not being identity and good faith in reporting not being total recall, one can never be sure where in the relayed text the line between the expression of the two voices can be drawn, and so one must be content with provisional instead of certain readings. That is to say, one must be content with readings that now have to accommodate critical *disponibilité*, readings that are made more consistent with Gide's values – which is the way it should have been all along anyway. We will now consider the parallels between Michel and his friend that allow confidence – but only provisional confidence – in the text.

First, adolescent relationships seem vital for both Michel and his friend. In showing how Michel can be viewed as experiencing a "generativity crisis," (that is, facing the psychological question "whether he will remain like a child, or follow his parents in orderly succession by raising children of his own," Porter, "The Generativity Crisis" 60), Laurence Porter observes that:

> Uneasy with the outcome [after the sacrifice of his career and possessions, and after the death of his wife, Michel] reactivates an adolescent pact and summons three school friends from distant lands to hear him. This narrative framework has been called awkward and artificial [by Lafille, *André Gide Romancier*, 23]. On the contrary, it is in keeping with the situation for Michel to revive adolescent relationships, dominant in his emotional life before his marriage. (Porter, "Generativity" 67)

But a pact is plural, and Michel was not the only one of his group of *anciens collégiens* to feel the pull of adolescent friendship, the appeal of which endured beyond school days. Addressing his brother, the narrator states: "Tu sais quelle amitié de collège, forte déjà, mais *chaque année grandie* [my emphasis], liait Michel à Denis, à Daniel, à moi. Entre nous quatre une sorte de pacte fut conclu . . ." (I, 369). The fact, moreover, that the three friends, "quittant tout" (I, 370) *à la Dumas*, did not hesitate to come running from afar at Michel's appeal to a bond formed long ago suggests that their adolescent relationship may have exercised, and indeed continued to exercise, a vital role in the emotional life of each of them. Michel at least concludes as much: "Mes chers amis, je vous savais fidèles" (I, 372). The narrator would seem all the more susceptible to the charms of the past evoked by the pact, since he, like the confused Michel, does not give the impression of having a distinct idea about what constitutes happiness for an adult: "Je ne suis ni triste, ni gai; l'air d'ici vous emplit d'une exaltation très vague et vous fait connaître un état qui paraît aussi loin de la gaieté que de la peine; peut-être que c'est le bonheur" (I, 369).

To the extent that Michel is undergoing an identity crisis,[24] the fact of the frame allows us to reckon that, *mutatis mutandis*, the crisis may be echoed within the narrator. (Unless of course, and very strictly speaking, it is not the other way around.) Let us consider, for example, the first sentences of *L'Immoraliste*. As was indicated earlier, we are left to believe that it was the powerful brother who originally wanted and asked for a written account of Michel's last three years: "Oui, tu le pensais bien: Michel nous a parlé, mon cher frère. Le récit qu'il nous fit, le voici. Tu l'avais demandé; je te l'avais promis; mais à l'instant de l'envoyer, j'hésite encore . . ." (I, 369). The (Racinian?) "Oui" that opens both his letter and the book, along with the imperfect "pensais" and the pluperfect "avais demandé, avais promis," evoke an entire earlier story, one in which, we may say with confidence, the narrator did not play the most satisfying role. The stark juxtaposition of the forms of *demander* and *promettre* in staccato phrases, and the tension between the narrator's hesitation to send off the letter on the one hand and the pressure that he feels to comply with his brother's wishes on the other, suggest the authority exercised by the impatient *Président du Conseil*. He is the one after all who, as the narrator compliantly indicates, is going to settle the question of Michel's future ("nous attendons ta réponse" I, 367). The potential for sibling tension seems high.

There is as well the following statement to take into account: ". . . lors [du] dernier passage [de Michel] à Paris, Denis était en

---

[24] Defined in the following terms by Porter: "That his father has made Michel's choices for him postpones but also intensifies his identity crisis. Erik Erikson pithily explains that this 'time of breakdown' and of 'acute identity diffusion' 'usually becomes manifest at a time when the young individual finds himself exposed to a combination of experiences which demand his simultaneous commitment to *physical intimacy*, . . . to decisive *occupational choice*, to *energetic competition*, and to *psychosocial self-definition*' (emphasis Erikson's) [Erik. H. Erikson, "The Problem of Ego Identity," in his *Identity and the Life Cycle. Selected Papers* (in *Psychological Issues* I, no. 1, 1959), p. 123]" (Porter, "Generativity" 59).

Grèce, Daniel en Russie, moi retenu, tu le sais, auprès de notre père malade" (*I*, 370). The least that can be said about this sentence is that its beginning shows how much a proclivity the four friends have for traveling, a proclivity, first of all, that would explain why the narrator seems to know Italy well ("[Michel's village] perche au haut d'un roc comme certains bourgs de l'Ombrie" *I*, 70) and why all of them had abandoned Paris for an extended time prior to Michel's return there with his wife (*I*, 422). Second, in its implication of romantic wanderlust, the proclivity would reinforce the impression that adolescent drives have been slow to leave the pact members. But what invites special attention is the end of the sentence: "moi retenu, tu le sais, auprès de notre père malade." An illness necessitating the presence of a son who would apparently much rather be off traveling is serious, serious enough to be – or to have already been – the harbinger of the death of his father. Michel's narrative of course gets its initial emotional thrust from his own father's death. Furthermore, our narrator – a man emotionally inclined to forestall the onset of adulthood and for whom a father's declining health cannot help but stir up awareness of the threat of death that grows with adulthood – must listen to his friend tell at length how death touched him with its wing (*I*, 380) and how it finally took away his young wife. Because of his father's ill health and possible death, then, the friend has been prepared to experience especially intense emotional resonance with Michel, already something of a soul-mate for him, raising the possibility that in the final analysis the health-illness dualism found by Fortier slides over from single to shared textual genesis. (In passing we should underline the significance of this for narrative reliability: it suggests that we are dealing with a narrator touched by deep, unsettling anxieties, that is, a narrator far removed from the sort of objective serenity presumably required for the flawless relaying of Michel's account that is taken as a given by traditional criticism.)

The words "tu le sais" tease with further, more fascinating implications. Since the letter's recipient – the narrator's brother – obviously must know about the father's illness, what point can there be in mentioning it? If we seek an answer within the possibilities permitted by the traditional assumption that Michel's text is the independent main text, then the preliminary, secondary frame may for instance introduce themes to be developed later – in this case threatened health – but may not challenge narrative priorities by becoming the focus of the scrupulously attentive reading that Gide's texts, that is, "main texts," deserve.²⁵ Within the framework of traditional critical practices, the words "moi retenu [etc.]," then, would be addressed more to the reader than redundantly to the narrator's already informed brother, allowing Gide to start developing his themes. But given all the preceding arguments about the primacy of the frame, we may pause to pay more attention to this redundancy for its own sake. Why repeat to a brother something that is only too well known, unless the narrator feels prompted to stress a point? Although inclined, as we have seen, to indulge in wanderlust like his four friends, the somewhat immature narrator had been obliged to stay put, all alone apparently, with an ailing father, presumably because his highly placed, powerful brother ("La haute position que t'ont valu tes grands mérites, le pouvoir que tu tiens . . ." *I*, 369) was busier than his "frivolous" brother, too busy at any rate to attend to a sick, possibly dying father. The words "tu le sais" would seem in this light then to be coming from pique and maybe resentment, a possible residue of fraternal rivalry. Furthermore, those feelings may well contribute to the formal, perhaps even frosty, character of the opening of the highly personal and unusual letter, a formality hardly required under the circumstances, however powerful the brother: "A MONSIEUR D. R., Président du Conseil; . . . mon cher frère" (*I*, 369). (The need of the reader to know something about this brother could have of course been just as easily served at other junctures, e.g, by fleshing out the later "le pouvoir que tu tiens" with "en tant que Président du Conseil.") In short, just as Michel in his "generativity crisis" was struggling with paternal authority over his identity, so too one can conceive how the narrator would be caught up in a psychological struggle with his brother who, because he is a *président de conseil* recognized by the four "boys" as the final arbiter of Michel's fate, stands out as the father figure par excellence of *L'Immoraliste*.²⁶

---

[25] See for example in "The Artistry of Gide's Onomastics," Pasco and Rollman's argument for the level of attention called for just by Gide's use of names.

[26] "Que signifient . . . ces initiales: *D.R.*? Doit-on y attacher une signification, ou conclure que le choix est totalement arbitraire – conclusion hâtive à mon sens étant donné la très grande attention qu'apporte Gide à *tous* les détails dans la composition de ses romans. . . . Monsieur D.R., ne serait-ce pas à l'occasion, *Deus Rex*, véritable président du Conseil, à qui l'on demande d'intervenir du haut de son pouvoir pour sauver une pauvre âme qui s'est fourvoyée aux enfers? Dans la Bible, l'Eternel

Finally, the similarity of the two voices suggested by the parallels between Michel and his friend becomes almost graphic at the end of the text, which does not at all resemble the misleading beginning, where the transition between the frame and the narrative is made to seem clear, through the printing layout. The opening frame and the beginning of Michel's story, separate and distinct in appearance, occur on different pages, and are marked off as well by suspension points and the title "PREMIERE PARTIE." But the deceptive impression of difference created at the beginning is less pronounced at the end, where one could expect the closing of the frame to stand out neatly from the end of Michel's tale. On the third from last page, expectations are initially raised by means of spacing thanks to which and following which Michel's self-conscious formal closing of his story abruptly presents itself ("J'ai fini de vous raconter mon histoire . . ." etc. *I*, 470). Following that, however, instead of distinction, one gets an indecisive blending. The two different narrative threads of the frame and tale are both taken up again, but run together without any sharp physical separation and with Michel's last comments enveloping those of the framer, and not vice versa. So as they both fall into silence, the two voices graphically show themselves to be what narrative structure, psychological parallels, and the narrator's sense of being an involved accomplice suggested they were all along, that is, very similar, but commingled and confused in their priority.

D) *Paradigmatic Value of the Frame in* L'Immoraliste

The indecisive status of Michel's relayed narrative leads in turn to an appreciation of the important paradigmatic value of framed narratives. Consider the illustration that they offer of what Frank Stanzel, in his magisterial *A Theory of Narrative*, has called *Mittelbarkeit* or "mediacy" (Stanzel 4). The distinguished German critic determines that mediacy characterizes and influences *any* narrative

---

parle du milieu du tourbillon, rappelle son serviteur à l'ordre et le restitue dans ses biens. Une telle solution est-elle envisageable pour *L'Immoraliste?* L'hypothèse est bien tentante lorsqu'on songe aux analogies bibliques – Pierre, le psalmiste, Job, et elle rentre parfaitement d'ailleurs dans les structures binaires du roman, dans la série d'oppositions qui sont soigneusement mises en évidence . . ." ( Oliver 46-47).

and that *every* narration can reach a reader only through a mediator, constituting:

> a sort of analogue to our [post-Kantian] experience of reality in general: [and here he quotes Käte Friedemann] "'the narrator' is the one who evaluates, who is sensitively aware, who observes. He symbolizes the epistemological view familiar to us since Kant that we do not apprehend the world in itself, but rather as it has passed through the medium of an observing mind. In perception, the mind separates the factual world into subject and object." (Stanzel 4)

We have here of course a philosophical version of Booth's narratological observation that each literary work is the product of an "implied author" (Booth, 71-77), and perhaps even of Compagnon's contention that all literature is ultimately quotation. Michel Butor gets at mediacy in the simplest language of all:

> Le monde, dans sa majeure partie, ne nous apparaît que par l'intermédiaire de ce qu'on nous en dit: conversations, leçons, journaux, livres, etc. Très vite, ce que nous voyons de nos yeux, ce que nous entendons ce nos oreilles, ne prend son sens qu'à l'intérieur de ce concert. (Butor 88)

However one couches such an understanding, a framed narrative such as *L'Immoraliste*, forthright and consequent in its mediacy, advances the insight by embodying it most concretely.

Narrative framing has psychological implications as well. To the extent that Heidegger and Lacan, for example, are correct in asserting language's power over us,[27] and to the extent that a text like Michel's framed account is mimetic, it offers a figuration of our

---

[27] "Man acts as if he were the shaper and master of language, while it is language which remains mistress of man.... For in fact it is language that speaks. Man begins speaking and man only speaks to the extent that he responds to, that he corresponds with language, and only in so far as he hears language addressing, concurring with him. Language is the highest and everywhere the foremost of those assents which we human beings can never articulate solely out of our own means" (Martin Heidegger, "... Dichterisch Wohnet der Mensch..." [1954], in Steiner x-xi).

"Le sujet aussi bien, s'il peut paraître serf du langage, l'est plus encore d'un discours dans le mouvement universel duquel sa place est déjà inscrite à sa naissance, ne serait-ce que sous la forme de son nom propre" (Lacan 251-52).

very persons that, like his at least in this, are accessible to the mind primarily as the narratives that our and others' voices allow them to become. Etymology is pertinent here. In his book *The Literary Persona*, Robert C. Elliot has marveled that the word, "person," "the term incorporating the moral essence of human beings" (Elliot 19) should come from the Latin *persona* (in turn borrowed, perhaps from the Etruscans), meaning the mask an actor wore on stage. Elliot quite rightly cautions his readers to remember that masks are mysterious things. In early Greek and Roman theater, and even today in so-called primitive societies, one puts on a mask less to hide identity than to become – not just to illustrate but to become – a mediator with a higher reality (Elliot 21-23), and perhaps even in fact to become the higher reality itself. So the mask is not a obvious matter, and neither are language or a person. But at the origin of the word for our personhood stands the metaphor – the mini-story – of a mediating mask, of a theatrical role, a theatrical story. Etymologically at least, to be a *person* is to put on an already scripted part. The question is: who or what does the scripting? A framed narrative suggests that, our efforts notwithstanding, the "lines" are not directly ours.

Both epistemologically and psychologically, then, framed narratives in general incarnate mediacy, and so illustrate the feature found by Stanzel to touch all narratives. It may, moreover, be precisely the framed narrative's paradigmatic value as such an incarnation that explains its perennial appeal, an appeal that might otherwise seem curious. As Paul Hazard has wondered in his study of the crisis in modern European awareness:

> La recette est toujours la même: on commence par l'histoire d'un manuscrit, transmis ou retrouvé miraculeusement: d'où vient que cette fiction n'a jamais cessé de séduire les écrivains, et qu'ils la reprennent effrontément les uns après les autres comme si elle était toujours fraîche? (Hazard vol. 1, 43)

In any case, mediacy is necessarily productive of uncertain narrative as it implies that access to any text (and so – in our language-based experience – to knowledge of reality and to self-definition) is, at a minimum, at one remove.

But these examples of paradigmatic value are illustrated not only in *L'Immoraliste* but also in many other framed accounts. What should especially interest us is what sets *L'Immoraliste* apart, namely, the way in which it gives the paradigm a characteristically Gidean twist. The twist lies exactly in the trait that typifies Gide and his works, *disponibilité*, the willful refusal to renounce for the sake of mere consistency the riches to be found alternately and alternatively in opposed, incompatible experiences. By pressing the frame for an appropriate global reading strategy, we will come to hear this call to refusal.

In spite of the earlier demonstration that *L'Immoraliste* is polyphonic, I personally have found it impossible to read it consistently and exclusively as such. True, I can at moments refuse to read steadily, and I can pause reflectively over words, or sentences, or even paragraphs in order to pick over them as relayed, double-voiced expressions. I am, moreover, certainly obliged infrequently but systematically to recognize the voice of the framer in the studied architecture created by the regular direct intrusions of the headings dividing the book into three parts with chapter sub-divisions. But if I yield to the urge to read on for any length at all, try as I might to focus on Michel's narrative as a necessarily imperfect reconstruction emanating and inseparable from his friend's voice, I inevitably fail: as I read the friend's version of Michel's story in any sustained, page-turning rhythm, I quickly and repeatedly yield to the impression of listening only to *Michel's* voice. Is the readerly habit of inference so strong, or is the very nature of language so inferential, that I am incapable of reading a first-person narrative without trying to construct an "I" to take responsibility for it? Whatever the case may be, if my failure to read what I know to be a polyphonic text as anything other than monophonic, derives from a quality in the text and not from my own shortcomings as a reader (and I assuredly am not alone in my monophonic reading, as even a perfunctory reading of the scholarship demonstrates), and if we accept that hundreds of earlier, satisfying studies of *L'Immoraliste* are not worthless for being logocentric, the creation we call "Michel" is then too captivating and enticing to be denied immediacy by the logic of the narrative structure.[28] David H. Walker has reached a similar reading regarding all of Gide's fictions:

---

[28] The seductive power of a logically inaccessible voice is hardly a discovery of Gide's. There are three philosophers – Plato, Descartes, and Kant – mentioned or alluded to in *L'Immoraliste*, each of whom put material reality into a situation not

> Il est vrai que l'écriture [of Gide] accuse sa propre incapacité à saisir le réel; mais elle aura quand même pour fonction d'inviter le lecteur à reconnaître, au-delà de l'écriture du personnage, un vécu qui lui a servi de prétexte tout en échappant à sa prise. Gide se donne pour but, non point simplement de communiquer l'impossibilité de récupérer tel ou tel détail, mais de créer, à partir de stratégies narratives particulières, ce que j'appellerais un "effet de référence," tout comme le linguiste Guillaume a baptisé de l'étiquette "effet de sens" ce mouvement de pensée qui précède l'établissement d'un sens particulier. Somme toute, l'écriture chez Gide ressemble au "quartz étrange" dont sont faits les boutons de manchette qui figurent dans *Les Caves du Vatican*. D'une part, cette "agate embrouillardée . . . ne laissait rien voir au travers d'elle"; d'autre part, pourtant, le narrateur précise qu'elle *paraît* transparente. (Walker, "L'Écriture et le Réel dans les fictions d'André Gide" 127)

I propose, then, that formally *L'Immoraliste* establishes initial conditions prohibiting the illusion of direct contact with the main character, only to go on to generate and sustain powerfully precisely that illusion. In a way, this confirms an enduring article by Elaine Cancalon ("Création et Destruction"), who demonstrated that the narrators of *Isabelle* and the three *récits* under discussion in this book are riven by the pull between creation and destruction. I would like to think that these pages make it plausible to suggest that her demonstration can be applied to *Gide*'s narrative strategies as well, that what she calls creation/destruction I would call mimetic illusion/narrative subversion of illusion.

We can be sure, moreover, that Gide was aware that the structure which he chose raises such issues: in an earlier version he had allowed the secondary narrator three months to write down Michel's account, and even more significantly, Gide had him recognize the muddying effects of narrative relaying. Whereas the published version reads: "Je t'adresse donc ce récit, tel que Denis,

---

dissimilar to the secondary position of *the* text in Gide's book. (The profound influence of Schopenhauer on Gide suggests how attracted he was to philosophic idealism in general, Angelet, *Symbolisme et Invention* 13-14.) Of those three, the Greek philosopher, in what is perhaps his masterpiece, *The Symposium*, showed impressive imaginative powers indeed in drawing attention to the problems of framed narrative, and was probably the first writer to do so. Plato and Descartes will be discussed more in the pages to come.

Daniel et moi l'entendîmes," an earlier version mentions the *récit* "tel que tous trois nous l'avons dû récrire, hélas! le déformant parfois par oubli, tâchant de lui garder son accent même" (Gide, *Romans* 1520). But the failure to resist Michel in spite of the text's narrative strategy is the sort of result that makes advisable Gide's decision *not* to include the narrator's explicit avowal of inadequacy. That is because the inclusion of words unequivocally expressing mediacy would reduce the impact of Michel's tale by obligating us, in spite of ourselves, to endeavor to fix attention on its inaccessibility. It would then more strongly encourage us to try to resist captivation and to maintain a highlighted distance between ourselves and his voice. While logically more true, it would have been, I would now like to propose, psychologically and linguistically more false.

On the one hand, let us recall that *L'Immoraliste* is an *ironic* treatment of bold individualism. In his attempt to become completely and purely what he called his authentic self,[29] Michel in effect kills his wife without understanding how or why, paradoxically ending up abulic, vacant, bereft of any sense of liberation, and – significantly and ironically – dependent upon his friends. Moreover,

---

[29] It is noteworthy that in one of *L'Immoraliste*'s key passages, Michel's moment of epiphany when he articulates his search for the authentic self, we find a microparallel of the narrative structure, in that he uses the image of the palimpsest, that is, a text contained by another text:

> Après que l'aile de la mort a touché, ce qui paraissait important ne l'est plus; d'autres choses le sont, qui ne paraissaient pas importantes, ou qu'on ne savait même pas exister. L'amas sur notre esprit de toutes connaissances acquises s'écaille comme un fard et, par places, laisse voir à nu la chair même, l'être authentique qui se cachait..................
>
> Et je me comparais aux palimpsestes; je goûtais la joie du savant, qui, sous les écritures plus récentes, découvre, sur un même papier, un texte très ancien infiniment plus précieux. Quel était-il, ce texte occulté? Pour le lire, ne fallait-il pas tout d'abord effacer les textes récents? (Gide 398-99)

Notice how, echoing the message of the narrative structure, Michel compares personality to layers of verbal entities, of texts. While recognizing that the outer ones are acquired and unauthentic, he asserts that inner ones exist independently and that they alone are originary and authentic. So on the one hand, he assumes the inference to be drawn from my understanding of the narrative structure, i.e., that his personality can be seen as a text, but on the other hand he has no sense of the implication (so important to, for instance, Lacan, and probably Bakhtin) that, illusion notwithstanding, the self has no functional social existence, authentic or unauthentic, that is independent of others' language.

In the pages to come, we will return in much greater detail to the image of the palimpsest.

in a no less futile linguistic equivalent of his would-be social individualism, he summons his friends to be present while he and he alone talks in order to tell his story, brooking little conversation, no questioning, no exchange, engaging only in self-statement:

> Michel nous a reçus sans témoigner de joie; très simple, il semblait craindre toute manifestation de tendresse; mais sur le seuil, d'abord, il embrassa chacun de nous trois gravement.
> Jusqu'à la nuit nous n'échangeâmes pas dix paroles....
> Quand ce fut la nuit, Michel dit:
> "Mes chers amis, je vous savais fidèles. A mon appel vous êtes accourus, tout comme j'eusse fait au vôtre. Pourtant voici trois ans que vous ne m'aviez vu. Puisse votre amitié, qui résiste si bien à l'absence, résister aussi bien au récit que je veux vous faire. Car si je vous appelai brusquement, et vous fis voyager jusqu'à ma demeure lointaine, c'est pour vous voir, uniquement, et pour que vous puissiez m'entendre. Je ne veux pas d'autre secours que celui-là : vous parler." (*I*, 371-72)

Nonetheless, just as Michel's social dependency is revealed to be unavoidable, so too is his linguistic dependency: within the fiction, his tale has life only because of his friend, only because it has been communicated through another. The etymology of his Hebrew name notwithstanding ("like God"), he cannot exist self-sufficiently as an independent *Verbum*. Thus, allegorically, his story would seem to affirm that we cannot free ourselves of social and linguistic dependency, being capable instead only of substituting one dependency for another, but in the effort toward independence doing violence to the Other in our lives.

That is on the one hand. But on the other hand, is the lived truth of Michel's sort of independence/dependence that simple, that easily repudiated? Is it not the case, on the contrary, that the sad psychological reality behind individualism is that time and again it generates the illusion of its own possibility? And is it not true also that time and again we yield to the illusion that it is ourselves alone that we express in our utterances? – as if language is not endlessly learned and borrowed from others, sustained and imprinted by others, as if language is not in fact inherently an exercise with others and in otherness itself. How could it *not* be freighted with the Other? It is precisely in developing and foisting on the reader those illusions *while* challenging them structurally, true to *disponibilité*, that *L'Immoraliste* attains full paradigmatic value. To be faithful to the paradox of individualism and of language (and so of first-person narrative) as they are lived in our experience, that is, victoriously seductive but utterly impossible as generally perceived, *L'Immoraliste* virtually requires a framed voice that does not allow attention to be drawn too decisively to its dependency on an enabling context, indeed, that does not allow attention to be fixed on that framed voice's consubstantiality with another voice, even while not repudiating that consubstantiality. Otherwise, *L'Immoraliste* would come across as a *roman à thèse*, a tidy demonstration of a fault held at arm's length and one to be avoided, instead of functioning as an implicating story of how a deceptive quality highly valued in our culture and narratives can become an ironic tool of misleading and destructive tendencies.

It is probably not coincidental that *L'Immoraliste* is also about suppressed sexuality leading up to death. If we project Freud's equivalency of pleasure-seeking and the death wish ("Beyond the Pleasure Principle") on to sexuality and death as operative in *L'Immoraliste* (and in much else of Gide's), would the equivalency not also embrace its textuality? What I mean is that as readers of the book we are touched by eros and thanatos, in that we are driven by a deluded yearning for *the* definitive text, which would of course be the death of meaning, the death of textuality. And yet, on the other hand, if a text is inaccessible in the fullest sense of that word – and therefore infinitely open to any and all interpretation – meaning and the text would seem to die again, this time in a centrifugal explosion fueled by uncentered personal reader whim.

Let us now consider an additional consequence of consubstantiality of voice: any reading of Michel's text must, upon reflection, *implicitly* take on an unavoidably and thoroughly provisional note, which is of course consonant with *disponibilité*. But that note rings *explicitly* as well, making itself heard in the account (Première Partie, Chapitre VII) of the early results of what Michel was convinced was his new-found capacity for physical-moral vigor. By rights, one would expect the account to be stirring, since it is prefaced lyrically with solar, verdant richness that closes out Chapter Six by describing his naked body after his plunge into an icy pool outside Ravello:

> Vite transi, je quittai l'eau, m'étendis sur l'herbe, au soleil. Là, des menthes croissaient, odorantes; j'en cueillis, j'en froissai les feuilles, j'en frottai tout mon corps humide mais brûlant. Je me regardai longuement, sans plus de honte aucune, avec joie. Je me trouvais, non pas robuste encore, mais pouvant l'être, harmonieux, sensuel, presque beau. (*I*, 402)

But the extremely short Chapter Seven opens immediately thereafter on a dissatisfied tone ("Ainsi me contentais-je . . . d'exercices physiques qui . . . ne me satisfaisaient plus pour eux-mêmes" *I*, 402). It then prepares its central, infelicitous moment by stumbling over Michel's acknowledgment of the silly disproportion ("à vos yeux ridicule peut-être," *I*, 402) between the allegedly monumental cause and the paltry effects: his grandiose "revolutionary new being" managed to . . . discover physical exercise and . . . to cut off its old beard while letting its hair grow long on its head!!! We can certainly sympathize with Michel's befuddled disappointment at this meager outcome. Exercise and cosmetics are poor testimonials to the "actes étonnants" that he was sure could have been performed by his prodigious new self. Why were the actual results so few and superficial? As we shall see below in my Section III, C, on the image of the palimpsest, the explanation is that the "revolutionary new being" is in fact non-existent. Self-delusion about its existence notwithstanding, his own dissatisfaction prompts an assertion that intimates the philosophic crux of the problem:

> Voilà tout ce que mon être neuf, encore désoeuvré, trouvait à faire. Je pensais qu'il naîtrait de lui des actes étonnants pour moi-même; mais plus tard; plus tard, me disais-je, – quand l'être serait plus formé. Forcé de vivre en attendant, je conservais, comme Descartes, une façon provisoire d'agir. (*I*, 403)

One marvels at how Michel's own embarrassing provisionality leads him to Descartes's provisionality, a comparison so appropriate that it is eery. Granted, there are profound differences. Descartes was working within a rigorously analytic approach and not from the emotional flush of a near-death experience like Michel, proceeding from thought and not sensation *cum* barely repressed eroticism. Too, he was seeking to preserve and justify received values not abandon them, etc. Nonetheless, even though Gide's *eiron* does not explore or perhaps even recognize it, Descartes's work had been a keystone in the philosophic construction of modern individualism so important to Michel.[30] Not only that, but it was the father of the *cogito* who fused modern philosophy and Western individualism in the erroneous intuition (central to Michel's experience) that the "I" has existence simultaneous with thought but prior to and autonomous of language. In his intuition of the isolated thinking "I," Descartes fails, among other things, to subject to the *doute méthodique* the very language (a communal, preexistent entity) that allows for the formulation (creation?) of the thinking "I." So unexamined language is inextricably bound up with the very entity that he assumes to discover in an originary intuition. This of course corresponds rather neatly to Michel's assumption of his own verbal independence, the assumption that the narrative frame shows to fail. It is only right that Michel, aspirant to a Cartesian state of intuited independence, has to follow the master in allowing slighted contingency to creep back in through an appeal to the provisional. What better context for an ironic Gidean voice to harken back to fundamental issues of self and language – issues at the heart of the text – than an allusion that ties them in with another Gidean preoccupation, situational ethics? It is done in such a way, moreover, that the pertinent philosophic, linguistic, and moral topics all intersect precisely in provisionality, a condition of *disponibilité*.

The allusion to Descartes is doubly appropriate since Michel's sentence about provisionality can be read as well to evoke the status of the text vis-à-vis the reader. Having created a reading dilemma through its narrative structure that renders the main voice logically inaccessible, the text hints here at a way out consistent with itself. Or to put it exactly as Gide himself did in responding to misguided readings of *L'Immoraliste*: "A vrai dire, en art, il n'y a pas de problèmes – dont l'oeuvre d'art ne soit la suffisante solution" ("Préface" *I*, 367). Faced with the tricky quality of Michel's voice (and of any would-be individual voice), instead of renouncing all possibility of meaning because of hopelessly entangled and receding signifying agents, we may heed the lesson summoned up in Descartes's example by committing ourselves to "une façon provisoire d'agir

---

[30] See for example Lacan: "... le *cogito* philosophique est au foyer de ce mirage qui rend l'homme moderne si sûr d'être soi dans ses incertitudes sur lui-même, voire à travers la méfiance qu'il a pu apprendre dès longtemps à pratiquer quant aux pièges de l'amour propre" (276).

*critique*," that is, "une façon provisoire de lire." We are then liberated from any necessity to identify *the* text, tantamount to a necessity for coming up with *the* reading. The lesson may be practiced, moreover, with little reservation, for – and here we find again the Gidean twist imparted to the paradigmatic values of framed (mediate) narrative – what reading of any narrative, first-person or otherwise, is *not* provisional? To appeal to the famous Heraclitian image (as Gide himself authorizes us to do, since his ars poetica, *Le Traité du Narcisse*, is largely built on it), can we ever come twice to the same verbal flow that is a literary text? So we can accept the pragmatic wisdom of Booth's general "rhetorical dimension" and of the particular convention of perfect memory in dealing with *L'Immoraliste*, the difference being a recognition of how *disponibilité* governs its narrative structure and of how much more willfully arbitrary that recognition requires our critical play to be. The sense is not so much to be found as made – and unmade – in an openness to narrative possibilities.

This of course sets our reading against the very explicit textual values of Plato, the other giant philosopher of presence alluded to – and so sucked into intertextual play – in *L'Immoraliste*. In what is perhaps his masterpiece, *The Symposium* – contested only by *The Republic* (Hamilton, in Plato 526) – Plato was probably the first writer (or philosopher or writer-philosopher) to draw attention – and emphatically at that – to the problems of framed narrative. Apollodorus recounts Aristodemus's recounting of the conversations and speeches that occurred at Agathon's dinner, to which Socrates among others had been invited. The master's speech, moreover, in Chinese box fashion, consisted of his recounting one of the dialogue-lessons given him by Diotima. As if that were not enough to raise the issues arising from narrative relaying, Aristodemus had been hung over when he relayed the tale and Apollodorus is telling his tale a second time, having had the opportunity to get "the story pretty pat" (*Symposium* 174c), that is, having had the opportunity to polish, change, and distort it. Doubtless Plato intended the narrative implications of such a form and situation, since he highlighted them twice ("so far as Aristodemus could remember," *S*, 176a, and "before I [Apollodorus] go on I must make it quite clear that Aristodemus did not pretend to reproduce the various speeches verbatim, any more than I could repeat them word for word as I had them from him," *S*, 178a).

But Plato's game is surely less narratological than philosophical (more narrowly, epistemological). To begin with, the form of *The Symposium* is remarkably appropriate for making the reader experience the indirect, elusive but nonetheless enticing character of the Ideas perceptible behind gross appearances, since the readers are following arguments that engage them, even though those arguments are necessarily transmitted in a form redundantly rendered glaringly imperfect. And then toward the end, the obstreperous crasher Alcibiades, even (more accurately, precisely) with a mind as clouded by alcohol as the minds of most seekers after the Good, the True, and the Beautiful are clouded by mental flabbiness, is made to reaffirm the Platonic insistence on full presence, for he rescues Socrates's thought from the chain of slippery signifiers by simply positing the existence of a securer level of access, one above language:

> Besides, when we listen to anyone else talking, however eloquent he is, we don't really care a damn what he says. But when we listen to you, or to someone else repeating what you've said, even if he puts it ever so badly, and never mind whether the person who's listening is man, woman, or child, we're absolutely staggered and bewitched. And speaking for myself, gentlemen, if I wasn't afraid you'd tell me I was completely bottled, I'd swear on oath what an extraordinary effect his words have had on me – and still do, if it comes to that. For the moment I hear him speak I am smitten with a kind of sacred rage, worse than any Corybant, and my heart jumps into my mouth and the tears start into my eyes – oh, and not only me, but lots of other men. (*S*, 215c-e)

So while we should not at all be surprised to see Michel allude to the two key philosophers of presence whose values would seem to validate his attempt at ontological self-statement, his falling back upon provisionality undoes it all. (So of course does the very fact of intertextuality – textual dependence, as we see next.) By citing derivatively Descartes's telling failure to attain ethical immediacy, he simultaneously underscores his own ethical lack and allows inadvertently reflection about the failed classical and neoclassical metaphysics at work behind his assumption of personal and textual immediacy.

Provisionality, the model of *L'Immoraliste* shows us, is as inevitable in narratives as it is useful for those who would read them accurately.

## III. Contradictions Inherent in the Accessible Voice

Much excellent, enduring work on *L'Immoraliste* has come from critics assuming what Booth calls the "rhetorical dimension" that calls for an accessible text. The preceding pages have tried to show, though, how that work has been flawed by its failure to take into account fundamental problems generated by Gide's narrative strategy. In the following pages, critical strategy will be reversed and the voice of *L'Immoraliste* will be treated as Michel's. Through an appeal to intertextuality and through a detailed exploration of one of the book's decisive images (the palimpsest), it will be shown that, notwithstanding the assumption of an accessible text, "Michel's voice" or "person," under the strain of its inherent contradictions, still fragments into polyphony and constitutive absence. The point of course is not to repudiate "the rhetorical dimension," but rather to use it in a spirit of *disponibilité*, to play it off against its critical opposite in the search for ever richer readings.

### A) *Michel, An Echo of Ménalque*

The above reading of the narrative structure of *L'Immoraliste* depends heavily on the way in which Michel's individualistic voice is undermined by the implications of its being entirely quoted. Among several corroborating features of *L'Immoraliste* (traditionally read) which suggests that the dynamics of quotation remain at the heart of the book no matter what, is one of the emphases made by its architecture (already a reminder of a narrative presence other than Michel's). The center of its ternary geometric structure (i.e., the second of three chapters in the second of three parts) is devoted to incidents dealing essentially with Michel's perplexity about how an individual and a society lives "authentically." Struggling with distaste for the conforming Parisian set that he finds in his salon and with uneasiness over Marceline's pregnancy, he discovers the condition for authenticity to be uniqueness:

> –[The guests in their Paris salon] se ressemblent tous, disais-je [to Marceline]. Chacun fait double emploi. Quand je parle à l'un d'eux, il me semble que je parle à plusieurs.

> —Mais, mon ami, répondait Marceline, vous ne pouvez demander à chacun de différer de tous les autres.
> —Plus ils ressemblent entre eux et plus ils diffèrent de moi.........
> ... [J]e restais un étranger parmi les autres, comme quelqu'un qui revient de chez les morts. Et d'abord je ne ressentis qu'un assez douloureux désarroi; mais bientôt un sentiment très neuf se fit jour. Je n'avais éprouvé nul orgueil, je l'affirme, lors de la publication des travaux qui me valurent tant d'éloges. Etait-ce de l'orgueil, à présent? Peut-être; mais du moins aucune nuance de vanité ne s'y mêlait. C'était, pour la première fois, la conscience de ma valeur propre: ce qui me séparait, me distinguait des autres, importait; ce que personne d'autre que moi ne disait ni ne pouvait dire, c'était ce que j'avais à dire. (*I*, 423-24)

But he gropes after and finally articulates this insight about how essential uniqueness is to authenticity – an insight couched moreover in terms of what he alone could articulate ("ce que personne d'autre que moi ne ... pouvait dire") – only to discover one month later someone else formulating the same thing, after having reached the same conclusion probably much earlier: Ménalque.[31] The renowned outsider provokes within Michel no less confusion than resentment when he declares to him:

> Ce que l'on sent en soi de différent, c'est précisément ce que l'on possède de rare, ce qui fait à chacun sa valeur – et c'est là ce que l'on tâche de supprimer. On imite. Et l'on prétend aimer la vie!
> Je laissais Ménalque parler; ce qu'il disait c'était précisément ce que le mois d'avant, moi, je disais à Marceline; et j'aurais donc dû l'approuver. Pourquoi, par quelle lâcheté l'interrompis-je, et

---

[31] Much the same experience may have befallen Gide vis-à-vis Nietzsche, it appears, shortly before he began writing *L'Immoraliste*: "Nietzsche me rend fou; pourquoi a-t-il eu lieu; j'eusse *follement* voulu l'être; je découvre avec jalousie une à une toutes mes secrètes pensées; je sais bien qu'un temps viendra où je ne serai plus sensible qu'aux divergences et que j'aurai contre lui presque uniquement alors de l'hostilité; mais aujourd'hui je me sens en l'écoutant comme Amphitryon après que Jupiter a passé... On m'accusera plus tard d'avoir été formé par Nietzsche; on dira même que c'est chez lui que j'ai appris l'anti-Wagnerisme etc." (letter to Marcel Drouin, dated only "Perouse 28 mars" and quoted by Ireland, *André Gide* 183, who argues that it was probably written in 1898). Holdheim (58-65), however, sums up admirably reasons for suspecting that Gide may have found it extremely difficult to assess accurately when and how he came to know Nietzsche. For the sake of prudence, then, we should restrict ourselves to saying that Gide *claimed* to see in Nietzsche what Michel saw in Ménalque.

lui dis-je, imitant Marceline, la phrase mot pour mot par laquelle elle m'avait alors interrompu:
  –Vous ne pouvez pourtant, cher Ménalque, demander à chacun de différer de tous les autres. . . . (I, 432)

This act of verbal repetition by Ménalque, already located within the central second chapter of the central second part, must be seen as a key moment, since it overdetermines itself, first by being set off precisely by another verbal repetition (Michel's retorting to Ménalque by quoting verbatim Marceline's objection to his own version of the sentiments expressed by Ménalque). It is then echoed in a strange passage four pages later. In one paragraph of that second moment, prose quotation aspires to an almost incantatory rhythm with the repetition of the words "Ah! Michel, toute joie" and "toujours," the effect of which is immediately extended twice by what is itself an expression of repetition, "est pareille à" (the emphases will be mine):

  –*Ah! Michel, toute joie* nous attend *toujours*, mais veut *toujours* trouver la couche vide, être la seule, et qu'on arrive à elle comme un veuf. – *Ah! Michel! toute joie est pareille à* cette manne du désert qui se corrompt d'un jour à l'autre; elle *est pareille à* l'eau de la source Amélès qui, raconte Platon, ne se pouvait garder dans aucun vase . . . Que chaque instant emporte tout ce qu'il avait apporté.

  Ménalque parla longtemps encore; je ne puis rapporter ici toutes ses phrases; beaucoup pourtant se gravèrent en moi, d'autant plus fortement que j'eusse désiré les oublier plus vite; non qu'elles m'apprissent rien de bien neuf – mais elles mettaient à nu brusquement ma pensée que je couvrais de tant de voiles, que j'avais presque pu l'espérer étouffée. Ainsi s'écoula la veillée. (I, 436-37)

How unique can individualism be when the fiercely counter-culture loner Ménalque is heard explaining himself by quoting the Bible and the author of the *Republic*? If indeed, as Michel himself recognizes, his outlandish friend's lapidary expressions[32] (heard before

---

[32] See also: "Il faut, répondait-il aux insultes, laisser les autres avoir raison, puisque cela les console de n'avoir pas autre chose" (425); "Mais je tiens la sobriété pour une plus puissante ivresse; j'y garde ma lucidité" (426); "C'est à soi-même que chacun prétend le moins ressembler" (431); "Le bonheur ne se veut pas tout fait, mais sur mesure (435)"; "On croit que l'on possède, et l'on est possédé (435)," etc.

his own account was written) revealed his thoughts to him as they engraved themselves on his awareness, to what extent is Michel's account not already an echo? The relaying frame letter doubles an apparently already doubled voice of would-be individualism.

(Like the frame itself, this doubling is not without precedent in Gide's *Le Traité du Narcisse*, in which Narcissus's framed dream takes in the story of a predecessor that is still another would-be individual, Adam, and then the story of the Poet who, like Narcissus, contemplates Paradise. We can ground doubling even more deeply in Gide's work, for from the very start of Gide's literary efforts quoting *was* literature,[33] which explains in part the prominence of quotations in, for example, his first [pseudonymously] published book *Les Cahiers d'André Walter* [containing pages of quotations], and in *La Porte étroite*, a work that takes its title and chief image from a quotation.)

### B) *Michel, An Intertext of Rousseau*

There are numerous ways to demonstrate how *L'Immoraliste*, even logocentrically read, undermines the individualistic voice by means of quotation. But none is more fitting than to consider the characteristically ironic action exerted upon Gide's *récit* by words cited from the French writer most identified with efforts to articulate the individualistic voice, Rousseau. That irony pervades *L'Immoraliste* is certain. This has been convincingly argued by critics such as Robert Goodhand, Allan H. Pasco, Martine Maisani-Léonard, Albert Sonnenfeld, and Monique Yaari who thereby corroborate the judgment of one of the more interesting readers of *L'Immoraliste*, Gide himself who declared (see above, 37) that all his books except *Les Nourritures terrestres* are ironic and that *L'Immoraliste* is a criticism of a certain individualism.

---

[33] "Immediately following her husband's death [in 1880],. . . [Gide's mother] took her son away from school and fled with him to the family home in Rouen. At the Henri Rondeaux' house in the rue de Crosne the boy met again his cousins, the children of his uncle Émile Rondeaux and his wife Mathilde. With the three girls – for he never had much to do with the boys – he embarked on his first literary undertaking: the foundation of a magazine in which the girls could publish their work. Gide tells us that his own contribution was limited to the transcribing of irreproachably classical texts; but his literary vocation had already begun to declare itself, for his unpublished notes for *Si le grain ne meurt* contain, for the year 1881, the mention: 'mes premiers vers' " (Ireland, *Gide* 15).

We should recall that Michel, the pursuer of that individualism, is a paleographer skilled in Latin, Greek, Hebrew, Sanskrit, Persian, and Arabic (*I*, 373); that as a precocious scholar, he had written a respected work on Phrygian religion (*I*, 373); and that he is, as Ménalque characterizes him, an "aveugle érudit," a "gros lecteur" (*I*, 426), comfortable in his explicit references to the Bible (*I*, 397, 467), Homer (*I*, 391, 465), Theocritus (*I*, 398, 462), Plato (*I*, 436-37), Descartes (*I*, 403), and of course to Jean-Jacques Rousseau (*I*, 386). So, in what is not the least of the ironies suffusing his narrative, Michel, this verbal sophisticate by profession and by inclination, claims at the very outset of his story that he wants to – implying indeed that he even can – tell his story "simply": "Souffrez que je parle de moi; je vais vous raconter ma vie, simplement, sans modestie et sans orgueil, plus simplement que si je parlais à moi-même" (*I*, 372).[34]

In its modern form, such a ploy goes back of course to Rousseau, the father of the sort of highly literate, would-be anti-literary self-exploration that Michel ends up practicing in spite of himself. We recall that in the famous *avertissement* and then in the opening paragraph of *Les Confessions*, Rousseau skillfully uses bold rhetoric to make sweeping claims indeed about his uniqueness and sincerity:

> Voici le seul portrait d'homme, peint exactement d'après nature et dans toute sa vérité, qui existe et qui probablement existera jamais. ("Avertissement," in *Les Confessions* 2)

> Je forme une entreprise qui n'eut jamais d'exemple et dont l'exécution n'aura point d'imitateur. Je veux montrer à mes semblables un homme dans toute la vérité de la nature; et cet homme sera moi. (*C*, 3)

---

[34] As if, furthermore, even the adverb "simplement" is clear and self-interpreting. In spite of a syntax in which, at first glance, the other adverbial expressions "sans modestie et sans orgueil" seem to act appositively to clarify, and so to encourage the interpretation of "simplement" to mean "avec simplicité," upon consideration one finds it difficult to eliminate ambiguity: "raconter ma vie simplement" could mean "raconter ma vie sincèrement," or even "raconter ma vie uniquement." See Maisani-Léonard, 79. See also Pasco, "Irony and Art": "The sentence forcefully contradicts the claimed simplicity through the smooth, carefully modulated members, the amplification, the repeated use of *parler*, the conduplication of *simplement*" 189. For a more extended treatment of Michel's artificial language, see Pasco's amplification of his article in his book, *Novel Configurations*.

This of course from a writer who read and knew for example his Augustine, his Montaigne, and perhaps Cardano (Jacques Voisine, "Introduction" ix-xiv, in Rousseau). But since Rousseau insists so absolutely that he has no forerunner and can have no successor,[35] one presses the position logically, and one could maintain that his supposedly unique sincerity in the printed word requires in principle a complete absence of anything literary, that is, of anything verbally imitated or imitable. One could even argue that Rousseau's claim ultimately precludes anything that does not bridge the chasm that the rest of us must know between word on the one hand and "nature"'s truth on the other. Rousseau therefore would have his readers believe that he will attain uniqueness because he alone will be making a "simple" union of word with "natural" truth. In fact, of course, among autobiographies Rousseau's *Confessions* have arguably gone unsurpassed in literariness, that is, in all those qualities that transcend verbal simplicity.

Small wonder and sizeable irony, then, that in *L'Immoraliste* – essentially a relayed confession – we hear Rousseau quoted precisely when Michel feels the need to verbalize the first steps in the discovery of *his* uniqueness. After spending the first chapter covering the consequences of his honeymoon trip – the mysterious tubercular disease that almost killed him – and after spending the second chapter describing the efforts made to regain his health, he devotes the third chapter to his then newfound awareness of the body, an awareness that will play a key role in his burgeoning individualism:

> Je vais parler longuement de mon corps. Je vais en parler tant, qu'il vous semblera tout d'abord que j'oublie la part de l'esprit. Ma négligence, en ce récit, est volontaire; elle était réelle là-bas. Je n'avais pas de force assez pour entretenir double vie; l'esprit et le reste, pensais-je, j'y songerai plus tard, quand j'irai mieux.

---

[35] Another measure of the extent to which *L'Immoraliste* refracts what it encompasses into new patterns of irony is the closed circle of reference created for *Les Confessions* by Michel's name. It had belonged earlier after all to Montaigne, another voice that claimed to be attempting to portray its self exclusively and sincerely to those with whom it felt close. ("C'est icy un livre de bonne foy, lecteur. . . . Je l'ay voué à la commodité particulière de mes parents et amis . . .," Montaigne, "Au Lecteur," in *Oeuvres complètes* 2.) Thus, in the light of *L'Immoraliste*, Rousseau's text, attempting to stand unprecedented and unmatchable, gets taken into a referential loop by the text of a Michel which postdates *Les Confessions* even while setting up echoes that predate them.

> J'étais encore loin d'aller bien. Pour un rien j'étais en sueur et pour un rien je prenais froid; j'avais, comme disait Rousseau, "la courte haleine." .... (I, 386)

While it is true that we are dealing merely with a three-word quotation, as Albert Sonnenfeld has observed: "André Gide, lecteur infatigable! On exagérerait difficilement l'importance des citations et du rôle qu'elles jouent dans son oeuvre.... Or Gide ne choisit que rarement ses citations à la légère ...," (Sonnenfeld, "Baudelaire et Gide," 79). Once accepted for scrutiny, the quotation from *Les Confessions* makes it possible for us to set in motion a process of literary comparison compelling enough to highlight still another irony, but one that stands out even in a book abounding in ironies: by allowing just these three words from Rousseau's autobiography, "la courte haleine," to penetrate his narrative directly, Michel's voice, a voice intent on avoiding literariness and absorbed to the point of blinding distraction in its own individuality and its own uniqueness (I, 423-24, 431-32), allows itself and many of its most important experiences to be turned into intertextual[36] echoes of Rousseau's voice and experiences. (Francis Jammes, although in-

---

[36] Let me note here what is meant in these pages by "intertextual." My definition starts from Gérard Genette's very practical description ("une relation de coprésence entre deux ou plusieurs textes, c'est-à-dire, eidétiquement et le plus souvent, ... une présence effective d'un texte dans un autre," Genette, *Palimpsestes* 8). So I view *Les Confessions* and *L'Immoraliste* as what he would call respectively "hypotexte" and "hypertexte" (Genette, *Palimpsestes* 11). But since, as we saw, Antoine Compagnon has persuasively maintained that the "grafting" of a quotation onto another text initiates within the reader's concept of the source document the dynamics of the potentially infinite regression of interpretants (described by Charles Pierce, Compagnon 60-61), in applying Genette's definition to the quotation from Rousseau, "la courte haleine," I will further assume that the regression sets up a Derridean "coabsence" in it as well. In addition, I presuppose with Michael Riffaterre an active reader for whom "le mode de perception [de l'intertexte] gouverne la fonction cognitive du texte" (Riffaterre, "La Trace de l'intertexte," 4). That implies, as Compagnon puts it, that "il n'est plus possible de parler de la citation pour elle-même, mais seulement de son travail, du travail de la citation" (Compagnon 36).

But Compagnon's perspective has an advantage, I believe, over Riffaterre's, in that it immediately opens up the possibility of reciprocal action between the quotation and the text onto which it has been grafted, an action that allows play as opposed to the necessity implied by Riffaterre's word, "gouverne." The notion of intertextuality as activity does not of course originate with Riffaterre or Compagnon, going back through Julia Kristeva, mother of the term, to at least as far as Mikhail Bakhtin. See Angenot, "L'Intertextualité."

sensitive to the distinction between Gide's and Michel's voices [see above, 30], was indeed sensitive to *L'Immoraliste*'s Rousseauan touches: "[*L'Immoraliste*] est . . . le sanglot d'un Rousseau lugubre," Francis Jammes, in Gide, *Romans* 1516.)

We can begin observing how attention to Rousseau's words can work upon Michel's narrative, by first recapitulating some of the main lines of Michel's story. It starts out recounting an austere childhood in a protestant household where, with the mother dead, the father and son share a passion for books. Later in his life, the boy-become-adult is gripped by wanderlust that develops after a brush with a life-threatening illness from which he recovered thanks only to the care of a maternally dedicated woman who happened to be Catholic. In large part as a result of this experience, he discovers that civilization, born of vital nature, scleroses into its constricting, destructive opposite. But each of these points, one of course realizes, can be found in Rousseau's story: *Les Confessions* recounts Jean-Jacques's motherless, bookish childhood with his father in Calvinist Geneva, the ministrations of a Catholic "Maman" (Mme de Warens) who saved Rousseau from his mysterious illness, the "manie ambulante" that characterized the rest of his life, and the articulation of the notion that civilization, while sprung from nature, is antithetical to nature.

Related to the subject of dependency on maternal women, there is the issue of independence which too draws Michel into Rousseau's biographical orbit. For instance, Michel attaches great importance to the stubborn cultivation of his own vigorous independence, to the point of readily offending Marceline when, out of devoted, tender concern, she offers her help. It is his visible hostility that rewards her, as it would reward God himself (*I*, 385-86). Of course, his independence blossoms only after Marceline's unflagging care has seen him past the critical phase of his illness (*I*, 380) and his "doctrine of the strong" (*I*, 459-460) takes form only after his dependency upon her ends and hers upon him has begun. Furthermore, after his justification of the need to suppress the "weak," facilitates Marceline's destruction, he nonetheless and revealingly is as quick to be tamed by Moktir (*I*, 469) as the latter's gentle rabbit. Moreover, this symbolic return to dependency is worthy of the "moral pioneer" who in the end asks his friends to take his life in hand. Can we not see reappearing here the twists and turns of the contrary and contradictory essence of the fierce independence of

Jean-Jacques (C, 429)? Of the two, he was the first to see himself as a moral pioneer (C, 2), finding repeatedly and easily situations in which to pursue his independence, but situations always arranged by others (Mme de Warens, Mme d'Epinay, le Maréchal du Luxembourg, et al.). He no less repeatedly and easily heaped hostile scorn on any suggestion that they had any rights over him. The independence of Rousseau stands as no less selfish than Michel's, whose repudiation of the tubercular Marceline is not without parallel to the earlier abandonment of the then wretched "Maman" (C, 463) by the (if we are to believe him) faithless scoundrel whose life she had saved (C, 256).

Once begun, then, the process of comparison of the two texts starts taking in far more than just key points from the story lines: one sees how many of Rousseau's very personality traits and habits of mind reappear in Michel, or to express it more accurately, how many of Jean-Jacques's traits and habits start making Michel's seem derivative and secondary. In addition to their resentfully dependent independence, there is also the inclination to view childhood experiences as a means of explaining adult conduct. At the start of his tale, Michel says:

> Le grave enseignement huguenot de ma mère s'était, avec sa belle image, lentement effacé en mon coeur; vous savez que je la perdis jeune. Je ne soupçonnais pas encore combien cette première morale d'enfant nous maîtrise, ni quels plis elle laisse à l'esprit. (I, 373)

For all its brevity and feeling of ground-breaking discovery, that kind of observation owes much to *Les Confessions*, in which Rousseau spends the entire first four books recounting his childhood and "première jeunesse" (C, 198), largely in an effort to explain Rousseau the unusual adult. Rousseau's attention to what we now feel comfortable calling the "formative years" helped make him an intellectual revolutionary in his time and a harbinger of modern values and assumptions. So reading *L'Immoraliste* with *Les Confessions* in mind helps work a transformation in one of the ways in which Michel may be perceived. To today's readers Michel often appears at first as an intellectual precursor (*L'Immoraliste* was published in 1902), because his sense of the importance of childhood experiences readily contributes to what more than one critic has viewed as the pronounced Freudian character of the narrative.[37] But observed in the light of *Les Confessions*, Michel turns in a traceable way into a specifically derivative Rousseauan thinker.

Among other traits and habits of mind, consider as well the following: the deep discomfort that both Michel and Jean-Jacques experienced on social occasions (*C*, 760, *I*, 422-23, 429-30), the feeling that "le vrai bonheur ne se décrit pas" (*C*, 271; "Que serait le récit du bonheur?," *I*, 408), the tendency to sleepless nights (*C*, 684, *I*, 385, 396, etc.), the difficulty in pursuing long-range projects (*C*, 490, *I*, 418, 438, etc.), plain even Spartan tastes in regard to material comforts (*C*, 78, *I*, 374), and an awareness of being judged contradictory by others (*C*, 229, *I*, 403, 432, etc.).

One shared trait that is not the least consequential of all and that indeed may generate in large measure many of those that we have just considered is the one recognized by Rousseau but not by Michel. Whereas Rousseau says (e.g., *C*, 373-74) that he tended to "donner le change" to sexual drives and so masturbated to "side-track" what he took to be his carnal need for women, Michel fails to acknowledge the subterfuges he uses to "side-track" the homoerotic attractions which he feels repeatedly. This difference in self-awareness notwithstanding, it is hard to refrain from ruminating about the extent to which sexual repression in both figures contributed to the other personality traits described above.

Since the intertextuality at first modestly established by the quotation "la courte haleine" penetrates Michel's narrative more deeply the more we scrutinize it in light of *Les Confessions*, we reach a point where we can even start to wonder if one of the most memorable scenes of *L'Immoraliste*, perhaps even its key scene, does not too stand in debt to Rousseau's autobiography. What careful reader of *L'Immoraliste* has not paid special attention when coming across Michel's words: "Un matin j'eus une curieuse révélation sur moi-même..." (*I*, 394)? That attention is well rewarded as Michel then recounts how he thought he was unobserved in watching furtively in his mirror the little Arab boy, Moktir, who was steal-

---

[37] See of course the landmark psychological study of Gide by Albert Guérard. Another distinguished study is David Steel's "Gide et Freud," in which Steele highlights the similarities in the thinking of the two men, while demonstrating that the Frenchman knew nothing of the Austrian's theories before the former's own mature thought had developed. Steele offers as well a useful list of psychoanalytical examinations of Gide's life and work.

ing Marceline's scissors and who thereby became Michel's favorite. Michel's almost instinctive attempt at deception by pretending to be reading, the narcissistic pose in front of the mirror, the fascination with the beautiful boy, the baffling but intense joy Michel knew because of this assault, however modest, on Marceline's property and so indirectly on Marceline herself, and finally his failure to appreciate his own obviousness (he had to be told later that Moktir saw how avidly the seemingly indifferent Michel was watching him in the mirror) – all the facets of this superbly representative scene coalesce in an image that creates a true moment of epiphany for *L'Immoraliste*. But if, as we saw, Michel's story and very personality can be seen to mimic Jean-Jacques Rousseau's, this scene too, communicating much of the essence of *L'Immoraliste*, can itself take on insinuating similarities with passages from *Les Confessions*. Admittedly, it reflects, not a single moment from *Les Confessions*, but rather two in combination: Rousseau the boy thief (who stole asparagus, the canonical ribbon, and the bottle of white wine, *C*, 35 ff, 91-95, 310-11) and Rousseau the awkward young lover who gets caught in a complicated game of (only apparently) secret glances and gestures with Mme Basile, a game that concludes when a mirror betrays him (*C*, 80-81). But as Michel stands before *his* mirror and sees and identifies with two figures, both the sexually provoked adult and the pretty, thieving boy, is he not combining eidetically for us (in spite of himself since he would sunder them) two facets of his psychic life that stand comparison to Rousseau's?

To introduce a final point in the argument on the progressive absorption by the Rousseauan *hypotexte* of Michel's attempt at simplicity, uniqueness and individuality, we can comment briefly on another aspect of *L'Immoraliste*'s narrative structure. John T. Booker, finding that critics misrepresent *L'Immoraliste* when they advance its synchronic, symmetrical narrative form, maintains that one gets closer to its true character by noting the diachronic, evolutionary flow of Michel's tale (Booker, "*The Immoralist*"). Booker observes the passage from the first part – a cool, abstracted account of events situated well in Michel's past – to the third and last part, which deals with tumultuous events ever closer to the time of narration, and so which takes on an accelerating air of disorder born of a passionate, not so easily abstracted present. While Booker has accurately described the narrative structure, he may be a little hasty in then seeing in it a sign of the narrative novelty of *L'Im-*

*moraliste*.³⁸ Was it not Rousseau who observed himself on several occasions caught up in the troubled, paranoid pages of the second part of *Les Confessions* that contrasts markedly with the organized nostalgia of the first part, and who, on one of those occasions, commented?:

> Plus j'avance dans mes récits, moins j'y puis mettre d'ordre et de suite. L'agitation du reste de ma vie n'a pas laissé aux événements le temps de s'arranger dans ma tête. Ils ont été trop nombreux, trop mêlés, trop désagréables, pour pouvoir être narrés sans confusion. (*C*, 736)

So the progressive emotional and verbal disorder to which Michel confesses takes on ironically the order of a pattern imitated, of an *hypotexte* asserting the structures of its original context.

It would, let us emphasize, be totally inappropriate to suggest fault with previous critics of *L'Immoraliste* for what some might

---

³⁸ It is true that Booker draws his conclusion within the purview of fiction alone. But in the first place, such a restriction implies a too exclusive separation of fiction and autobiography, or at the very least of their techniques. In the second place, there is a further hint that Michel's narrative evolution and *diachronie* are less revolutionary than Booth claims, if one takes epic poetry into consideration. The narrative breakdown between the first and third parts of *L'Immoraliste* can stand comparison with Homer's *Odyssey*, which Michel had read in the Greek, apparently frequently, since mention is made twice of its being in his pocket (391, 465). The comparison would apply more specifically to what happens between the first account of some of his adventures offered by Odysseus himself in Book VII and the second one in Books IX-XII. The first is flat, laconic, painful ("achnúmenós . . . katélexa," "grieving . . . have I told [these things]," VII, 297), whereas the second is spell-binding ("Hos᾿ éphath', hoi d'ára pántes akên egénonto siopê,/Kêlêthmô d'èschonto . . .," "Thus he spoke, and then they all, in silence, fell hushed, and they were spellbound . . .," XIII, 1-2) and is a fabulation as rich as it is highly structured. Significantly, the events related (the encounters with the Cicones, the Lotus-eaters, Cyclops, etc.) are chronologically anterior to those in Book VII, thus allowing more psychological distance for Odysseus, even though they appear later in the narrative). The contrast is all the more striking since in Book VII Odysseus repeats in less than sixty lines (241-297) a sizeable story – the seven years spent with Calypso, the preparations for his departure, the catastrophic voyage itself, the perilous arrival at Scheria, home of the Phaeacians, his meeting with Nausicaa, her care of him, and his introduction by her to the palace of the king – that Homer himself has just told with *éclat* and subtlety in books V and VI. Odysseus, then, who in a sense is making an act of confession before the Phaeacians in order finally to liberate himself from the misdeeds keeping him from returning to Ithaca, experiences a narrative devaluation caused by his attempt to tell about a too immediate present.

Regarding Booker's claim, the narratological moral would seem to be that in the presence of apparent literary originality one should never underestimate the claims of intertextuality.

consider a glossing over of Rousseau's intertext, or a failure to appreciate the influence of *Les Confessions* on *L'Immoraliste*. To do so would imply that there exists a definitive *L'Immoraliste* in which certain literary products lie about passively, awaiting only a sufficiently diligent eye in order to be discovered. One would be much better advised to see the parallels mentioned above for what they are intended to be, namely, points generated by a comparative reading that attempts very deliberately to derive one text from the other. This study deals not with product but with production, that is, the sort of action at work in any framed/inter-text, be it huge or minuscule.

We have then solid ground for extending a point made above earlier: active, dynamic intertextuality and copresence/coabsence (or *différance*, if you will), which intersect in any quotation, must intersect in a truly essential way for all of *L'Immoraliste*, since quotation (through the frame) is its massive constitutive narrative structure. As I have previously proposed, the slighted problem of the play between the overlaid narrative voices of Michel and of his friend in *L'Immoraliste* is of the essence in this work, a work, let us not forget, in which one of the very explicit central images is that of the palimpsest (*I*, 398-99), i. e., of overlaid texts.[39]

It is not, therefore, peripheral or merely interesting that we can see what passes for Michel's "simple," unique, and individualistic voice getting ironically absorbed, with compounding complexity, into the deceptive voice of the father of modern autobiography. And if we recall that *haleine* has been one of the most venerable tropes for artistic in*spir*ation, it is hardly trifling that both Rousseau and Michel, trying to articulate the solitary, exclusively self-derived voice, experience the vital insufficiency expressed in "la courte haleine."

From the action of intertexts involving Ménalque and Rousseau, we may conclude again, therefore, that the "simple" literary voice is a myth, profoundly logocentric no doubt. More generally, this cor-

---

[39] This mutual mirroring between narrative form and key image suggests that *L'Immoraliste* was profoundly touched by the same Gidean instinct that led to the self-reflexive *mises en abyme* of his earlier *Paludes* and later *Les Faux-Monnayeurs*. For a definitive study of Gide's *mises en abyme*, see Dällenbach. Using the latter's framework, we can say that between the frame and the palimpsest there exists an example of *réduplication simple* ("fragment qui entretient avec l'oeuvre qui l'inclut un rapport de similitude," Dällenbach 52).

roborates earlier arguments that attempts at narration, even at unique self-narration, must always be exercises in intertextuality, in quotation,[40] and it is consistent with the working of the framed narrative in *L'Immoraliste*.

### C) *The Palimpsest*

Still assuming for the sake of argument the "rhetorical dimension," we will see that the image of the palimpsest just mentioned above offers another way to see how inaccessibility weaves its way through *L'Immoraliste*. The image appears in Michel's description of the key moment of his life, in the aftermath of his nearly fatal illness. He says that during his recovery, upon reevaluating his life, he suddenly and joyfully sensed what he calls his hidden *être authentique* (I, 398), repressed beneath the *être secondaire* (I, 399) that he asserts had been forced upon him. Comparing himself to a palimpsest, he speaks metaphorically and blissfully of the joy of discovering "sous les écritures plus récentes," "un texte très ancien infiniment plus précieux" (I, 399). While he does recount with power and beauty the promise of what he anticipated in the search for his authenticity, the conclusion must be drawn that this search is gravely flawed, since it leads rather directly to the death, one might almost say murder, of his wife Marceline.

One can explain the flaw in terms of Derridean supplementarity, whereby the supplement, the secondary, is at the heart of the primary or of what Michel called the "authentic," for as Derrida tells us:

---

[40] One last note of irony: the foregoing section treats the voice of the fictional Michel and the voice of the real Rousseau as if they were ontologically equal. To the degree that such apparent parity is found convincing (that is, to argue within the limits of reader impressions), one sees actualized one more subversion by *L'Immoraliste*: the so-called "real Rousseau" of the reader's imagination is no more real than Michel and the fictional Michel no more fictional than "Rousseau," each one being a "person" in the etymological sense discussed earlier. Even in taking the matter outside the realm of reader impressions into the realm of, say, history, the Rousseau of *Les Confessions* is of course in no way – physically, metaphysically, phenomenologically, etc. – the equivalent of the historical Rousseau. In such matters, it helps to remember that biography and autobiography started and remain intertwined with fictional biography and autobiography.

> ... le supplément supplée. Il ne s'ajoute que pour remplacer. Il intervient ou s'insinue *à-la-place-de*; s'il comble, c'est comme on comble un vide. S'il représente et fait image, c'est par le défaut antérieur d'une présence. Suppléant et vicaire, le supplément est un adjoint, une instance subalterne qui *tient-lieu*. (Derrida's emphasis, *De la grammatologie* 208)

We see at work in Michel's image:

> ... la logique de la supplémentarité, qui veut que le dehors soit dedans, que l'autre et le manque viennent s'ajouter comme un plus qui remplace un moins, que ce qui s'ajoute à quelque chose tienne lieu du défaut de cette chose, que le défaut, comme dehors du dedans soit déjà au-dedans du dedans, etc. (Derrida, *De la grammatologie* 308)

In this perspective, then, the outer text of the palimpsest presents itself as "un accessoire originaire et un accident essentiel" (Derrida, *De la grammatologie* 286).[41]

(Not coincidentally, this logic has already proven itself, in that it was behind what we have seen above regarding the framing, "supplementary" narrative of the anonymous friend: Michel's would-be individualistic voice, with its pretense of being fully direct and present, suffers from a lack that necessitates the addition of the framing voice, which thereby becomes "an originary accessory and an essential accident" that casts into doubt the very possibility of an individual voice.[42] Moreover, there exists a link between supplements and the intermediate:

---

[41] As Walker points out (*Gide*, 186, note 53), Frederic Jameson does a Derridean reading of the palimpsest in *L'Immoraliste*. But Jameson reads it instrumentally, to illustrate the image of textual decipherment in Derrida and Freud, not to analyze the nature and role of the image itself in Gide's text (Jameson 177-78).

[42] Need we add that the document, the entire letter, is in its turn supplemented, raising further questions of origin and lack: did the narrator finally send the letter?; to his brother? and if so, what did his brother do with it? if not, who "relayed" it and to whom?; since the letter ultimately became a book, how did that happen?; who is speaking in the "Préface"? (Ireland shows that it is not André Gide [Ireland, "Le Jeu des 'je' " 70-73]); what impact on the letter is exercised by all the "paratexts" such as the epigraph, the dedication, the title, and who should be considered responsible for them? (See Genette, *Palimpsestes* 9-10.) To look at the matter a little differently, where does one arbitrarily set the frontiers of the reading conventions that effectuate the passage into and out of fiction and why at that point? What does the setting tell us about the text's and our aspiration to presence?

> A travers cette séquence de suppléments s'annonce une nécessité: celle d'un enchaînement infini, multipliant inéluctablement les médiations supplémentaires qui produisent le sens de cela même qu'elles diffèrent: le mirage de la chose même, de la présence immédiate de la perception originaire. L'immédiateté est dérivée. Tout commence par l'intermédiaire, voilà ce qui est "inconcevable à la raison." (Derrida, *De la grammatologie* 226)

That link allows the conclusion that supplementarity, mediacy, and framing derive from the forces behind *différance*.)

Michel's "secondary being" or "recent text" (*I*, 399) is the repressive product – he says – of books, teachers, and parents, and perhaps more accurately, he admits, of his own efforts:

> Ce fut dès lors *celui* que je prétendis découvrir: l'être authentique, le 'vieil homme,' celui dont ne voulait plus l'Évangile; celui que tout, autour de moi, livres, maîtres, parents, et que *moi-même* [my emphasis] avions tâché d'abord de supprimer. (*I*, 398-99)

That final admission of his own suppressive role would offer then a clue to the flaw in his being. To wit, it suggests that the core of his true self is a lack of authenticity, one psychologically resonant, we may surmise, with his refusal to acknowledge his homoeroticism. The true self is in fact the secondary self, while the authentic self is a product created by the lack which lies at the heart of derived being and which prompts the concoction of the subsequent originary self. We can go so far as to say that the lack in the secondary being which allows itself to be overlaid by the contrived authentic being can be characterized as a constitutive absence of authenticity, a profound need to deceive, even to the point of suppressing what is most intimately and personally genuine in itself.[43]

---

[43] Both the apparent and the real dynamics of Michel's image of the palimpsest can also be found at work in his course, in his projection of the similar image of a usurping, secondary secretion on to civilization at large: "A propos de l'extrême civilisation latine, je peignais la culture artistique, montant à fleur de peuple, à la manière d'une sécrétion, qui d'abord indique pléthore, surabondance de santé, puis aussitôt se fige, se durcit, s'oppose à tout parfait contact de l'esprit avec la nature, cache sous l'apparence persistante de la vie la diminution de la vie, forme gaine où l'esprit gêné languit et bientôt s'étiole, puis meurt. Enfin, poussant à bout ma pensée, je disais la Culture, née de la vie, tuant la vie" (*I*, 424). The apparent dynamic – the Rousseauistic myth of the "people's" perfect contact between the

This paradox is hardly long in appropriating Michel's text, for while in full lyric flight over the consequences of his discovery of "authentic being," he abruptly denies that he had the thoughts that he just suggested he had at the time he just suggested he had them:

> Aussi bien n'étais-je plus l'être malingre et studieux à qui ma morale précédente, toute rigide et restrictive, convenait. Il y avait ici plus qu'une convalescence; il y avait une augmentation, une recrudescence de vie, l'afflux d'un sang plus riche et plus chaud qui devait toucher mes pensées, les toucher une à une, pénétrer tout, émouvoir, colorer les plus lointaines, délicates et secrètes fibres de mon être. Car, robustesse ou faiblesse, on s'y fait; l'être, selon les forces qu'il a, se compose; mais, qu'elles augmentent, qu'elles permettent de pouvoir plus, et . . . Toutes ces pensées je ne les avais pas alors, et ma peinture ici me fausse. A vrai dire, je ne pensais point, ne m'examinais point; une fatalité heureuse me guidait. (I, 399)

This demurral poses serious problems. What exactly is the extent of the adjective *toutes* in "toutes ces pensées je ne les avais pas alors"? If the word is applied broadly to Michel's entire discussion of his discovery of his authentic self, it means that his rebirth *as described* took place only at a subsequent moment, in fact perhaps at the time of narration. Even if we could for the sake of argument peremptorily limit the application of that comprehensive word only to the paragraph in which it appears, and so only to his thoughts specifically about an increase in vitality above and beyond mere convalescence, those thoughts seem so intimately tied to the entire preceding section, that one can only with difficulty conceive discounting the former without discrediting the latter. And besides, the emphatic negation in "je ne pensais point" seems to warrant a broad application of "toutes."

At the very least, Michel underscores the question of his narrative reliability by showing how he could be confusing the thoughts

---

mind and nature now lost through vaguely urban ("cultured") faults – cannot hide the reality that Culture more likely derives from anguishing absence, as in the lack of a completely reliable or constantly present food source, metaphor of our own mortality. That much is suggested by the agrarian etymology of 'culture,' and by the related and widespread allegory of the death of the seed (e.g., Ceres's daughter Proserpine, Dionysus, Christ), 'culture' and 'cult' deriving from the same Latin root 'colere.' Nature and life, because of their lack, spark the myth of (desire for) natural plethora and superabundance.

he is having as narrating subject in the present with those he had had as narrated object in the past. But even an analysis of this generous appraisal leads back to misrepresentation. Jonathan Culler, in explaining how Derrida's understanding of iterability undoes Austin's and Searle's appeals to intentions as a ground for some of their key distinctions (constative-performative, serious-nonserious, intended-unintended), makes the following observation:

> When questioned about the implications of an utterance I may quite routinely include in my intention implications that had never previously occurred to me. My intention is the sum of further explanations I might give when questioned on any point and is thus less an origin than a product, less a delimited content than an open set of discursive possibilities linked to the consequences of iterable acts and to context that pose particular questions about those acts. (Culler 127-28)

So Michel may not so much be lying as merely being scrupulously honest in trying to describe his past motivations: the attempt at description changes the thing described, à la Heisenberg. But since efforts to explain past intentions routinely generate extrapolations, refinements, and indeed additions, it becomes possible to see any such retrospective efforts as de facto misrepresentations. Or as semiotics would have more decisively had it in the first place, lying is a condition of language (which passes off sign as reality), and so a condition of description. The next, inevitable semiotic question – à la Epimenides – is then, what of Michel's lying description of his lying description? In short, for both the charitable and not so charitable reader, the truth of this and other examples of Michel's intentions slips away no less than the text built on those intentions.

Consequently, the possibility arises distinctly that Michel, in admitting that these key thoughts did not occur at the time he has been saying they occurred, is in effect turning those allegedly seminal reflections – reflections that in the course of his narrative will become implied justifications of actions in his recent past – into *ex post facto* additions to his story that belong not to the "le temps de l'histoire" but more likely to the "temps du récit" (Genette, *Figures III* 77 ff). That is to say, then, that what had been offered here as source, upon examination turns out to be supplement.

This conclusion, at first intimidating in its paradox, in fact builds confidence that we are not being glib in our understanding and application of the mechanisms of repression: seeing Michel's "authentic being" as the supplementary product of the repressive "secondary being" is in keeping with, for instance, Freud's understanding of the dynamics of repression. Concerning his extensive psychoanalysis of the so-called "wolf-man," Freud maintains that:

> scenes from early infancy, such as are brought up by an exhaustive analysis of neuroses [. . .] are not reproductions of real occurrences, to which it is possible to ascribe an influence over the course of the patients's later life and over the formation of his symptoms. It [Freud's interpretation] considers them rather as products of the imagination, which find their instigation in mature life, which are intended to serve as some kind of symbolic representation of real wishes and interests and which owe their origin to a regressive tendency, to an aversion from the problems of the present ..................................................................
> We should say to the patient: "Very well, then; your neurosis proceeded *as though* you had received these impressions and spun them out in your childhood. You will see, of course, that that is out of the question. They were products of your imagination, and were intended to divert you from the real problems that lay before you. . . ." (Freud 521-22; Freud's emphasis) [44]

The possibility that Michel's "authentic being" is constructed afterwards by the repressive imagination of the "secondary being" warrants our going back to the beginning of the text to determine if indeed the "authentic" continues the negative action of the "secondary," instead of predating and differing from it. At its most fully

---

[44] Regarding the unconscious, Jonathan Culler says: "Freud emphasizes that the unconscious is by no means simply a layer of actual experiences that have been repressed, a hidden presence. It is both constituted by repression and the active agent of repression. Like [Derrida's] *différance*, which designates the impossible origin of difference in differing and of differing in difference, the unconscious is a nonoriginary origin which Freud calls primary repression (*Urverdrängung*), in which the unconscious both initiates the first repression and is constituted as repression. If the discovery of the unconscious is a demonstration that nothing in the human subject is ever simple, that thoughts and desires are already doubled and divided, it turns out that the unconscious itself is not a simple hidden reality but always, in Freud's speculation, a complex and differential product.........................................................
[Freud's term] *Nachträglichheit* [or deferred action] names a paradoxical situation that Freud frequently encounters in his case studies, in which the determining event in a neurosis never occurs as such, is never present as an event, but is constructed afterwards by what can only be described as a textual mechanism of the unconscious" (Culler 162-63).

developed, the "authentic" Michel is, we must assume, represented by the post-illness, post-search individual who has shaken off his past and who is retrospectively narrating his whole story. It is that Michel who begins by addressing his three solicitous friends in these terms:

> Mes chers amis, je vous savais fidèles. A mon appel, vous êtes accourus, tout comme j'eusse fait au vôtre. Pourtant voici trois ans que vous ne m'aviez vu. Puisse votre amitié, qui résiste si bien à l'absence, résister aussi bien au récit que je veux vous faire. (*I*, 372)

This formal, affectively forbidding style is of a piece with the description of him made on the previous page by his anonymous friend:

> Michel nous a reçus sans témoigner de joie; très simple, il semblait craindre toute manifestation de tendresse; mais sur le seuil, d'abord, il embrassa chacun de nous trois gravement. Jusqu'à la nuit nous n'échangeâmes pas dix paroles. (*I*, 371)

The frame closes on no less flat a description:

> Il avait achevé ce récit sans un tremblement dans la voix, sans qu'une inflexion ni qu'un geste témoignât qu'une émotion quelconque le troublât.... (*I*, 470-71)

Such pinched-lip emotional restraint ought not be attributed to a desire for an uncharacteristic, objective, factual tone, or to a momentary aberration brought on by the unusually intense circumstances being experienced here by Michel. It is true that, having buried his wife three months earlier, he is seeing friends who have come to help him after a three-year absence from his life. One could conceivably argue that it is a surfeit of emotion that blocks its own expression here. However extraordinary these circumstances, the voice and portrait of Michel's "être authentique" are nonetheless entirely in keeping with the emotional state of what must be considered the "être secondaire" at its most developed, that is, the Michel described in the account of the marriage immediately predating the psychosomatic crisis and putative rebirth. For that

Michel too, there was notable emotional flatness, a striking disjunction between event and emotional response, strongly suggestive of psychological repression. Concerning his own wedding, he says:

> La dernière fois que nous nous vîmes, c'était, il m'en souvient, aux environs d'Angers, dans la petite église de campagne où mon mariage se célébrait. Le public était peu nombreux, et l'excellence des amis faisait de cette cérémonie banale une cérémonie touchante. Il me semblait que l'on était ému, et cela m'émouvait moi-même. (I, 372)

The word "banale" shocks, of course, since it is applied to a ceremony meant to join together – usually in love – two people for life, as even Michel recognizes (I, 373), and at which all of one's important friends feel impelled to gather, even if, as is probably the case in this particular marriage, most of them have to come from the four corners of the globe (I, 370). Wonder though we may, however, about exactly what made the ceremony banal for him, he himself seems unaware of the need to offer an explanation. His silence on the matter becomes all the more exasperating in retrospect when we learn that, as a famous philologist and historian (I, 373-74) who filled a vacant chair at the Collège de France (I, 408), he is not – one assumes – incapable or heedless of verbal precision. The exasperation grows as we must deal with the "authentic" Michel's proclivity for flabby language (such as, on I 379, "une sorte d'irritation," "comme un instinct," "une sorte de rage") at those very instances when one has the impression of reaching a key moment of his psychological drama. Not that great verbal intelligence cannot be linked with an incapacity for self-analysis, but when it is, it often suggests a lack of affect. That possibility seems assured in Michel's case when one considers the full implications of the toneless observation of emotional parasitism that had followed on the heels of "banale": "Il me semblait que l'on était ému, et cela m'émouvait moi-même" (I, 372).

Not at all inconsistently, he recognized no feelings for "celle qui devenait ma femme" (I, 372), the bloodless expression used first to introduce Marceline, avoiding the more personal use of her name:

> Je connaissais très peu ma femme et pensais, sans en trop souffrir, qu'elle ne me connaissait pas plus. Je l'avais épousée sans

> amour, beaucoup pour complaire à mon père, qui, mourant, s'inquiétait de me laisser seul. (*I*, 372)

One may at first see in this filial compliance a tendency to submissiveness presumably rejected by the later "immoralist." But suspicion about the alleged distinction between Michel's "secondary" and "authentic" being alerts us to the significance of his later deference to the authoritative Ménalque, his virtual surrender to the will of Moktir, his continued dependence on his three friends, and ultimately his submission once again to a father-figure, the *Président du Conseil*. As he says sweepingly and bluntly to his friends at the end of his story: "Arrachez-moi d'ici à présent, et donnez-moi des raisons d'être" (*I*, 471). All this reinforces the conviction that in comparing moments of submissiveness in the "secondary" and "authentic" Michels we are dealing, not with two isolated instances of emotional, authority-dependant self-repression, but rather with an invariable trait. Regarding self-repression, one cannot avoid taking into account Michel's repeated refusal to acknowledge his glaring homoerotic impulses, a refusal made all the more grating for readers because of his making fidelity to one's true self a prominent refrain in his narrative.

On the level of diction, moreover, Michel gives signs of a tic that betrays the extent to which self-repression is his first, nearly instinctive, usually only partially successful response to strong emotion: on no fewer than five occasions of intense emotion, he makes use of the expression "ne pas/ne plus y tenir." The first example appears in his account of the honeymoon trip, shortly after his arrival in North Africa. Having hidden from his wife Marceline all the evidence of the copious blood that he had spit up at the nocturnal onset of his illness, he admits to the irritation that he felt rising within himself at her ignorance:

> Je me sentais injuste, il est vrai, me disais: si elle n'a rien vu c'est que je cachais bien; n'importe; rien n'y fit; cela grandit en moi comme un instinct, m'envahit... à la fin cela fut trop fort; je n'y tins plus; comme distraitement je lui dis: – J'ai craché le sang, cette nuit. (*I*, 379)

It is shortly thereafter that Marceline happens to introduce Michel to Bachir, the first of the Arab boys to whom he will feel powerfully attracted. Of the next day, the one following the first awkward meeting, Michel relates: "Le lendemain, pour la première fois, je m'ennuie; j'attends; j'attends quoi? je me sens désoeuvré, inquiet. Enfin je n'y tins plus: – Bachir ne vient donc pas, ce matin?" (*I*, 382). At least three other comparable examples of "ne pas/ne plus y tenir" can be found,[45] examples that reverberate in similar uses of *retenir*, such as "je ne pus retenir mes larmes" (*I*, 376) and "crachats [de sang] que je ne retins plus" (*I*, 378). That tic finds semantic resonance in numerous comparable expressions: "*Je me repris*, me cramponnai, finis par *maîtriser* [my emphasis] mon vertige . . ." (*I*, 378); and ten pages later: "Et puis, parler aux enfants [arabes], je ne l'osais pas devant [Marceline]; je voyais qu'elle avait ses protégés; *malgré moi* [my emphasis], mais par parti pris, moi je m'intéressais aux autres" (*I*, 388); five pages later: "Sentant sous les ciseaux tomber ma barbe, c'était comme si j'enlevais un masque. N'importe! quand, après, je m'apparus, l'émotion qui m'emplit et que *je réprimai de mon mieux* [my emphasis], ne fut pas la joie, mais la peur" (*I*, 403), etc.

Attempted self-repression is not the only indication that the prior "acquired text" functions as the origin of Michel's subsequent "original text" and lends it all its traits. One of the more interesting psychological indications of this is his response to maternal figures. It is transparent that Michel's mother and wife tend to merge in Michel's awareness as representatives of the mother figure. The numerous associations tying together mother, la Morinière, Marceline,

---

[45] "–J'ai tant prié pour toi, répond-elle [Marceline]. –Elle dit cela tendrement, tristement; je sens dans son regard une anxiété suppliante . . . Je prends le chapelet et le glisse dans sa main affaiblie qui repose sur le drap, contre elle. Un regard chargé de larmes et d'amour me récompense – mais auquel je ne pus répondre; un instant encore je m'attarde, ne sais que faire, reste gêné; enfin, *n'y tenant plus*:
–Adieu, lui dis-je – et je quitte la chambre, hostile, et comme si l'on m'en avait chassé" (*I*, 439).
"Le dernier soir que nous restions à Naples je prolongeai jusqu'au matin cette débauche vagabonde. En rentrant je trouvai Marceline en larmes. Elle avait eu peur, me dit-elle, s'étant brusquement réveillée et ne m'ayant plus senti là. Je la tranquillisai, expliquai de mon mieux mon absence et promis de ne plus la quitter.
–Mais, dès la première nuit de Palerme, *je n'y pus tenir*; je sortis . . . . . . . . . . . . . . . . . . . . . .
–Com'è bella la Signora! dit-il [un cocher italien] d'une voix charmante en regardant s'éloigner Marceline.
–Anche tu sei bello, ragazzo, répondis-je; et, comme j'étais penché vers lui, *je n'y pus tenir* et bientôt, l'attirant vers moi, l'embrassai" (*I*, 462).

and maternity[46] – all those letter Ms! – argue that convincingly. It is no less transparent that the "authentic" Michel harbors an ill concealed and unacknowledged rage against the mother figure, as is seen repeatedly in his conduct toward its most frequent embodiment, Marceline: his first reflex is to hide from her his true feelings and thoughts, to lie to her, and to heap on her barely contained hostility (*I*, 378, 385, 388, 389-90, 395, 403-04, 459-60, 461). It is seen as well, of course, in his immediate, unquestioned preference jubilantly bestowed on Moktir when the boy indirectly attacks Marceline by stealing her scissors (*I*, 394-95). That preference carries over to Moktir's doubles: Athalaric who "se révolte contre sa mère Amalasonthe" (*I*, 407); the Heurtevent men who regularly revile women (they used to beat the mother who – typically for mothers in *L'Immoraliste* – died, they rape and corrupt the servant, they have incestuous relations with the daughter, *I*, 446); Alcide who does violence (and in a sense *viol*) to La Morinière; and the little Arab boy who at the end manages to make Michel banish the older (i.e., maternal) sister from Michel's bed (*I*, 471-72).

But one could be led to believe that this hostility was felt only by the "authentic," not the "secondary," Michel, since the opening pages portray the latter as favorably disposed toward his mother:

> le grave enseignement huguenot de ma mère s'était, avec sa belle image, lentement effacé en mon coeur; vous savez que je la perdis jeune. Je ne soupçonnais pas encore combien cette première morale d'enfant nous maîtrise, ni quels plis elle laisse à l'esprit. (*I*, 373)

These opening lines on the childhood of the "secondary Michel" convey an impression of happy memories of the all too brief time

---

[46] –"Je regardais ma femme cependant [qui avait fait monter des enfants arabes]; elle était maternelle et caressante" (*I*, 389-90).
"[La Morinière], propriété que possédait jadis ma mère, où j'avais avec elle passé quelques étés de mon enfance, mais où, depuis sa mort, je n'étais pas retourné" (*I*, 408).
"Marceline, une semaine après notre arrivée [at La Morinière], me confia qu'elle était enceinte ..............................................................................
Nous allions nous asseoir près du bois, sur le banc où jadis j'allais m'asseoir avec ma mère ..............................................................................
Nul doute, pensais-je, que l'exemple de cette terre, où tout s'apprête au fruit, à l'utile moisson, ne doive avoir sur moi la plus excellente influence" (*I*, 410).

spent with his mother. Because of the play of association, one is readily persuaded that since the image of the mother was "belle," Michel found her "grave enseignement huguenot" no less comely. This seems especially so since he claims to have been profoundly influenced by it (although to his apparently mild surprise), and since he misses the woman who taught it to him, as is suggested by the words that are *de rigueur* for a good child recalling with emotion a lost parent: "je la perdis jeune." She left a "belle image" that, having been erased only slowly and apparently regretfully from his heart, presumable cast by association its favorable glow on her "grave enseignement huguenot." Similarly, the later "authentic Michel" gives voice to the fondest of memories of the dead "Marceline, ma femme, ma vie" and of the life-saving help that she gave him (*I*, 380).

But it does not take long for a retrospective pluperfect describing the nascent "authentic" being to cast doubt on the favorable opinion held by the "secondary" being of his mother, and to suggest that once again repression has been working on his feelings:

> la ressemblance de ces brochures [popular treatments of medical questions] avec les petits traités moraux dont on avait agacé mon enfance, ne me disposait pas en leur faveur. . . . (*I*, 384)

Since what he calls his "childhood" basically covers the years when he was under the apparently complete tutelage of his mother (before he turned fifteen and before she died, *I*, 373), the pronoun *on* fails to work as a dodge to avoid naming the grating purveyor of the tracts he resented (it was certainly not his atheistic father, *I*, 373). His mother, it becomes apparent, was not the tender presence implied by the earlier passage. Her "beautiful" image having suddenly taken on irritating hues, there arises a possible explanation of why Michel seemed somewhat surprised to realize "combien cette première morale d'enfant nous maîtrise": he probably did little except to fight it.

The attempted dodge looms large, first because it shows that the seemingly novel pattern of hostility toward the mother on the part of the "primary" personality derives from a condition better concealed but nonetheless extant in the "secondary" one. Next and more importantly, notwithstanding the impression of naive simplicity spun by the opening pages, deceitfulness laced with hostility is seen to mark the "secondary" Michel's attitude toward the women in his life. That deceitfulness is of a sort capable of producing the fiction of a hidden "texte infiniment plus précieux," "plus fruste et difficile à découvrir mais d'autant plus utile à découvrir et valeureux" – the better to hide itself and the constitutive lack at the center of Michel's personality.

Given this penchant for roiling deceitfulness, which, if pronounced, would have important implications for fundamental narrative reliability, it is disturbing to find other signs of it, for instance, the description of the life led by the "secondary" Michel, before marriage:

> Une autre chose que j'ignorais [before his marriage], plus importante encore peut-être, c'est que j'étais d'une santé très délicate. Comment l'eussé-je su, ne l'ayant pas mise à l'épreuve? J'avais des rhumes de temps à autre, et les soignais négligemment. La vie trop calme que je menais m'affaiblissait et me préservait à la fois. (I, 374)

When one keeps in mind what extensive travel at the turn of the century could entail, then the delicate, untested health, and the enfeebling, too calm life just portrayed would seem incompatible with, say, the rigors of travel later embraced feverishly by the tempered, stronger Michel. After all, was Michel's first, desperate physical crisis not precipitated by the unfamiliar strains of traveling (I, 374-378)? Or so the demands of making the "acquired" Michel appear markedly different from the "authentic" Michel would lead us to believe, for, having created that impression, Michel's account goes on to add, but only in passing, that before his wedding he had indeed actually travelled extensively:

> Je ne m'étais accordé jusqu'alors [the time of his marriage] que de courtes vacances. Un voyage en Espagne avec mon père, peu de temps après la mort de ma mère, avait, il est vrai, duré plus d'un mois; un autre, en Allemagne, six semaines; d'autres encore – mais c'étaient des voyages d'études; mon père ne s'y distrayait point de ses recherches très précises; moi, sitôt que je ne l'y suivais plus, je lisais. *Et pourtant* à peine avions-nous quitté Marseille, divers souvenirs de Grenade et de Séville me revinrent, de ciel plus pur, d'ombres plus franches, de fêtes, de rires et de chants. (I, 375; my emphasis)

"Et pourtant"?! – as if he were surprised at . . . what?: from the time he was fifteen years old, vacations that were not vacations, well, at least not for his father but perhaps in fact for him; vacations that were short, well, except for the one to Germany lasting six weeks and another to Spain lasting "more than" a month; vacations that were presumably infrequent, well, except for "d'autres encore"; vacations during which all that Michel did was read, well, except for those unspecified vacation experiences that impressed on him memories "de ciel plus pur, d'ombres plus franches, de fêtes, de rires et de chants." Furthermore, concerning the most skimpily mentioned trips ("d'autres encore"), how frequent and how long had they been? And to where? Since they were allegedly undertaken as working trips by his father who was an expert in Phrygian rites, why would Michel and his father not have spent time in Mediterranean regions such as Asia Minor and Rome where those rites had been propagated, and other similar but taxing regions of the South that, as Michel will subsequently admit, dazzle him? (And where the little boys dazzle him. Hopelessly speculative but intriguing questions stir regarding his companion-father's anxiety at the prospect of dying before he could get his son married.) In short, after scrutinizing the second mention of Michel's travel experience, we cannot continue to accept the impression created – how intentionally? – by the first. At best, it appears contrived of Michel – stout member, let us recall, of an adolescent brotherhood given over to wanderlust – to state that he had never put his health to the test because he had led only a calm and sheltered life closed, he implies, to travel.

At worst it calls into sweeping question Michel's veracity. Because of that, because of the hostile deceit that characterizes his relationship with the maternal figures that make up so much of his story, and because of his subsequent casual demurral over his own tendency to fabricate ex post facto explanations of his conduct (see above, 83), there has to be addressed the question, and a Gidean one at that, of the point at which psychological self-repression crosses over and straddles the line separating it from lying about oneself. For Fortier too, *L'Immoraliste* has to be read with the possibility kept in mind that Michel may have lied in places when he told his story to his friends (Fortier 35, ff.). But Michel's mendacity goes beyond mere details, details that would, for instance, put him in a bad light. In a passage dealing with his dissimulation toward his wife that undermines once and for all any narrative reliability that Michel may have enjoyed, he integrates his repressive instincts with so vast a (to use his word) "natural" capacity for lying that truth itself, and at its broadest, becomes the chief object of his repression:

> Ma dissimulation même (si l'on peut appeler ainsi le besoin de préserver [from Marceline] ma pensée), ma dissimulation . . . augmentait [his love for her]. Je veux dire que ce jeu m'occupait de Marceline sans cesse. Peut-être cette contrainte au mensonge me coûta-t-elle d'abord; mais j'arrivai vite à comprendre que les choses réputées les pires (le mensonge, pour ne citer que celle-là) ne sont difficiles à faire que tant qu'on ne les a jamais faites; mais qu'elles deviennent chacune, et très vite, aisées, plaisantes, douces à refaire, et bientôt comme naturelles. (*I*, 403-04)

We should note that in spite of this admission Michel had been growing into deceit long before he acknowledges it – as one has every right to expect. Even in opening his account, he recalls a "supercherie" (373) committed as a young man, whereby he and his father had passed off Michel's *Essai sur les cultes phrygiens* as his father's work. The frame, then, in still another act of echoing, duplicates the status of his very first text, in that both deceive and deny him authorship. In addition, if we reflect on the meaning of 'supercherie' (the substitution of the false for the authentic), the incident and choice of word harmonize with, and perhaps prefigure, Michel's appealing to the image of the palimpsest: in both cases one is dealing with a deceptive substitution. Etymologically, *supercherie* (\**superculus*) may even offer a scabrous anticipation of *palimpseste*.

The consequences of his attitude toward lying would be unsettling enough had it touched "only" his life with Marceline following his recovery. But if, as the preceding pages argue, the "authentic" Michel, the one in question here, is merely an imagined product of the "secondary" Michel that shares its traits, such an attitude would not be novel and restricted, it would not have impacted only moments of his rapport with his wife, but rather his whole account, his whole life. Repression works in Michel comprehensively then, touching veracity in narration as well as eroticism, emotions, and Marceline's physical being. But to say that a narrative's fundamental veracity has been profoundly and diversely tainted is to say that one has a tenuous hold indeed on it.

Because then of intertextuality on the one hand and the palimpsest on the other, we conclude confidently that even a reader comfortable in logocentrism can at no time be assured of direct contact with the main character's authentic voice, the usually presumed object of study in *L'Immoraliste*, which lack of contact helps to confirm the validity of the *disponible*, deconstructive insistence on the implications of the frame. But the effect of such a conclusion is not to cut us off from reading (on the contrary, I hoped to have shown), but rather to oblige us to recognize the arbitrariness of our readings of both texts and "persons." Another effect of our decentered conclusion is to expand the available critical space of *L'Immoraliste*, by finding cause to explore more attentively the story of the anonymous friend who relays Michel's story.

In addition, we have seen that, to the extent that mimesis obtains in the *whole* text of *L'Immoraliste* (framed *and* framing sections), Gide's text offers a trope on one of the central issues of *L'Immoraliste*, individualism. The proposed reading has brought out the problems encountered by any voice trying to attain complete individuality, which ultimately means, does it not?, trying to attain originary status. Recalling that Michel's name means "like God" in Hebrew offers us the occasion to see how bold indeed such aspirations are and how miserably they must fail. Perhaps Heidegger and Lacan got it right in asserting that, instead of being the masters of language that our acts show we assume we are, we are its creatures and serfs. Perhaps language is our Derridian supplement.

Moreover, having lost direct contact with the main character's voice, we find ourselves of necessity pushed back from his story of events to questions about the story of the telling, questions that subvert the mimetic illusion, first, because we cannot possibly evaluate even the story of the telling without a hold on the tale, and, second, because to be reminded of the teller telling is to be reminded that any story, however captivating, is just a version of events, a creation, a fiction, that is, a deception. But again, what reader has not been led by Gide's art, even back from an appreciation of the void of indeterminacy, to feel drawn by Michel's elusive voice, that is, caught up as a vague accomplice – not unlike Michel's relaying friend himself – in what can only be the illusion of his acts and his person?

CHAPTER TWO

## *LA PORTE ÉTROITE*

*La Porte étroite* is a torment of semantic openness. Consequently, discerning critics (see, for instance, Kapetanoviç, Helbo, Sonnenfeld ["On Readers and Reading"] Shorley, Greene) have for some time now already established the grounds for what I am calling the void of this text, with the result that some of the following pages will read like an *état présent* of relevant scholarship. But to position that void within the bi-polarity of *disponibilité*, I will argue that despite semantic openness, despite *La Porte étroite*'s being the unreliable Jérôme's text, despite even the mutilation of Alissa's letters and diary at the hands of the obtuse Jérôme, it is her voice that establishes a counterpresence to textual inaccessibility. The method employed will be to press the narrative gambit of *La Porte étroite*, just as insistently I did that of its *livre jumeau*, *L'Immoraliste*: in this case, if "Jérôme" wrote this text, we should see what we discover in reading it first as if "he," not Gide, is responsible for all its features. That will lead again to the indeterminacy resulting from the framing and relaying of the principal voice by another (Alissa's by Jérôme's), and from their mutual "in-living." It will as well lead down what I hope will be interesting byways, not the least of which is a consideration of the impact of Jérôme's narcissistic proclivities on the writing of his text.

I. Jérôme as Editor

A) *Jérôme the Misquoting "Author"*

It is an astonishing symptom of the blind faith lent to narrative authority that few if any critics have ever commented on (much less explored) the fact that Jérôme completely misquotes the biblical verses that are at the heart of the book and that give it its very title:

> Le pasteur avait d'abord lu tout le verset: *Efforcez-vous d'entrer par la porte étroite, car la porte large et le chemin spacieux mènent à la perdition, et nombreux sont ceux qui y passent; mais étroite est la porte et resserrée la voie qui conduisent à la Vie, et il en est peu qui les trouvent.* (*La Porte étroite*, in *Romans* 505)

No such verse exists in the Bible.

But even Robert W. Greene, in his magisterial article "Fading (Sacred) Texts and Dying (Guiding) Voices in Gide's Early *Récits*" which dissects the mischief of quotation in *La Porte étroite*, makes nothing of this misquotation. Asserting that the "title . . ., as the text's epigraph reveals, comes straight from the Gospel according to Luke" (Greene 82), he apparently assumes that Jérôme has cited accurately. Consequently, even though eminently aware that little if anything "comes straight" in *La Porte étroite*, his assumption allows him to misstate the reality of the title's source: it comes from both the epigraph *and* Jérôme's misquotation. Where it comes from, then, is far less "straight" than it appears. Nor is this the first time that Gide has one of his characters mangle an important, well known quotation, making it even less likely that he could have been merely careless about so central a citation. Lines from Mallarmé's "Brise Marine" fare no better in *Paludes* (Fillaudeau 184-85 and Apter, 51) than does Luke in *La Porte étroite*. On the other hand, his characters could get words from holy writ right when it suited his purposes: Michel quotes the letter of the Bible accurately (*I*, 397), as does the Pastor usually. So if Jérôme misquotes the Bible that Gide spent so much of his life pondering, there should be a high level of confidence that his character's mistake has esthetic significance.

What Jérôme calls "un verset" actually is an amalgam made up of expressions from both Luke and Matthew. Beginning accurately with Luke's "Efforcez-vous d'entrer par la porte étroite,"[1] the rest

---

[1] As translated by Louis Segond, whose version of the French Bible was preferred by Reformed Churches at the turn of the century. See "La Bible," *La Grande Encyclopédie*.

In their entirety, verses 23-30 of Luke XIII read as follows: "Quelqu'un lui dit: Seigneur, n'y a-t-il que peu de gens qui soient sauvés? Il leur répondit: Efforcez-

of the so-called verse then leaves the more succinct Luke to rework slightly the more elaborate Matthew's second sentence of chapter VII, verse 13 ("Car large est la porte . . ."), returning to greater (if not complete) precision with the rest of Matthew's verse 13 and all of his verse 14 ("Mais étroite est la porte . . ."). [2] The choice seems far from idle, for the result is an emphasis on the need for effort, so dear to the austere, elitist Jérôme. Such emphasis is accommodated better by Luke's "Efforcez – vous d'entrer" than by Matthew's "Entrez." But in Luke's subsequent (and missing) language, his opening remarks turn inclusive, to Jérôme's dislike we may be sure, for by the time that the catholic Luke's 29-30 are reached, the emphasis on the exclusion of the "many" is, if not repudiated, at least enormously softened. Luke's Christ turns the "few" of the question put to him ("n'y a-t-il que peu de gens qui soient sauvés?") into what comes to appear as a various and growing horde: "Il en viendra de l'orient et de l'occident, du nord et du midi; et ils se mettront à table dans le royaume de Dieu" (Luke, XIII, 29-30). Not surprisingly, Jérôme veers away from Luke's characteristically universalist development, to accommodate Matthew's subsequently more demanding view of an ascetic handful of the chosen, a view that con-

---

vous d'entrer par la porte étroite. Car, je vous le dis, beaucoup chercheront à entrer, et ne le pourront pas. Quand le maître de la maison se sera levé et aura fermé la porte, et que vous, étant dehors, vous commencerez à frapper à la porte, en disant Seigneur, Seigneur, ouvre-nous! il vous répondra: Je ne sais d'où vous êtes. Alors vous vous mettrez à dire: Nous avons mangé et bu devant toi, et tu as enseigné dans nos rues. Et il répondra: Je vous le dis, je ne sais d'où vous êtes; retirez-vous de moi, vous tous, ouvriers d'iniquité. C'est là qu'il y aura des pleurs et des grincements de dents, quand vous verrez Abraham, Isaac et Jacob, et tous les prophètes, dans le royaume de Dieu, et que vous serez jetés dehors. Il en viendra de l'orient et de l'occident, du nord et du midi; et ils se mettront à table dans le royaume de Dieu. Et voici, il y en a des derniers qui seront les premiers, et des premiers qui seront les derniers." For those interested in pursuing the depths at which textual crosscurrents may be working in *La Porte étroite*, it is curious to note that Luke, whose text Jérôme will alter, openly set out to write his gospel "d'une manière suivie" (1, 3), that is, with a deliberate sense of narrative structure and order unlike the alleged patch-work and simple quality that Jérôme envisions for his account.

[2] Compare Jérôme's "Efforcez-vous d'entrer par la porte étroite, car la porte large et le chemin spacieux mènent à la perdition, et nombreux sont ceux qui y passent; mais étroite est la porte et resserrée la voie qui conduisent à la Vie, et il en est peu qui les trouvent," with Luke's "Efforcez-vous d'entrer par la porte étroite. Car, je vous le dis, beaucoup chercheront à entrer, et ne le pourront pas," and with Matthew's "Entrez par la porte étroite. Car large est la porte, spacieux est le chemin qui mènent à la perdition, et il y en a beaucoup qui entrent par là. Mais étroite est la porte, resserré le chemin qui mènent à la vie, et il y en a peu qui les trouvent."

tinues to resonate better with Jérôme's personality. (It would be interesting to know if the Pastor quoted by Jérôme had gone on to include Luke's conclusion: "Et voici, il y en a des derniers qui seront les premiers, et des premiers qui seront les derniers" [Luke, 13, 30]. That is of course an unsettling message for the spiritually self-righteous, such as Jérôme, and the exclusion of that message would seem typical of Jérôme's selective memory. But we cannot, of course, determine if it was Luke that the Pastor had been citing in the first place.)

The implications of the critical oversight regarding this misquotation seem enormous. If it is profoundly askew that Jérôme presents the quoted basis of the meditation that provides the single most important image for his and Alissa's goal in life and so for their story, then what possible confidence can be attached to the way in which he tells the other, less important details? It would be one thing for him to quote key expressions here and there from his recollection of the parable, or to paraphrase its sense. But it is quite another to misquote seemingly verbatim (i.e., in a sizeable quotation) what Jérôme calls "tout le verset," an extensive text so readily verified. It makes sense, then, to affirm the appropriateness of *La Porte étroite*'s taking its title from this hash of verses, for – in form and substance – the book *is* misquotation. Not only that, but the eponymous verses are a seamless conflation of two different voices and opinions on the "strait gate" – an anticipation of the final status of Jérôme's and Alissa's narrative roles since, under scrutiny, their voices will be seen to merge.

His stunning misrepresentation takes on complicating texture in light of his mention five pages later that he and Alissa had memorized long passages from the Vulgate Bible. It could be argued indulgently that, being more self-assured than precise, his memory inadvertently cobbled together from two sources the expressions that had pleased him more. Or it could be argued more harshly that such early, detailed knowledge of the Bible put him into a position to discern better than most the differences between Matthew and Luke. So when he remembers, Jérôme is either capable of inadvertent, self-serving reconstructions (a rather common problem) that are grossly idiosyncratic (less common) or else he is given to breathtaking effrontery in deliberately reworking even easily corroborated details. To give the latter possibility its worst formulation, Jérôme may be a narrator who deliberately misrepresents, that is, who lies.

While it cannot be proven one way or the other, this less likely prospect cannot be dismissed out of hand. Gide in his "excesses" could turn to a demonstrable liar as a narrator, as we saw in *L'Immoraliste* and as we will see in the next chapter when we consider *La Symphonie pastorale*. The putatively "depoeticized" Alissa (*PE*, 573-74), moreover, saw fit to lie to Jérôme about her true feelings. Could the resentful, less than magnanimous narrator have felt that turnabout is fair play? But no matter what the exact case for *La Porte étroite*, this example of Jérôme's untrustworthiness as a narrator dealing with a – *the?* – decisive moment of his life compromises substantially and indeed perhaps irremediably the fit between his *histoire* and his *récit*.

Those are the implications just for the reading of *La Porte étroite*. What of the implications for received critical attitudes regarding first-person narratives in general? Why has so significant and revealing a misquotation by Jérôme not been raised as an issue before? Has Gide's epigram from Luke XIII, 24 lulled critical watchfulness by in effect vouching for at least the opening words of Jérôme's quotation? (Pressing narrative convention, we could exculpate Gide by moving this paratextual accomplice from Gide's purview to Jérôme's.) Perhaps partisan Gideans who recognized the "verse" for what it was but who overlooked "Jérôme's" responsibility for the misquotation, tolerantly forgave Gide for what they assumed was his mistake. Or did Gide somehow have Jérôme stitch together a patchwork from Luke and Matthew that seemed so quintessentially right that no one felt the need to take pause over its accuracy or to verify it? Or perhaps a taboo is at work? Could it be that no one had bothered to check because of a vague uneasiness about dealing with sacred texts in profane criticism? Or could the taboo be that the verse was sensed to be too central for interrogation, too much like the text itself to have what it lacks revealed? Or could the taboo be an esthetic one that bans double-voicedness from consideration? It may be that tradition has somehow communicated the understanding that the quotation, like the text, had to be an authoritative given, lest readerly *vertige* ultimately result.

Whatever the explanation, the situation is reminiscent of critics' glossing over Michel's acknowledgement of his easy lies or of his whimsically passing off an amalgam of past and present impressions as an historic account of his past. (See above, 83-84.) We recall how to admit Michel's consequent and sweeping lack of narrative trustworthiness confronts the reader with the poorly tolerated absence of a manageable story, ultimately leaving instead only the play of Michel's verbal caprice, just as the frame leaves the reader awash in indeterminacy of voice. We will now try to show how *vertige* cannot be avoided in *La Porte étroite* either, this "twin in excess." First, Jérôme's misquotation will be shown to be thoroughly typical of him as a narrator, so much so that he loses any reliability whatsoever as a narrator, leaving only Alissa's letters and diary as documents that invite our credence because of their objective status (Jérôme merely copies them). But then Jérôme's unreliability, this time in the form of editing, will be seen to pervade even those seemingly trustworthy texts, so that once again, as in *L'Immoraliste*, the reader will have been lured by impressions of an accessible text that under scrutiny retreats into unfulfilled promises; once again, in the final analysis, the reader will have to confront the tension of an exceptionally compelling, present-seeming voice (Alissa's), the logical absence of which undermines the foundation of first-person narrative as traditionally conceived.

As in the preceding chapter, the demonstration will push the limits of a narrative convention. Or to put it less aggressively, we will respect Gide's gifts more and received reading strategies less. As we have seen, reading and critical conventions operative at the time of publication of Gide's *récits* allowed for identifying his voice and intentions with those of his characters, a logical and aesthetic muddling that irritated Gide more than once. That explained the tone of bare containment found in the preface to l'*Immoraliste* noted in the previous chapter. And we observed that time has led to reading conventions that are more sensitive to the distinction between authors and their narrative voices. But such conventions still frequently allow for considerations about the author to interact with – and sometimes even to intercept – critical probing of narrators' limits. Not that this is always bad, on the contrary, but Gide took enormous pride in what he called his "profound sympathy" that permitted him to attain and communicate the "objectivity" of his narrators, especially in the case of Jérôme:

> ... déjà l'on m'avait pris pour l'Immoraliste; soyez bien assuré que, si je vis, l'on me prendra pour plus d'un autre encore. Je suis Protée. Garder son style propre à travers ces déroutantes transformations, voilà le hic. Mais je crois que ce qu'il sied d'ad-

mirer le plus ici, ce n'est pas le style, c'est la transformation (si toutefois je ne fais rien que m'y prêter, si je ne m'y compromets pas) et que mon meilleur gît dans un don de sympathie profonde. Ou je reste étranger, ou, si je pénètre dans autrui, c'est par le souterrain. De là, du reste, mon besoin de mettre mes récits à la première personne.

Ce "je" est pour moi le comble de l'objectivité. Dans *La Porte étroite*, je tiens que ça a été un véritable tour de force, une clownerie d'homme-serpent qui se coule dans un verre de lampe; ce fut ma porte étroite à moi, d'où je suis sorti quelque peu courbaturé, pas trop disloqué après tout, merveilleusement assoupli et tenace à moi-même. . . . (Letter to Christian Beck, 16 October 1909, quoted by Décaudin, "Sur trois récits d'André Gide" 132)

Why not then play Gide's game to his declared strengths and push the limits of Jérôme's status as a character "objectively" independent of his creator? While critics have long acknowledged many of Jérôme's responsibilities as narrator, they have done so intermittently and inconsistently, that is, without attempting a reading from which Gide's narrative responsibilities have been preliminarily excluded. There has been no systematic effort to pursue the ramifications of Jérôme as exclusive author. So for as long as we can, let us now read as if responsibility for the text found in *La Porte étroite* belongs to Jérôme alone, as if all the features of the narrative proper derive solely from him.

B) *Narrator vs. Editor*

Imagining then that Jérôme, not Gide, put every feature of the text together, will first lead us to see that his role as narrator is colored by, converges with, and indeed is supplanted by that of editor. (By "narrator" will be meant one who tells a story in one's own right, by "editor" one who makes significant use of others' texts to put a story together but who has the power to alter those texts.) Few would contest the coloring or converging of his narrating by and with his editing, since Jérôme uses Alissa's letters to get his chronology straight (*PE* 541), and then lets selected documents of hers that he has in his possession gradually become the dominant texts in sheer physical dimensions alone.

i) *Narrative Unreliability*

Explanation is called for, however, in asserting that in *La Porte étroite* editing supplants narrating. It is not just that Jérôme the narrator is unreliable, but he can be shown to be so singularly unreliable throughout his tale that the only hope left of arriving at an understanding more faithful to the diegetic "what happened" than his version of it is the material he edits: the trustworthiness of his memories and judgments pales in relation to the credibility of the documents that he passes along to his reader.

Even Zvi Lévy, the most vigorous defender of Jérôme's narrative role (see below, 116 ff.), has to emphasize the latter's limitations. Reading Jérôme's opening paragraph carefully, he concludes astutely:

> ... le prologue procure une image de la situation du personnage narrateur; et, plus précisément une image de sa situation morale: toute sa force dépensée et toute sa vertu usée dans le vécu de Jérôme personnage, il ne reste qu'un Jérôme narrateur moralement épuisé et intellectuellement incapable de juger lucidement les événements de son *Récit*, les comportements de ses partenaires ni même sa propre vision des choses. (Lévy 110)

Lévy asserts nonetheless that the account by the worn out narrator stands "conforme à la réalité des événements dans leur déroulement originel . . ." (Lévy 110). Such confidence seems misplaced. We have only to compare Jérôme's opening statement of narrative selection ("Ce ne sont pas mes premiers souvenirs que je prétends écrire ici, mais ceux-là seuls qui se rapportent à cette histoire," *PE* 497) with the staggering implications of the understated qualifier that appears a mere paragraph later, "autant qu'il m'en souvient," or with the implications of the aside two pages later, "Un jour de cet été – ou de l'été suivant, car dans ce décor toujours pareil, parfois mes souvenirs superposés se confondent" (*PE* 499-500, echoed later, as we just saw, on 541, when he resorts to Alissa's letters to get his chronology straight). In other words, Jérôme will base his story on relevant memories alone but, unfortunately for his readers, he may not remember everything relevant, and when he does, may jumble it together with other (relevant? irrelevant?) memories.

As if to certify this understanding of his opening remarks,

Jérôme demonstrates subsequently a characteristic penchant for highlighting his narrative shortcomings himself, confessing explicitly on more than one occasion to colossal inattention to important comments made by other characters. For instance: "Sont-ce là précisément ses paroles [of Alissa's sister Juliette]? je ne puis l'affirmer, car, je vous le dis, j'étais si plein de mon amour qu'à peine entendais-je, auprès, quelque autre expression que la sienne" (*PE* 519). And later that night, when alone: "Ah! triste aveugle que j'étais, cherchant mes torts en tâtonnant, de n'avoir pas songé un instant que les paroles de Juliette, que j'avais si mal écoutées et dont je me souvenais si mal, Alissa les avait peut-être mieux entendues" (*PE* 520). These comments fairly guarantee that we do not know what Juliette said when she and Jérôme were probing how he viewed Alissa's and his future. They raise the unsettling possibility that we do not even know the sense of what she said. Her words may have been of capital importance in light of Alissa's stunned reaction (*PE* 520) at overhearing their remarks: was Alissa overcome by the overt broaching – finally – of the subject of engagement, or by Jérôme's refusal to consider getting engaged, or indeed by Juliette's possible hints – denied to us – at her manifest love for Jérôme and even, conceivably, hints at her resentment towards Alissa?[3]

Another example of inattention occurs in Jérôme's version of his last meeting with Alissa. As Babcock remarks:

> During their last meeting, Jérôme suddenly kisses Alissa, who responds passionately but, seemingly recovering herself, pleads, 'Aie pitié de nous, mon ami! Ah! n'abîme pas notre amour.' Jérôme adds: 'Peut-être dit-elle encore: N'agis pas lâchement! ou peut-être me le dis-je moi-même, je ne sais plus . . .' (*PE* 577), quite openly alluding to the capacity of his memory, and his *récit*, for inaccuracy. (Babcock, *Portraits of Artists* 44)

And a different kind of inattention is betrayed when Alissa, in a terse but brief statement (*PE* 565), makes the declaration, considered by Loring D. Knecht crucial to the whole book, that holiness is an "OBLIGATION": Jérôme merely asks: "Qu'ajoutai-je [to his earlier letter to her] qui pût la pousser à répondre ceci" (*PE* 565). What indeed! Of an allegedly long letter, he lets us see only the few

---

[3] See Lévy, 32-58, for this latter view of Juliette.

sentences from it – quoted from memory no less – that he claims he recalls.

This inattention contributes to an explanation of what can be called the patchiness of Jérôme's narrative. It certainly could be a necessary aspect of recollection per se, as he himself tells us and demonstrates in the first chapter through his use of recalled "lambeaux" (hardly a term to instill confidence). But starting in the second chapter incompleteness looms as something more than that, achieving the status of a multi-faceted motif. First, and characteristically of the whole chapter, we are made to join Jérôme in his effort to piece together the fragments of the conversation he overheard between Alissa and her father (*PE* 508-10). Second, allied with this effort and parallel to its effects, there are the feelings aroused immediately afterwards by the teasingly incomplete conversation (*PE* 511) between the adolescent Jérôme and his mother about his feelings for Alissa. Third, we have to deal with the implications of two sets of suspension points that lop off parts of Alissa's first reported letter to him, on the occasion of the death of his mother (*PE* 512). Fourth, as we have just seen, in the especially intense scene that gets to the central question of when and indeed if Jérôme will ever marry Alissa, he had been so thoroughly "amused by his artifice" of making florid declamations to Juliette about love as a means of addressing the near-by Alissa, that he had become oblivious to Juliette's relevant comments. Fifth, uneasy curiosity is piqued – but not satisfied – by Alissa's father's allusion to "events" that "turned" his sister. This is an ominous evolution fraught with consequence because, of course, "Félicie ressemblait beaucoup à ce qu'est à présent Juliette" (*PE* 515):

> Tout ce qui vous déplaît en ma pauvre soeur, elle le doit à des événements que je connais trop pour pouvoir la critiquer aussi sévèrement que vous faites. Il n'y a pas qualité si plaisante de la jeunesse qui ne puisse, à vieillir, se gâter. Ce que vous appelez: agitation, chez Félicie, n'était d'abord qu'élan charmant, primesaut, abandon à l'instant et grâce. . . . (*PE* 515)

Sixth, as Albert Sonnenfeld has explained, there are telling lines from Baudelaire's "Chanson d'automne" that do *not* make it into Jérôme's second chapter (Sonnenfeld, "*Strait is the Gate*: Byroads in Gide's Labyrinth" 118-32).

While Gide's hand is doubtless at work here on considerations above and beyond the range of awareness and action attributable to his character Jérôme, one may learn to appreciate better the author's achievement of "objectivity" in Jérôme by exploring the latter's "responsibility" for the motif of patchiness before invoking the former's. In this instance, that appreciation comes when one realizes how the motif itself acts in the service of Jérôme's very conscious portrait of himself as a fourteen-year-old at the time, with which *he* chooses to open his account in chapter two and which the rest of it serves to illustrate:

> Sans doute, comme un enfant de quatorze ans, je restais encore indécis, disponible; mais bientôt mon amour pour Alissa m'enfonça dans ce sens. Ce fut une subite illumination intérieure à la faveur de laquelle je pris conscience de moi-même: je m'apparus replié, mal éclos, plein d'attente, assez peu soucieux d'autrui, médiocrement entreprenant, et ne rêvant d'autres victoires que celles qu'on obtient sur soi-même. (PE 506)

Can it be that Jérôme *wants* to be, and to remain, the adolescent he thinks he was in the circumscribed world of Fongueusemare that he recalls imperfectly?

The self-absorbed adolescent described after the colon ("je m'apparus replié, [etc.] . . .") could not help but have only partial awareness of what was going on around him. The older Jérôme, at times fully cognizant of his youthful inattentiveness and self-absorption (e.g., his conversation with Juliette), at others less so (e.g., his conversation with his mother), could therefore have articulated an account where narrative incompleteness becomes a motif, precisely because of his sense of what he had failed to notice when younger.

But it could also be because the adult author takes pleasure and comfort in resurrecting his adolescent self in as much detail as possible, including the undeniable "faults." Apropos, we ought not to forget that he had not specified in his opening paragraph the exact nature of "le dernier plaisir" (PE 495) that he hoped to find in recounting his memories. Was it to relive a shared past whose memory would resurrect Alissa, or was it more to relive his own past, the memory of which would resurrect instead his youthful self? Ominously, the description of those real shortcomings does not read negatively (from Jérôme's perspective) because they culminate in what he considers his saving strength, his proof of spiritual election: "ne rêvant d'autres victoires que celles qu'on obtient sur soi-même." The retrospective writer of the second chapter seems entirely consistent with the individual who (later, at the end of the *histoire*, but prior to the start of writing) caused Juliette pain when he barked out his determination to remain faithful, not to the memory of Alissa, but to the memory he believed she had had of *him*:

> —Asseyons-nous, dit-elle en se laissant tomber dans un fauteuil. Si je te comprends bien, c'est au souvenir d'Alissa que tu prétends rester fidèle.
> Je fus un instant sans répondre.
> Peut-être plutôt à l'idée qu'elle se faisait de moi. . . . (*PE* 597)

Keeping in mind that the many readings which he had recommended to her had helped shape her idea of him considerably in the first place,[4] we have reason to suspect that this bookish nostalgic, in his faithfulness to Alissa's/his text-determined view of himself, and in his written efforts to revisit his past, is to a significant degree a Narcissus returning to beloved textuality in search of his own image. That would help explain "his" decision to have such an unflattering portrait of himself published. True, although few readers would find in it any justification whatsoever of his conduct, he appears undiscerning enough to see in it more than ample justification. But there is the more intriguing chance that, as a self-absorbed, text-dependent Narcissus, he was driven to enter into material, verbal contact with his self image. Intense self-preoccupation could explain both his sketchy writing, his failure in the present to fix on anything other than his self and what reflected it (i.e., a skewed view of a derivative Alissa). It could also explain his sketchy attention in the past, when he failed to fix on words other than his own, be they direct or indirect (e.g., through Alissa the compliant reader).

---

[4] "Ainsi que je me l'étais promis, je lui écrivais très longuement chaque dimanche; les autres jours, me tenant à l'écart de mes camarades et ne fréquentant guère qu'Abel, je vivais avec la pensée d'Alissa et couvrais mes livres favoris d'indications à son usage, soumettant à l'intérêt qu'elle y pourrait prendre l'intérêt que moi-même y cherchais" (*PE* 530).
". . . [J]'avais pris l'habitude, en effet, de semer mes livres et ceux d'Alissa de la première lettre de son nom, en regard de chacun des passages que j'aimais et voulais lui faire connaître" (*PE* 545).

Seen in the light of this possibility, there is a telling incident, in that some of its details evoke strikingly those of the traditional Narcissus myth. A bucolic, attractive female distracts the young Jérôme: "J'éprouvais un singulier malaise auprès de ma tante [Bucolin, from the verdant Martinique], un sentiment fait de trouble, d'une sorte d'admiration et d'effroi" (*PE* 499). The figure of the reflecting pool, central to the myth, penetrates our awareness in three metonymic displacements: first, in the small mirror usually carried (*PE* 499) by the seductress (in Jérôme's mind at least)[5] and into the circle of which she pulls together the image of his and her face (*PE* 500); second and at a farther remove, the water-associated sailor shirt that she starts to open (*PE* 500); third and back to a more straightforward evocation, the little tank of water to which Narcissus-like he flees to try to wash away her touch (*PE* 500).

Not surprisingly, the incident reads like a primal scene, due in large portion to the highly charged description of the putative attempt at seduction by the very carnal, beautiful maiden/mother (e.g., "... plus encore que l'ardente couleur des écharpes que ma tante jetait sur ses épaules nues, ce décolletage scandalisait ma mère. Lucile Bucolin était très belle," *PE* 497-98). It is due even more to the striking use, atypical for *La Porte étroite*, of the present tense. Commenting on the appearance of several verbs in the present that occasionally arise in Jérôme's retrospective account, Eric Marty observes:

> Leur fonction serait donc de briser l'anesthésie monocorde de l'imparfait, mais aussi de donner à entendre, de plus près, les scènes fondatrices du récit. Ce sont, en effet, les épisodes marquants, qui, comme des souvenirs trop brûlants, reviennent, et sont revécus et marqués par là d'un sceau inhabituel: les caresses de la mère d'Alissa à Jérôme, ses crises obscènes, les consolations que Jérôme prodigue à Alissa.... (Marty 84)

---

[5] Roy Jay Nelson observes that there could be many reasonable alternative explanations (other than adultery) of Lucile's ultimately unexplained flight from her family. (See below, 129-30) Nelson also astutely observes that the final explanation, whatever it was, was available to Jérôme but assiduously kept by him from the reader. This underscores the tendentiousness of Jérôme's account. Consequently, because he assumed (but did not show) that her putting her hand down his shirt was "dirty" (could she not have been just tickling him?), the salacious but unstated assumptions underpinning his account of her flight have been passed on successfully to virtually every critic of *La Porte étroite*. In studies of *La Porte étroite* where one reads 'Lucile,' the epithet 'adulterous' either appears or is usually understood.

The incident does indeed read like a "scène fondatrice," all the more so for my purposes of establishing Jérôme's text as a narcissistic mirror, since one of its contexts is books, the source of so much of his sense of himself. For instance, what Lucile was attempting to distract Jérôme from was a book that he wanted to read: ". . . j'entre au salon chercher un livre; elle y était. J'allais me retirer aussitôt; elle qui, d'ordinaire, semble à peine me voir, m'appelle . . ." (*PE* 500). Moreover, Jérôme keeps a portrait of her as she was at the time, a portrait that shows her characteristically holding a book.

It seems odd that he has kept over the years a picture of a woman whom he reproaches for having done so much harm (*PE* 499). But that is no more odd than a particular quality of Alissa, to whom he feels so attracted: she resembles her mother very much (*PE* 501). She also happens to resemble Jérôme's mother (*PE* 515), meaning that the three important women in his life resembled each other. There is reason then to postulate oedipal anxieties on his boyhood part regarding all three of these key women in his life: the first memory which Jérôme chooses to record is one combining his father's death when he himself was a pre-pubescent eleven-year-old (*PE* 495), that is, on the threshold of active sexuality; the second memory is his attempt to restrain his mother's physical appeal by insisting that she continue to wear the black ribbon of death instead of the more vibrant mauve. (It seems permissible to wonder if Jérôme's taste for masochistic mortifications of self-denial does not owe a lot to guilt over what could appear to a child to be a death-wish successfully directed at his father. If so, he would share an apparent taste for expiation with Alissa, who gives signs of trying to make up for the sins of her mother.) Viewed in this Oedipal light, the contradictory quality of his distancing courtship of Alissa is then a reprise of his erotic yet (to him) death-dealing responses to the two mothers who look like her and each other. He is drawn to the seductive, frightening mother whose picture he carries around, while insisting that the other incarnation of the mother not break out of her unthreatening "air également doux et triste" (*PE* 495): death is at stake. Such may be the anxieties feeding his narcissistic uncertainties and need to ponder a fabricated, textual pre-adolescence of innocence.

Given then the tight interplay in Chapter Two *as written by "Jérôme"* between the motif of incompleteness and the issue of youthful self-awareness suspiciously narcissistic, it is small wonder that his account at this point betrays an apparently heightened receptivity to recollections involving mirrors and reflected images, especially since one of them entails a broken one (" – Mes enfants, dit-il [Jérôme's uncle], même brisée Dieu reconnaîtra son image." *PE* 515) To be sure, images of reflection reappear beneath Jérôme's (as opposed to Gide's) pen simply because he likes them, as two of the examples suggest ("Car nous nous souvenions du mot de Goethe qui, parlant de Mme de Stein, écrivait: 'Il serait beau de voir se réfléchir le monde dans cette âme,' *PE* 515; "Oh! si seulement nous pouvions, nous penchant sur l'âme qu'on aime, voir en elle, comme en un miroir, quelle image nous y posons!" *PE* 518). But Jérôme's inclusion of the image of the mirror (see also *PE* 520), especially one broken on occasion, suits especially well the goal and atmosphere of this, his second chapter.

In retrospect, then, one can also retrieve the rich significance of Jérôme's description of the Bucolin house at Fongueusemare from the almost exclusive purview of the author's direct relationship with readers. Critics do well to comment on the obvious symbolism of the varying opacity of the window panes, of the "bouillons" in some of them, and of the perspective-restricting house (having blind walls on the north and south) into which the windows are set:

> [The house] ouvre une vingtaine de grandes fenêtres sur le devant du jardin, au levant; autant par derrière; elle n'en a pas sur les côtés. Les fenêtres sont à petits carreaux: quelques-uns, récemment remplacés, paraissent trop clairs parmi les vieux qui, auprès, paraissent verts et ternis. Certains ont des défauts que nos parents appellent des "bouillons"; l'arbre qu'on regarde au travers se dégingande; le facteur, en passant devant, prend une bosse brusquement. (*PE* 496)

Discussions of this description assume that the symbolism works only beyond the narrator's ken, that is, ironically. But what happens to our understanding of the working of the symbol, if we keep prominently in mind that Gide would have us pretend that Jérôme chose what to describe, that Gide wrote this while in "Jérôme's skin"? What happens, in other words, if we remain attuned to the latter's recognition of his own inattentiveness, and to his sense of the unsatisfactory nature of his earlier memories? We realize that his including among so few and so brief physical descriptions the "blindered" house and its distorting windows is consistent with *his* insistent awareness of his narrative shortcomings. He may even have included it for the same reason he felt compelled to draw attention to his fragmentary awareness and memories, that is, out of a knowing sense that he was missing something central in his understanding of himself, something like the Oedipal tragedy that we surmise in his childhood. To an understanding such as his, his description of the house might even serve to excuse him by showing how objective, how natural limits of vision are. In fact, he may well have approved such blindered awareness, because as we just saw, he takes it as a sign of his selection, of his being a member of the spiritual elite too preoccupied by lofty concerns to be attentive to the quotidian. His awareness does function, even though, much like his understanding of story-telling (*PE* 495), he would have us believe that it gives every sign of working "simply" (for instance, he assumes that his memories are in tatters "only" occasionally – "par endroits" – and are therefore fundamentally trustworthy). From the start then, Jérôme, far from being completely ignorant of his closed perspectives and distorted memories, has reason to be sensitive to what the house suggests in itself and to him as he resuscitates the imperceptive youth that he was (and, one senses early on, that he would remain). The irony of the symbol continues to function, but now at an additional level that leavens our understanding of Jérôme.

The subject of understanding brings us back to the larger point under development in this opening section: the patchiness, blindness, and limited perspective of his account have a devastating effect on his narrative reliability, an effect that his awareness cannot mitigate, but merely underscores. Not only are his recollections unreliable because admittedly spotty and biased, but as the closing scene between Jérôme and Juliette suggests, the adolescent personality responsible for their generation continues to be responsible for their very redaction and for that of more recent memories:

> If *La Porte étroite* does not have universal appeal, it may well be in part because it has little movement. It is static (see Brée, [Germaine Brée, *Gide* (New Brunswick, N.J: Rutgers University Press, 1963)], p. 159), but precisely because it had to be, because the character that Jérôme had to be stifled all normal movement. This substantive reality is admirably reflected in the tempo that

Gide has given to the work. All progression is either illusory or artificial. We remain at the static point of Jérôme's arrested development. (Knecht 648)

So the far from subtle narrative irony is that the qualities reflected in his adolescent self-portrait by the words "replié, mal éclos, plein d'attente, assez peu soucieux d'autrui, médiocrement entreprenant," obtaining throughout his life, have obtained throughout his narration.

In "external" corroboration of his narrative weaknesses are the references to his extraordinary unreliability, conveyed (by him) in the comments of others, for instance in Abel Vautier's remarks on his blindness regarding Juliette (*PE* 523, 528, 537). We may then assert in complete confidence that from its opening lines and in a variety of noteworthy ways Jérôme's own text calls into question his value and so function as narrator.

### ii) *The "Main" Text*

Jérôme's editing also challenges the primacy of his narrating, in that, as five persuasive appraisals of *La Porte étroite* will entitle us to claim, Alissa's journal, not Jérôme's narrative, is the main text. (The expression "main text" can be a troublesome one, especially regarding a book as elusive and narratively complex as *La Porte étroite*. A definition will be proposed inductively, after the following examination of pertinent views of Alissa's diary.) To the degree that one accepts that her text does in fact function as the "main text," Jérôme's "main" role becomes less that of narrator and more that of editor.

The most succinct statement of the status of Alissa's document can be found in an article by Michel Lioure:

> Par sa situation romanesque, sa qualité littéraire et sa densité spirituelle, le *Journal d'Alissa* est le sommet de *La Porte étroite*. Gide assure en être "très content" (Lettre à A. R., printemps 1909, citée dans A. GIDE, *Romans*, La Pléiade, 1549), et sa constante prédilection témoigne de l'importance esthétique et morale de ce *Journal* où s'illuminent soudain le secret d'Alissa et l'énigme de son sacrifice. Mal satisfait de la "flasque prose"

qu'implique le "flasque caractère" du narrateur Jérôme, Gide savoure au contraire dans ces pages privilégiées les "amandes" d'un "nougat" romanesque dont le "mastic" lui semble "pâteux" (*Journal*, 7 novembre 1909, édition de la Pléiade, 1955, p. 276). (Lioure 39)

This incisive paragraph is useful for those of us who have read the book repeatedly, because through its effective recapitulation of the main features of Alissa's diary it helps us to recall and understand the sense of sudden illumination brought on by first exposure to it. That experience, together with the diary's features as listed by Lioure, argue well for its primacy.

In much the same vein, Christian Vandendriessche finds that the diary "drives" the entire book, imparting to it its true character:

> Si quantativement, le Journal d'Alissa occupe, au sein du récit de *La Porte étroite*, une place relativement restreinte, il ne constitue néanmoins la partie motrice, celle qui motive tout un comportement..................................................................................
> La minutieuse reconstitution du chassé-croisé entre récit et journal permet d'affirmer que les deux modes d'écriture se complètent sans jamais se superposer. . . . Le récit, livré d'abord, est une épure, à laquelle le journal rend ses véritables dimensions, pour faire de l'oeuvre une figure achevée. (Vandendriessche 107)

G. W. Ireland reaches a compatible conclusion by asking whether the story told by Jérôme is fundamentally his or that of Alissa, and whether it is he or she who achieves what Ireland argues to be the desired outcome of any first-person narrative, the constitution of an "I" that enters into an intersubjective relationship with the reader. To both questions his answer is Alissa.[6] Ireland's observation that

---

[6] "Revenons à la question centrale. Il est peu évident que l'histoire racontée par le frère du Président du Conseil [in *L'Immoraliste*] est très peu *son* histoire à lui. Dans quelle mesure l'histoire racontée par Jérôme est-elle son histoire?
   Comme j'ai dit, tout récit commence par un Je. Mais tout récit est en même temps constitutif d'un Je qui en est l'aboutissement.
   Nul doute que la fonction profonde de *L'Immoraliste* est de permettre la réalisation en premier lieu d'*un* Je: d'obtenir que le lecteur consente à écouter ce que dit ce Je dans un état de totale suspension d'incrédulité, de se laisser muer lui-même en cours de route en un Je qui participe non moins intensément à l'aventure qui est la fiction que cet autre Je qu'il faut trouver, accepter, *reconnaître*. Ce dialogue dont je vous parle s'établit plus ou moins facilement et est maintenu à des degrés très va-

Jérôme tells Alissa's story, not his own, should perhaps be buttressed by noting how Jérôme excises from his account much that he knows about himself, but apparently little of what he knows about Alissa. For instance, after saying that he will include "[les souvenirs] seuls qui se rapportent à cette histoire" (*PE* 497), Jérôme excludes many of the details concerning his life away from Alissa, that is, his studies in Paris, his experiences while traveling to Italy, while living in Greece, etc.; he incorporates into his narrative several of her letters but only one of his own, and so on.

Elaine Cancalon, moreover, has done a study, one of the conclusions of which lends support to Lioure's, Vandendriessche's, and Ireland's positions. Even though at a later point in her argument she offers the insight that the main character of *La Porte étroite* is better viewed as Jérôme and Alissa taken as a couple (Cancalon, *Techniques et Personnages* 81, an observation that will harmonize nicely with the "in-living" of their voices that I will assert below), this perceptive *Gidienne* nonetheless includes only Alissa when she lists those characters from Gide's five principal *récits* who share the traits of protagonist:

> Les protagonistes (André Walter, Michel, Alissa, Gérard, le Pasteur) des cinq récits que nous examinerons représentent des variantes d'un même type de caractère dont les traits sont établis par certaines idées générales présentes dans chaque oeuvre. Les thèmes principaux qui relient tous les héros et qui déterminent leur caractère sont les suivants:
> 1) la recherche de l'absolu
> 2) le refus de la réalité
> 3) le refus des contradictions de la nature humaine

---

riables d'intensité: quasi nul par exemple entre le lecteur et le frère du Président du Conseil, il est sporadique mais quelque fois assez fort dans le cas de Marceline. Mais on sent pourtant très nettement que le centre même du livre, c'est le Je qu'arrive à prononcer Michel.

Il n'en va évidemment pas tout à fait de même de *La Porte étroite*, puisque Jérôme, dans une certaine mesure, parvient lui aussi, du moins formellement, à se constituer en Je narrateur. Mais la différence ici ne me semble toucher que très peu à ce que j'ai appelé la structure profonde du livre. Car en fait, la position centrale du livre, le lieu privilégié où un Je narrateur pleinement constitué dialogue directement avec un Je lecteur à ce niveau d'inter-subjectivité est, en fait, accaparée tout entière par Alissa" (Ireland, "Le Jeu des 'je'" 79).

4) l'opposition entre la liberté et la contrainte
5) l'opposition entre l'esprit et le corps.

(Cancalon, *Techniques et Personnages dans les récits d'André Gide* 5)

The text of the protagonist can lay strong claim to being the "main" one.

Moreover, in a later article written in 1990, responding directly to Zvi Lévy's argument that Jérôme's text is the main one (see below, 116), Cancalon triangulated on Alissa's narrative role, by using the theories of Gérard Genette (*Le Discours du récit*) and Roland Barthes (*S/Z*), and Jean Rousset's insights into the epistolary novel. Explaining the ironic metadiegetic status of Alissa's letters and diary, the way *she* (not Jérôme) sets the puzzles of the text's hermeneutic code, and how her writing constitutes the only significant act of the book, Cancalon insists convincingly that we should still view Alissa as the protagonist of *La Porte étroite*. It is Alissa who "pulls the narrative strings" (Cancalon, "*La Porte étroite: ou le triomphe du métadiégétique*" 71), because it is *her* correspondence that stimulates the growing curiosity about her family and about her apparent refusal of Jérôme's love, and *her* diary that assumes final narrative authority.

The expression "main text," then, obviously has nothing necessarily to do with being the longer one. Nor should it suggest the better written in an absolute sense: "flasque prose" revealing a corresponding personality that nonetheless compels reader interest is no less — and perhaps more — a literary accomplishment than sensitive prose revealing a tortured, interesting soul. But within the conventions of the book, pretending that "Jérôme" — not Gide — wrote certain pages and "Alissa" — not Gide — others, Lioure's judgment of the diary's literary and spiritual superiority stands. His using as a criterion of importance its "situation romanesque," Vandendriessche's using its driving force, Ireland's using intersubjectivity, Cancalon's demonstrating that Alissa "pulls the narrative strings," all those criteria merit acceptance. (That is, within the conventions of the book, we must again acknowledge. For it took Gide's laborious elaboration of "Jérôme"'s text and the interplay of the letters to prepare the *coup* of the diary's impact; it took his skill to delineate the two characters in a way that made "Alissa" more engaging and more narratively manipulative in spite of her limited access to the reader and that made the more directly present "Jérôme" a reluctant conduit to a stronger reader relationship with "Alissa.") Finally, the "main text" comes from the protagonist, that is, from a character incarnating questions and values that are both the fulcrum and focus of the book's creative energies. In short, and viewed from its effect on the reader, the "main text" turns out to be the more seductive one, Alissa's.

("Main text" in the sense of a definitive text is only a working hypothesis for any novel. It does not – cannot – exist of course. In *La Porte étroite*, this makes itself felt in the fact that even if Jérôme had passed along to the reader every page of the diary and letters that he had gotten from Alissa, that would not be everything because she herself had destroyed one of her notebooks [*PE* 590]. Taking possibilities one step further, had she left for him every single word that she had ever written, that would not suffice either because here too, many of her texts were written not for her but for him [*PE* 594], that is, were not *her* texts in the sense of ones transmitting exclusively her voice, her story. Even among the pages that may have been written exclusively for and by her she excised those that seemed to be too well written [*PE* 588].)

But Zvi H. Lévy, in the most highly detailed, painstakingly informed study to date of Jérôme's role in *La Porte étroite* (but one not without detractors),[7] will have none of considering Jérôme as anything less than the source of the main text. For him Jérôme is *the* narrator and his narrative, not Alissa's diary, is the main text:

> Du fait des limites chronologiques de sa rédaction, de la restriction de l'espace dramatique qu'il occupe par rapport au *Récit*, de l'"évacuation" hors de son propre récit d'un nombre important de données dramatiques déterminantes, on peut dire qu'Alissa, en fonction de narratrice, et le *Journal* en fonction de récit, restent loin de deçà de ces mêmes fonctions pour Jérôme et son *Récit*. Ceci ne veut pas dire qu'on ne peut pas tracer un portrait d'Alissa sur la base de l'ensemble des données du *Récit* et du *Journal*, sur la plan de la "description psychologique du personnage" et sur celui de son comportement "dynamique" dans l'action; ni même qu'on ne puisse – assez paradoxalement – obtenir un portrait plus complexe que ne le serait celui de Jérôme; mais c'est un portrait qui ne peut être tracé qu'à l'intérieur de la nar-

---

[7] See for instance reviews by David H. Walker, Michael Tilby, and Alain Goulet. For other, earlier, extensive studies of *La Porte étroite* see Davies, and Trahard.

ration de Jérôme et que le cadre narratif du seul *Journal* ne permettrait en aucun cas d'élaborer. On peut ajouter encore que les éléments fournis par le *Journal*, en sus de ceux fournis par le *Récit* (où l'on inclut, bien sûr, les lettres d'Alissa) sont relativement peu nombreux et sans signification suffisamment considérable pour changer l'image procurée déjà par le *Récit*. (Lévy 108-09)

One of the problems with Lévy's position is that, ironically enough, it does not adequately take into account Jérôme's role as relayer of information. First of all, there is a gradual erosion of Jérôme's narrative authority throughout his account, and it occurs not just in his relationship with Alissa's text:

> ... from early in Chapter II, [Jérôme's voice] is noticeably muted as other voices make themselves heard: Jérôme's summary of events gives way increasingly to dialogue; and the brief snatches of direct speech of Chapter I are succeeded in Chapter II by a series of ten conversations – mostly of an extensive nature – wherein the role of the narrator is significantly reduced. Accordingly, the reader is now less the confidant of Jérôme than a privileged eavesdropper gaining access to the confidences which pass between the characters. All in all, in narrative terms, a crucial shift has taken place. (Shorley 23)

Second, it is not that one has to deal with the "données [...] du *Journal*" and "les éléments fournis par le *Journal*," but rather that one is reduced to dealing with the "data" and "the elements provided by Alissa's diary *such as Jérôme provides them.*" In other words, the reader is not pitting Jérôme's *discours* against Alissa's – the presupposition made by Lévy – but rather Jérôme's against Jérôme's version of Alissa's. While this would seem initially to strengthen Lévy's hand, it paradoxically highlights an important facet of Alissa's relayed texts, their seductiveness, a feature that advantages her words over Jérôme's. Alissa's truncated text, as the more absent one (a quality heightened by the voice offering it *d'outre-tombe*), turns out to be the one that stirs more curiosity and reader desire, all the more so because of its concentrated intensity. So the decisiveness that Lévy tries to locate in the status of the two characters and their texts seems inadvisable (all the more so since it is at odds with the elusiveness of this first-person narrative, much commented on by recent critics). One of the few things that *is* certain for most readers is the imposing way in which Alissa's diary manages to exert its seductiveness, Jérôme's editing of it notwithstanding. That resistant seductiveness alone, while not dramatically standing Lévy's position on its head, would be enough to corrupt its basis.

Moreover, to slip momentarily out of the restraint of viewing Jérôme alone as responsible for the text, resistant seductiveness may be the main source of a tension that Gidean *disponibilité* calls for, in that it counteracts the logically determined inaccessibility of the diary, tugging it back toward "real-seeming" contact with the reader. To put it another way, the seductiveness places the main text where Robert W. Greene posits Gide's early *récits*, on the stress lines between reflexive and realistic fiction (Greene 75-76). It would, after all, be out of keeping with Gide's values if the narrative structure of *La Porte étroite* did not somehow restore the "balancement de la disponibilité" away from simple inaccessibility of its main text, the diary. Consequently, the diary provokes and necessitates readings such as Lioure's, Vandendriessche's, Ireland's, and Cancalon's that more fully take into account the impact of the diary upon readers, invalidating a more neutral, simplifying description like Lévy's that cannot address the affect at work.

Lévy's position, moreover, glosses over the enriching complications of the narrative structure of *La Porte étroite*, for instance when he argues that Jérôme's vision of love is echoed by Alissa's diary. Alissa wrote:

> Parfois j'hésite si ce que j'éprouve pour lui c'est bien ce que l'on appelle de l'amour – tant la peinture que d'ordinaire on fait de l'amour diffère de celle que je pourrais en faire. Je voudrais que rien n'en fût dit et l'aimer sans savoir que je l'aime. Surtout je voudrais l'aimer sans qu'il le sût. (*PE* 584)

Lévy observes:

> Cette vision de l'amour, formulation qui annule toute l'expérience antérieure (comme Alissa annule son passé), reprend la vision de l'amour chez Jérôme après la vision de la chapelle: "[Je pensais] la mériter mieux en m'éloignant d'elle sitôt" (*PE* 506), et le vécu de cet amour: "travail, efforts, actions pies, mystiquement j'offrais tout à Alissa, inventant un raffinement de vertu à lui laisser souvent ignorer ce que je n'avais fait que pour elle" (*PE* 507). (Lévy 96)

If one looks at the similarities between the two quotations exclusively from the perspective of the reader's time, then Lévy is correct to say that Alissa's vision "reprend la vision de l'amour chez Jérôme après la vision de la chapelle."

But here as virtually everywhere in *La Porte étroite*, in pursuing the alluring "what happened?" of *histoire* through cross-checking, one must first disentangle *histoire* from discourse coming from not just one character but two, from not one but at least four or five kinds of discourse. Christopher Shorely delineates perceptively what he calls the five "narrative modes" in *La Porte étroite*: Jérôme's "monologue" in the opening pages where he uses his own words, his slipping into dialogue in Chapter Two when he starts quoting more and more conversations, and of course his own letter, Alissa's letters, and then her diary. His first two categories, while appropriate and well founded, are part of an approach that views the resulting structure as Gide's (Shorley 31). Emphasizing as I do "Jérôme's" responsibility for the structure, I see both the monologue and the dialogues as emanating from his memory, and so sharing a status radically different from that of the contemporaneously written documents that he subsequently draws upon. Be they four or five, the kinds of discourse, emanating from the perspectives of two different characters, do offer the (merely apparent) hope that by cross-checking, readers can get a better hold on story than would be the case in a typical first-person narrative told from one perspective and in one narrative mode. But as readers of *La Porte étroite* try – and are encouraged – to patch together the story by negotiating the tangle of modes and sources of discourse, it becomes all too easy to lose sight of the chronology of the discourses.

Once attentive to that chronology, instead of to the usual diegetic chronology, we realize, as Sonnenfeld has underlined ("On Readers and Reading"), that Alissa's diary must have come – and been read by Jérôme – well before any of his narrative. In writing it, Jérôme speaks of the time of composition ("aujourd'hui") as one in which he is making an effort to relive past events: "... encore aujourd'hui que je reviens en arrière pour revivre tout ce passé ..." (*PE* 579). Since Alissa died less than a month after the events recounted on that same page, it is highly unlikely that Jérôme would have described them as past, or indeed that he would have wanted to relive them, unless considerable time had intervened. That would help explain why the last few pages, dealing with his visit to

Juliette ten years after the death of Alissa, follow the diary pages naturally without a break, without any indication that he had had to resume composition to append the last pages to an earlier version, etc. Since he had gotten the diary about a month after Alissa's demise, the "today" of composition must have taken place at least ten years later, when he started writing. So the diary came first. Nonetheless, Jérôme, who had read it and the letters (once? more than once?) ten years before he took up the pen (and read them how many times thereafter, and then how many times during writing?), presents them second, after having partially interlarded them into his own discourse. But during the decade between the time he first read her diary and the time he started writing, her concrete, seductive pages had ample opportunity to guide and influence his not so accurate memory and less than penetrating understanding. This makes it probable that, to the contrary of Lévy's position, Jérôme "reprend la vision de l'amour chez" Alissa. While he certainly experienced his own reaction to the sermon on the narrow gate before Alissa knew or wrote about it, he himself did not write about it until long afterwards, until some time after having been the susceptible reader of her hypnotic texts – and Jérôme offers abundant evidence that his bookish personality inclines him to let his reaction to texts, read aptly or otherwise, articulate the way that he sees things. (For example: ". . . appréciations, discussions, critiques [of favorite books] ne m'étaient qu'un moyen d'exprimer ma pensée," *PE* 530.) Moreover, as Lévy has done (55-56, 106), much can be read into the moment of the last recorded event (and so *before* he started writing), when Jérôme had declared to Juliette that his goal for the rest of his life was "peut-être" (!!!) to remain faithful to the idea that he thought Alissa had of him. That idea was most tangibly and faithfully incarnated in her diary. Consequently it is not farfetched to assume that his understanding of her vision of him *peut-être* colored Jérôme's subsequent rendition of events, so that the latter would be more in keeping with the former. The subject that Lévy invites us to scrutinize is then not a vision of love, but the *written expression* of a vision of love *remembered* better from writing than from direct experience. That expression is therefore the product of, among many other things, forces of intertextuality and tendentious reading.

Lévy's well-documented argument to the contrary has considerable importance for my position, however, because the difficulty of challenging its strengths has led to an appreciation of an "in-living" of voices similar to what we found at work in *L'Immoraliste*. Since Jérôme's written vision of events has been shaped to one degree or another by Alissa's, and since, on the other hand, Alissa's opinions were strongly influenced by Jérôme and his recommendations about reading, one cannot be sure whose vision is relaying whose. As in the framed and framing voices of *L'Immoraliste*, in the apparently distinct voices of Jérôme and Alissa we have a mutuality that blurs the frontiers of their separateness:

> *De livre en livre je le fuis et le retrouve. Même la page que sans lui je découvre, j'entends sa voix encore me la lire. Je n'ai goût qu'à ce qui l'intéresse, et ma pensée a pris la forme de la sienne au point que je ne sais les distinguer pas plus qu'au temps où je pouvais me plaire à les confondre.* (PE 588)

Arguing that Alissa's diary is the main text leads us as well down interesting byways. Assuming that Jérôme physically wrote the text, in which Alissa's correspondence and diary, as quoted documents, had to be italicized or underlined, we see that he was obliged to bestow on her words that same physical sign of authority that was called for when he quoted the Bible, Baudelaire, Racine, Dante, Shakespeare, *et al.* True, his own words are accorded that same authority – but only once, and briefly at that, in the two-paragraph selection from the only letter of his quoted directly but partially (*PE* 560). Those two paragraphs are dwarfed by the number and size of quotations from Alissa. Thus, both Jérôme the reader and Jérôme the writer would appear inclined to lend authority to Alissa's documents. Indeed, on one occasion he himself recognized his susceptibility to (and irritability at) Alissa's more "living and triumphant" language ("*chacune des phrases d'Alissa, contre lesquelles je m'insurgeais d'abord, restait en moi vivante et triomphante après que mes protestations s'étaient tues*" *PE* 573).

In another very physical sense, Jérôme underscores the power of her language upon him because of the extent to which, starting slowly in the second chapter, he progressively allows Alissa's letters and then her diary to crowd out his words. Although he starts quoting her letters only in Chapter Two where he inserts just one of them, and that in truncated form, by the time he reaches Chapter Five her correspondence reaches a peak by taking up much of its first third and then most of its last two-thirds, finally comprising 70 % of the whole chapter, a peak later surpassed by the diary. (Shorley 27). In all, her letters make up 15 % of the text in its entirety, with the diary making up still another 15 % (Cancalon, "*La Porte étroite*" 74). In consequence of the way in which they appear, both her letters and her diary, while only 30 % of the total text, turn their growing importance to appropriate the driving narrative force that was supposed initially to be his. That progression culminates in the symbolic position that he assigns to her sizeable diary, leaving to her quite literally the last word in the account of their common past. (He was, we note, sensitive to the significance of one's having the last word, having commented earlier: "[Abel] me plaisanta pour ce que je n'avais pas su poser mon dernier mot [vis-à-vis d'Alissa], comme il disait....," *PE* 522.)

Another outcome of his reading the diary and pondering it for ten years may have been encouragement in his editing ways, for in the diary Alissa too evidences the desire and the practice of excising parts of her writing (not to mention her life).[8] In Albert Sonnenfeld's highly respected article on reading in *La Porte étroite*, he proposed that as editor Jérôme practices a "rhetorical strategy toward his own reader analogous to the projected self of Alissa in her *Journal*" (which she had edited in several ways), a strategy that, like more than one aspect of his account, may have resulted from reading and being influenced by her text before starting his own (Sonnenfeld, "On Readers and Reading" 178-79). On the other hand, Jérôme had modeled editing for her much earlier, in his habit of marking passages for her special attention in the books that he recommended for her. To emphasize passages is, of course, a subtle cutting-away of others from an equal field of attention. Significantly, however, he claims to have let the passages that he thought would interest her guide his own interests: "... soumettant à l'intérêt qu'elle y pourrait prendre l'intérêt que moi-même y cherchais"

---

[8] "Like Gide who wrote his book by a series of excisions, Alissa eliminates everything living from her life: she sends Jérôme away and consents only reluctantly to reunions with him (meanwhile he too is eager to undergo separations in order to impress his own virtuousness on her); she discards her piano and her beloved books, retaining only vulgar works of edification written by 'simple souls.' Finally, she withdraws even from Fongueusemare into a bare nursing-home; a self-imposed imprisonment is a preparation for a worthy death" (Sonnenfeld, "*Strait is the Gate*: Byroads in Gide's Labyrinth" 127).

(*PE* 530). This textually/psychologically mutual "inter-editing" parallels rather tightly even the selection of subjects and books from which the *morceaux choisis* came:

> Nous nous étions procuré les Évangiles dans le texte de la Vulgate et en savions par coeur de longs passages. Sous prétexte d'aider son frère, Alissa avait appris avec moi le latin; mais plutôt, je suppose, pour continuer de me suivre dans mes lectures. Et, certes, à peine osais-je prendre goût à une étude où je savais qu'elle ne m'accompagnerais pas. Si cela m'empêcha parfois, ce ne fut pas, comme on pourrait croire, en arrêtant l'élan de mon esprit; au contraire, il me semblait qu'elle me précédât partout librement. Mais mon esprit choisissait ses voies selon elle, et ce qui nous occupait alors, ce que nous appelions: pensée, n'était souvent qu'un prétexte à quelque communion plus savante.... (*PE* 510-11)

Jérôme himself, then, correctly sees editing as a "sort of" interaction – "quelque communion plus savante" – for Alissa and himself, an imprecise but appropriate status that paves the way for positing in this *récit* what I called in my discussion of *L'Immoraliste* the Bakhtinian "in-living" of two different voices, more specifically in this case two editing and edited voices. In this is realized the thematic promise of the conflated biblical verses that produce the book's very title.

So against Jérôme's list of editorial excisions must be set Alissa's. For example, in her sixth piece of correspondence to Jérôme, dealing with her reaction to Racine's fifth *Cantique spirituel*, Alissa cannot help but transcribe what she calls "des strophes tellement belles," which include the first four lines of the first verse (the lines to be found on the Christmas card that Jérôme at age twelve had sent to her), and the second, third, and sixth verses. Interestingly enough, she skips the fourth and fifth verses entirely. While it could be that those verses simply did not strike her as being as beautiful as the others, one notices that both of them highlight the worthiness of humanity, making points at odds with her dour, masochistic religiosity: the poet marvels that the God whose Word "Fit éclore l'univers" "daignes/Jusqu'à moi rabaisser," taking on and dignifying human flesh in order to "Apprendre à l'homme coupable/Sa véritable grandeur." Since an appreciation of human importance and grandeur deriving from the Word-become-flesh would challenge the sexual anxiety and self-hatred underlying Alissa's stark interpretation of the "strait gate," the two verses have been removed from her version. Such acts are numerous on her part.[9]

The very least, then, that can be said about the relationships of anteriority and dependency between Alissa's and Jérôme's discourse is that they are far more problematic when one begins taking into account Jérôme's relaying of Alissa's texts, something Lévy does not adequately do, but that readings of earlier critics (Lioure, et al., Sonnenfeld) and a later rereading (Cancalon's) would allow for. Consequently, the earlier arguments maintaining that Alissa's diary is the main text still prevail, with the understanding that, like Michel's account, this main text slides into an indeterminate relationship with its frame.

### C) *Critical Yield*

But aside from the issue of the intrinsic value of seeing how Jérôme's shortcomings and the primacy of Alissa's diary undermine his importance as narrator, draw attention to his role as editor, and position both their voices in a dynamic dependency, there is the question of its further practical value. There would appear to be a critical "yield" to be earned by viewing him as an editor, as was implied by some of the preceding speculative byways. We can explore a point already mentioned in the opening paragraph of this chapter and *passim*, but passed over quickly: the diary as main text relayed by Jérôme serves as one more means of tying *La Porte étroite* to its

---

[9] "*A peine ai-je pu prier, depuis que je suis ici* [Aigues-Vives]: *j'éprouve le sentiment enfantin que Dieu n'est plus à la même place. Adieu; je te quitte bien vite; j'ai honte de ce blasphème, de ma faiblesse, de ma tristesse, et de l'avouer, et de t'écrire tout ceci que je déchirais demain, si le courrier ne l'emportait ce soir . . .*" (553); "*J'ai déchiré cette lettre, il est vrai; mais je te la récris à présent, presque la même.*" (559); "De nombreuses feuilles [of the diary] ensuite avaient été arrachées; sans doute relataient-elles notre pénible revoir du Havre. Le journal ne reprenait que l'an suivant (584); '*J'ai déchiré toutes les pages qui m'ont paru bien écrites. (Je sais ce que j'entends par là.) J'aurais dû déchirer toutes celles où il est question de lui. J'aurais dû tout déchirer . . . Je n'ai pas pu.*'" (588); "Ici s'achevait le premier cahier de ce journal. Sans doute [is Jérôme right?] un cahier suivant fut détruit; car, dans les papiers laissés par Alissa, le journal ne reprenait que trois ans plus tard, à Fongueusemare encore – en septembre – c'est-à-dire peu de temps avant notre dernier revoir." (590); "*Déchiré ma lettre* [after their last encounter]; *puis récrit. . . . Ma lettre ne partira pas*" (593).

"*livre jumeau,*" *L'Immoraliste*. It makes apparent that in both works the basic narrative structure involves a secondary character transmitting the voice of the main character. But given the differences (for example and most prominently, Jérôme has a narrative and diegetic role vastly more visible and important than that of Michel's anonymous friend), it suggests an evolving, comparative exploration of identical narrative issues on Gide's part. Whereas we saw how he suppressed in the final version of *L'Immoraliste* many but not all of the overt indications of narrative distortion that nonetheless come into play, in *La Porte étroite* we see the same sort of distortion, but forefronted and sustained in several ways by Jérôme's narrative. It is as if Gide wanted to work out more leisurely the implications of the frame that were passed over in silence in the earlier work. In the "*livres jumeaux,*" then, he took the same narrative strategy, working its potential first implicitly and then explicitly.

Furthermore, at least four investigations have concretely demonstrated the value of the theme of editing by articulating insights into *La Porte étroite* based on that theme. We have just seen Albert Sonnenfeld's comments on Jérôme's imitation of Alissa's editing strategies. On a larger scale, Arthur E. Babcock's book on reflexivity in Gidean fiction helps advance part of its argument on *La Porte étroite* by raising the issue of Jérôme's editorial selection in putting his text together (43-44). Robert W. Greene, making his case (mentioned above, 118) for including Gide among the giants of fiction who reconcile reflexive and realist narrative modes, argues for the reflexive side of the *La Porte étroite* by highlighting "Jérôme's status as the sole, unreflective and rather arbitrary redactor of the entire text that we are reading" (Greene 83-84). And in his study of narrative modes in *La Porte étroite*, Christopher Shorley has shown how Jérôme's status as editor who repeatedly mentions his need to choose what he considers relevant

> is both an appropriate analogue to the perspective of Jérôme the shy, embarrassed young protagonist, quite unable to penetrate the surface of things, and a skillfully restrained introduction serving to heighten, by contrast, the immediacy of what is to follow. (Shorley 22-23)

i) *Editing and Jérôme's Personality*

There is additional "yield" to be realized in pursuing further an attempt such as Shorley's to relate the theme of editing to Jérôme's personality. In the terms used in these pages, Jérôme the editor challenges Jérôme the narrator also because editing (in the sense of excising some of a story's details as one puts it together) suits – and reveals – his personality more than does narrating (in the sense of communicating as much of the story as possible).

Germaine Brée was one of the first to object to one of his capital excisions from his own account of events, attributing it however to Gide's need for suspense in his story and not to Jérôme's character:

> Gide dans *La Porte étroite* a voulu "éclairer" de façon plus complexe l'histoire racontée. Il le fait grâce à une fiction, permise, certes, mais dont le naturel savamment préparé cache une invraisemblance réelle; le côté construit, apprêté, de l'oeuvre transparaît. Le récit de Jérôme, en effet, est suivi du journal d'Alissa, qu'à la fin il s'incorpore. Ce journal permet de faire certains recoupements dans l'histoire de Jérôme, créant des perspectives troublantes, trouant en somme la ligne si unie d'un récit où il n'y a point de ces "lambeaux" annoncés [dans le 1er paragraphe]. Mais ce journal, Jérôme, d'après son récit, l'aurait eu en sa possession depuis dix ans. Comment en ferait-il abstraction lorsqu'il entreprend de raconter l'aventure même que ce journal éclaire? Gide a fait cette abstraction pour son personnage, car il en avait besoin. (Brée 194)

While Brée rightly emphasizes the discrepancy between what Jérôme knows and what he tells at the beginning of his account, her argument slights the possibility of explanations attributable to "Jérôme." Gide surely cultivated suspense in his book, and wanted readers to experience the same sort of shock of discovery that he had Jérôme go through upon the discovery of Alissa's diary, and those sensitive to the narrative discrepancy do well to situate one of its explanations among the author's considerations. But that is not to say that it is a therefore a shortcoming in Gide's art, on the contrary, for the narrative tactic is both a good one on his part, and a revealing one "on the part of" the narrator. Leland Chambers takes

Brée's alert response to Jérôme's narrative oversight that one step farther by working into it an appreciation of the latter's personality:

> Jerome's discovery of an unsuspected Alissa in the entries of her journal motivates his decision to "set down [his] recollections" of their thwarted relationship "quite simply." Gide does not allow Jerome to reveal the contents of Alissa's journal until late in the narrative even though, as narrator, Jerome possesses all pertinent information at the outset of his tale; instead, with the object of eliciting a similar response from the reader, Gide brings Jerome to re-create the context of passive ignorance which had made the disclosure of Alissa's real passion such a shock to him. Thus Jerome's decision to tell his story as he does betrays a more important aesthetic concern than his expressed desire to set things down "quite simply." Not caring to magnify the contrast between his narrator's impression of actuality and that actuality itself into one of the central concerns of the novel, as Ford later does in *The Good Soldier*, Gide does not emphasize Jerome's qualities as narrator, but focusses instead on him as a person who is naive, deluded, and essentially unchanged by his experience. Jerome's dispassionate manner of narration would seem incredible after the revelations of Alissa's journal if Gide had not underscored the tragic irony of Alissa's sacrifice by reiterating Jerome's obtuseness and emotional unresponsiveness in his final brief encounter with Juliette. (Chambers 305-06)

But a few things about *La Porte étroite* may not be as obvious as Chambers appears to imply, for instance, that "Jerome's discovery of an unsuspected Alissa in the entries of her journal motivates his decision to 'set down [his] recollections' of their thwarted relationship 'quite simply.'" If this is so, why did Jérôme not start to set down his account until more than ten years after first reading Alissa's diary? The decade of delay suggests a more tangled motivation behind his setting the story down "simply." Since the diagetic event closest to composition was his visiting Juliette "l'an passé" (*PE* 596), would not *it* be the more likely stimulus? And would not the desire to "revivre tout ce passé" (*PE* 579) that is behind his taking up the pen have been aroused to the point of action after all those years by the three virtual flashbacks he experienced in her house in Nîmes?: 1) the sight of the aged Juliette (". . . Juliette vint me rejoindre. Je crus voir la tante Plantier: même démarche, même carrure, même cordialité essoufflée," *PE* 596); 2) Juliette's sudden and unexpected request that he be the godfather of her latest child, who is named after and who is said to look like Alissa (*PE* 597); and 3) the memorial in which Juliette had recreated Alissa's room, each object of which "semblait revivre et raconter à mi-voix son passé" (*PE* 598), and which opens out, not onto the city, but "sur une sorte de préau planté d'arbres" (*PE* 597), very much à la Fongueusemare. Such flashbacks would have occurred all the more easily because they were eagerly sought after: ". . . je cherchais des yeux, inquiètement, ce qui pouvait rappeler le passé. Je reconnaissais bien, parmi le mobilier neuf du salon, quelques meubles de Fongueusemare; . . . ce passé . . . frémissait en moi . . ." (*PE* 596). Nor can we ignore the possibility that Jérôme started his account also to defend himself from Juliette's final reproach ("Allons!, fit-elle, il faut se reveiller . . .," *PE* 598), assuming – mistakenly – when he started writing and before Alissa's texts imposed themselves that he could recreate what he imagines to be an idyll gone curiously wrong.

Similarly, Chambers's position that Gide did not care "to magnify the contrast between his narrator's impression of actuality and that actuality itself" would be hotly contested by critics who view *La Porte étroite*'s distinctive interplay between various types of discourse as doing exactly that.[10] And these pages of course have been arguing that Gide's book *does* emphasize that contrast. But Chambers's principal point remains fundamental and convincing: there is a bond between Jérôme's character and the way he narrates. He could indeed tell his story *as if* he were not cognizant of Alissa's diary, at least partly because he is the sort of creature that he is, which is to say, "naive, deluded, and essentially unchanged by his experience," and suffering from "obtuseness and emotional unresponsiveness."

Another alert critic has recently brought to light a more subtle but nonetheless significant symptom of the Jérôme's failure to have his past interact with his present. Reading the description of Fongueusemare with considerable attentiveness, Marie Wégimont has noted three stylistic quirks: "le ton étrangement neutre du narrateur, son effort pour capter le regard de son enfance, l'irruption dans le présent de trois visions jaillies du passé enfantin" (Wégimont, "Description du jardin de Fongueusemare" 51). While she

---

[10] See Greene, Helbo, Kapetanoviç, Shorley.

has every reason to argue as she does that this failure owes much to Gide's personal attempt in *La Porte étroite* to understand the inadequate communication plaguing his own relationship with his wife, and while she concludes on a note that emphasizes the author's role,[11] her findings do not preclude the heuristic effort proposed in these pages to see Jérôme initially as exclusively responsible for the text. Indeed, Wégimont herself at several points winds up stressing points that make her overall reading quite compatible with that effort. For example:

> Jérôme-adulte ne pourra atteindre son but [capturing lost childhood images] que s'il retrouve non seulement les images de l'enfance mais surtout le regard vivant de l'enfant qu'il fut. Il y avait jadis dans le jardin une beauté lumineuse que Jérôme-enfant voyait et que Jérôme-adulte a du mal à re-voir, une beauté sans laquelle Fongueusemare est un jardin "pas très beau, que rien ne distingue de quantités d'autres jardins normands. . . ." Bref, la structure de cette description est dans la recherche du regard de l'enfance par le narrateur en vue de reconquérir la beauté lumineuse d'un paradis qui a été perdu. (Wégimont, "Description du jardin" 47)

This is of course another way of asserting that Jérôme's narrative is molded by his personality, one marked by a preference for the past and a resistance to letting it intermingle psychically with the present. Wégimont's whole argument is as well a refined, indirect demonstration of how, true to his most important, very revealing words, Jérôme is writing "pour revivre tout ce passé" (*PE* 579).

Furthermore, regarding his stylistic quirks, he demonstrates on a more general level a clear habit of editing out explanations for many of the other characters' acts and even of suppressing causative connectives throughout all of his account. In a very satisfying study Roy Jay Nelson has shown how Jérôme strains to allow for his infrequent use of causal conjunctions (*parce que, puisque*), causal prepositions (*de*, for instance), expressions of time or degree evoking causality, etc. Regarding the point of how Jérôme omits ex-

---

[11] ". . . [L]e narrateur n'est pas un être purement fictif, parfaitement distancié de l'auteur et se distanciant de l'histoire qu'il raconte par son 'discours.' Ici comme dans tout le reste du récit le point de vue du narrateur n'apparaît jamais de façon tout à fait distincte de celui de l'auteur ou du héros [the younger Jérôme]" (Wégimont, "Description du jardin de Fongueusemare" 51).

planations of other characters' acts, Nelson brings out, for instance, questions that can arise from a close scrutiny of the account of the unexplained abandonment of her family by Jérôme's aunt, Lucile Bucolin:

> Departure with a lover is plausible, but so is flight to escape the insidious boredom of Le Havre and Fongueusemare, or even to avoid recrimination, now that the secret is out (*PE* 504) of the possibly unadulterous but surely suspicious rendez-vous [between Lucile and the soldier in the presence of two children]. Considering the ease with which we could have been informed of Lucile's purposes and ultimate fate – two or three well-placed words would have left no doubts – one begins to suspect there is conscious suppression of causal connectives. (Nelson 52)

Doubtless, there are several ways to explain that type of suppression on Jérôme's part. Surely one of them is fear of having to – or inability to – face the causal connections between his and Alissa's past actions on the one hand and the catastrophic present on the other. In its turn, that fear or inability may have been an extension or repetition of his psychological defense in the face of the Oedipally charged memory that opens his account, the (wished for?) death of his father.

We need not go too far afield to find other examples of Jérôme's personality pushing him to edit subsequent events out of any interaction with the past that fixates him. I will limit myself to two more. My first example, involving Juliette, parallels Jérôme's insulating attitude toward Alissa's diary commented on by Germaine Brée. (We note in passing that the fact of the parallel makes it even more unlikely that as scrupulous a craftsman as Gide was sloppy in the verisimilitude of the book's narrative tactics, as charged by Brée.) The example occurs in the rendition of a conversation between Juliette and Jérôme just shortly before she decides to rush headlong and headstrong into an immediate marital engagement with the persistent but seemingly ill-matched wine-merchant Edouard Teissières:

> –Je [Juliette] comprends qu'elle [Alissa] veut te laisser libre.
> –Mais est-ce que j'y tiens, moi, à ma liberté! Et tu comprends pourquoi elle m'écrit cela?
> Elle me répondit: Non, si sèchement que, sans du tout pressentir la vérité, du moins me persuadai-je dès cet instant que Juliette n'en était peut-être pas ignorante. (*PE* 525)

While Jérôme may or may not have had at the time of the story any presentiment of the truth, he certainly knows it at the time of writing. But he fairly refuses to include it. Or to put it more accurately, I think, so precious to him is the past exactly as *he* had experienced it (and not as it may have been for another or "in reality") that he will not let his reliving it through writing it be altered by subsequent information. It starts to become apparent here that the question for Jérôme, then, is not so much whether to share or not share explanations with readers. The question is rather, as with the diary, how he can facilitate what he has recognized as his primary goal, to "revivre tout ce passé" as he and he alone had experienced it. Narcissus does not yearn after knowledge, and even if he had it, he certainly would make little effort to share it with bystanders. He is too consumed by his need to get a secure hold on his youthful, innocent self, assuming erroneously that it can be embraced in the image that he is generating. Consequently, regarding Chambers's portrait of Jérôme, mentioned above, as "naive, deluded, and essentially unchanged by his experience," and suffering from "obtuseness and emotional unresponsiveness" (Chambers 305-06), regarding the three stylistic quirks found by Wégimont in the description of Fongueusemare ("le ton neutre, l'effort pour capter le regard de l'enfance, l'irruption de visions du passé enfantin"), and regarding Jérôme's suppression of causative explanations in describing events, we can postulate anxious narcissistic self-absorption as the stem from which those qualities bloom.

Moreover, Jérôme's narrative occlusions do not occur just concerning major issues such as Alissa's diary, Juliette's rapport with her sister, and his style. For instance, he continues being reluctant with potentially illuminating details, almost gratuitously so, two pages after his description of Juliette (*PE* 527 ff), when he recounts the details of the less than crucial incident involving his friend Abel who waxes expansive about his feelings for Juliette: although Jérôme the writer knows fully what is in store for Abel's amorous expectations, he says nothing to his most important reader, himself, nor to any other eventual reader. The hand of the suspense-minded Gide working on behalf of his readers? Without a doubt. But merely that? Not terribly likely.

Let us consider a second major example showing Jérôme editing out events occurring after the formation of his cherished vision. It develops (on page 573) by means of very effective indirect free style, which is most readily evidenced by numerous exclamation points and rhetorical flourishes, plus an absence of introductory expressions such as *je croyais, je me disais*, etc. In the passage in question, he communicates the resentment he had felt upon discovering what he calls the "depoeticized" Alissa, who, it turns out later, was so only in appearance. The power of the passage is in fact such, that the reader can readily get caught up in it, experiencing its contents as a lingering present moment. That is, we can react to the Alissa of this passage as if indeed she had been and *remained* the limited and limiting woman that Jérôme – who subsequently learned better – thought he had seen at that moment:

> Eh! sans doute elle avait raison! je ne chérissais plus qu'un fantôme; l'Alissa que j'avais aimée, que j'aimais encore n'était plus . . . Eh! sans doute nous avions vieilli! cette dépoétisation affreuse, devant quoi tout mon coeur se glaçait, n'était rien, après tout, que le retour au naturel; lentement si je l'avais surélevée, si je m'étais formé d'elle une idole, l'ornant de tout ce dont j'étais épris, que restait-il de mon travail, que ma fatigue? . . . Sitôt abandonnée à elle-même, Alissa était revenue à son niveau, médiocre niveau, où je me retrouvais moi-même, mais où je ne la désirais plus. Ah! combien cet effort épuisant de vertu m'apparaissait absurde et chimérique, pour la rejoindre à ces hauteurs où mon unique effort l'avait placée. (*PE* 573-74)

But as the diary shows and so as Jérôme knows at the time of his writing, the Alissa of that apparently atypical moment was more than ever herself (whence the problem for the narcissistic Jérôme needing only idealized self-reflection), the "depoetization" was only a ruse on her part that was both sublime and diseased. There had been no return to the "natural," and never had she aspired more to the "heights." But a reader unaware of the diary at this point (as every first reader of *La Porte étroite* must be) runs the strong risk of coming away from this passage – which, to repeat, offers no corrective to its mistaken judgment – with a searing, unfavorable impression of Alissa, an impression that is difficult to erase completely even after reading her diary. The captivating indirect free style demonstrates as well as anything how against knowledge, against fairness, against reason itself Jérôme, hunched over his own self-absorbed memories of the past, will not let in the light of subsequent events independent of his inverted compusions.

More damning still, it makes Jérôme's narcissistic posture rather clear. His fury in the face of Alissa's rejection of his role for her is too enduring in its vivid immediacy to be attributed solely to his obtuse efforts to remain in the past. (And if he in fact remains enraged with, and so distant from, Alissa over what he knows at the writing *not* to be the case, what reason other than self-absorption can there be to remain in the allegedly common past that he offers as his motivation? Incidentally, it is highly unlikely that his resentment of her can be explained by her refusal to marry him. Such thinking, widely accepted before 1967, became essentially untenable in that year, after Loring D. Knecht's landmark article, "A New Reading of Gide's *La Porte étroite*," showed that it was Jérôme who, in act and in language, was reticent to approach marriage. Critics continue, moreover, to find corroborative details for Knecht's argument. See Babcock, *Portraits*, 35-36.) Nor can the persistence of his hostile reaction be written off as narrative fidelity in portraying his putative pre-diary reaction to her "depoeticization." What he had been after all along – "tout ce dont j'étais épris" – was never the tragically noble Alissa that her diary proved her to be, and that he knew her to be at the time of writing, but the obliging, "poeticized" Alissa, reflecting submissively and mirror-like his aspirations toward a idealized, innocent self. For Jérôme as he wrote, the account of her magnanimous rebellion in lying could only be a harbinger of the independent grandeur to be evidenced in the diary, and his anger at the latter, which demonstrated both her autonomy and her superiority, may well have strengthened instead of dissipating the otherwise inexplicable tenacity of the resentment betrayed by this passage. He does well to point out (and so to cause us to try to explain) his inability to identify the cause of the "haine vague contre ce que j'appelais encore 'vertu' " and of the "ressentiment contre l'ordinaire occupation de mon coeur" (*PE* 573) that at the beginning of the passage he says filled his heart. Jérôme's inability notwithstanding, thoughtful reading detects that much of that hostility must have arisen initially because his spiritual and literary echo/Echo had distracted him with an image not of himself.

His search for his youthful self in the mirror of his language may also contribute to an explanation of the unattributable *vous* that Jérôme addresses seven times in the course of his narration. While Babcock properly states that "the *vous* turns *histoire* into *discours*" (*Portraits* 32), it does not always do that. Maisani-Léonard points out that in two instances Jérôme's use of the pronoun ironically counteracts his discursive role as narrator (57-58). More comprehensively, then, and with the resulting ambiguity taken into account, the *vous* turns *histoire* into *discours* into *miroir*, that is, into an uncertain, shimmering surface that reflects Jérôme's use of language (and so Jérôme himself, since he is for the reader nothing but his use of language). Because of the formal function of that pronoun in French, Jérôme's use of it connotes the objective other (which is of course strengthened by the almost binary distinction of *vous* from the more familiar, subjectivity-laden *tu*). But the reader's inability on seven occasions to connect the *vous* to any referent, together with Jérôme's inconsistent use of the pronoun, offers an analogue to the imprecision with which Jérôme viewed others throughout all his life (and throughout his account). Recalling that he had exceptional difficulty in paying attention to and understanding the comments and feelings of others because he was too concerned with his own spoken and written words, and recalling the other signs of self-absorption, we conclude that his language itself goes beyond the usual limits of narcissistic impulses that everyone deals with, that his imprecise *vous* betrays his disinclination to focus on others, and in so doing sensitizes us even more to his excessive proclivity to project his self onto verbal representations of others. That, of course, is precisely what explains the striking disparity between the Alissa of the diary and the one of his narration, the latter representing the values and aspirations of Jérôme, i.e., more Jérôme than Alissa.

While in his language *narrateur* and *narrataire* may reach out to each other, they cannot of course merge, whence more frustration. When viewed as an aspect of Jérôme's (vs. Gide's) document, language's undeniable turning in on its own inadequacies throughout *La Porte étroite* takes on a dimension supplementary to those brought out by critics mindful of this *récit* only as Gide's document: it offers an "unconscious" analogue (on "Jérôme's level") – and perhaps even an example of "psychological displacement" – of the inevitable frustration of the narrator's emotional in-turning. (The analogue appears all the more convincing if one accepts Lacanian parallels between language and the unconscious.) Like Narcissus's pool, his words invite yet frustrate his attempt to clutch his past, i.e, his self – an image that can only seem to him not surface-generated, that can only seem to him not fracturable at the slightest analytic touch, that can only seem to him not the product of alterity.

But so unwarranted, so wilfully obtuse is the abiding hostility with which he bristles regarding the woman he claims to love, that one can only wonder if it takes in more than just his narcissistic reflexes. Can what is seen here be the uncontrolled effect of still another kind of narrational reflexivity on his part, which is conscious but unacknowledged (and so operating in bad faith)?[12] Jérôme's resentment of Alissa may have been sharpened by the burgeoning, undeniable impact of Alissa's letters and diary, those OTHER magical texts which his story forces him to rely on and to incorporate more and more, to the detriment of his self-absorbed visions. (He is forced to the extent that he cannot give up all pretense of sincerity and accuracy, without falling short even in his own eyes – and without taking himself outside the Gidean pale.) *We*, then, are watching Jérôme, who wants to relive his vision of the past through his writing, apparently growing in ornery but unadmitted resentment as *he* watches Alissa's texts and past take on increasing power and authority, in spite of his deepest desires and in spite of his power as editor. The misleadingly "depoeticized" Alissa becomes a target of opportunity for his multi-layered resentment.

One may therefore draw the conclusion that the conscious and unconscious narrative reflexivity of this *text*, "Jérôme's" text first, is appropriate for communicating a sense of the reflexive *personality* of this editing, obtuse, not completely insincere Narcissus.[13] We ex-

---

[12] Jérôme's bad faith should need no demonstration. To mention some of the more obvious examples, one could list, for example, how often he just "happens" to "overhear" or to "spot" others in private moments (his mother protesting to her brother about Lucile's "comédie," 501; the clowning of the soldier in Lucile's room, 502-503; Alissa's questions to her father about Jérôme and his father 508-09; etc.).

[13] If we put aside momentarily the effort to view the text as belonging exclusively to Jérôme, it becomes possible here to glimpse an allegory of Narcissistic authorship pertinent to Gide. Emily Apter has pointed out how Gide's anguish over a writer's block in 1890 led him to sketch precepts of a "doctrine of manifestation" dealing with the writer's obligations toward his text. She postulates this "doctrine" by appealing to Gide's diary (for instance: "Se considérer soi-même comme un moyen; donc ne jamais se préférer au but choisi, à l'oeuvre," *Journal* 18) and to *Le Traité de Narcisse* ("Les Vérités demeurent derrière les Formes-Symboles. Tout phénomène est le Symbole d'une Vérité. Son seul devoir est qu'il le manifeste. Son seul péché: qu'il se préfère," *Le Traité de Narcisse*, 8). Jérôme may have been guilty in Gide's eyes of violating that "doctrine." If Alissa, Jérôme's Beatrice (501), is his inspiration on the level of story, her text therefore representing inspiration on the level of discourse, his text then becomes a negative, menacing symbol for artistic texts, because it represents the artist's ability to chose a narcissistic vision of self over pure text, pure inspiration. The inspiration towers over the vision of self, but a

perience his narrative awareness as it struggles unsuccessfully both against the progressively intrusive, complicating power of OTHER texts, and we get a feel for his unconscious disarray as he struggles with the inversions of language that parallel yet betray his own emotional inversion. We have further cause, then, for maintaining that in reading *La Porte étroite*, we should, as argued at the opening of this section, look for the fit between his personality and editing as he practices it.

Moreover, the literary flip side of reflexivity – representation, mimesis – is thereby very well served, as is the larger metaphoric value of *La Porte étroite*, for how much of modern culture has not been driven by men struggling resentfully, reflexively but obtusely, both against the growing power of women's voices rising above the status of echoes/Echoes and against all that is implied by language stripped of its ontological equivalences, i.e., implied by the play of language reduced to signs. Moreover, in the face of contemporary criticism preoccupied by Gide's self-reflexivity, we should recall again the role of *disponibilité*. In each and every one of his works Gide has been the apostle of "availability" both in morals *and* esthetics. It is doubtful that his *disponibilité* would allow his own art to dismiss representation or even to downgrade it vis-à-vis reflexivity. By looking then at *La Porte étroite*'s text as first Jérôme's, we anchor the valuable, indeed essential, study of this reflexive text where such studies have belonged since *Quixote*, in the interplay between verbal mimesis and language's mind-games.[14]

The variety and yet fundamental similarity among 1) Jérôme's approach to Alissa's diary, 2) his memory of her and of Fongueusemare, and 3) his treatment of the Juliette-Abel story, and 4) of causality, lead to the conclusion that he has a clear tendency to editing, a tendency productive of an occlusive pattern in his narrative acts. So pronounced is the tendency and so frequent its manifestations, moreover, that to ponder it is to be lead to the realization that his excising proclivities influence more than just his narrative acts, going on to touch even his daily interactions with others. For a small instance, he stood by unresponsively when Abel tells him:

---

writer like Jérôme has the power to deny readers complete and immediate access to the former by indulging in the latter.

[14] Regarding that interplay, see Robert Alter, *Partial Magic: The Novel as Self-Conscious Genre*, especially his discussion of *Les Faux-Monnayeurs* 159-79.

"Ce consentement d'Alissa, que tu n'es pas capable de décrocher, je te l'obtiendrai par la force de notre exemple . . ." (that of Juliette and himself getting engaged, PE 529). He could have, and clearly should have, interrupted Abel to tell him that it was he Jérôme, not Alissa, who had created much of the situation himself by being the first to express a strong preference for not getting engaged (PE 517-18). He chose instead to keep that bit of information out of their conversations and planning. For a large instance, he evidences what verges on a compulsion to excise, when it comes to editing Alissa's reading. He not only guided her choice of books (and so her rejection of other books) but also discretely urged her in effect to skip those parts of the recommended readings that had not received his full approval (indicated by her initials, which he would jot in the margin of sections of the text that he deemed worthy of attention).

Furthermore, the suspicion arises even that it is in Jérôme's excising personality that there can be found part of the explanation for the appeal of this irritable, self-centered, insensitive, stylistically and morally flabby man to not one, but two young women. Indeed, one of them preferred him to no fewer than two other suitors, each having considerable if wildly divergent *attraits* of his own. To go on a search for an explanation of love is of course to go on a fool's errand – when one is dealing with life. In literature, however, an "explanation" of love can mean no more than a plausible rationale (see Lévy 131, note 60). Moreover, Jérôme's very patent *lack* of appeal – indeed, unsavory tepidity – incites, almost requires, an effort, however inadequate, at understanding why Alissa and Juliette were attracted to him.

One might maintain that part of their cousin's appeal for Alissa and Juliette could be only a sign of the workings of a small introverted world within what is already France's Protestant minority, looking exclusively to the few members of its own tight little community for emotional bonding. That part of the explanation takes added strength from the unhealthy inclination exhibited by the characters in *La Porte étroite* to see younger generations repeating the lives of older ones:

> Nous n'étions pas bien différents, je vous assure, de ce que vous paraissez aujourd'hui. J'étais assez pareil à toi, Jérôme; plus peut-être que je ne le sais. Félicie ressemblait beaucoup à ce qu'est à

> présent Juliette... oui, physiquement même – et brusquement je la retrouve, ajouta-t-il [Jérôme's uncle] en se tournant vers sa fille [Juliette], dans certains éclats de ta voix; elle avait ton sourire – et ce geste, qu'elle a bientôt perdu, de rester comme toi, parfois, sans rien faire, assise, les coudes en avant, le front buté dans les doigts croisés de ses mains.
> Miss Ashburton se tourna vers moi, et presque à voix basse:
> –Ta mère, c'est Alissa qui la rappelle. (*PE* 515)

Alissa and Juliette, of course, both see the next generation echoing their own, Alissa when she offers Jérôme her amethyst cross for a future daughter of his, and Juliette when she names her own daughter Alissa. Given such inclinations, one can speculate that the mysterious events in Félicie's life which (according to her brother, Jérôme's uncle Bucolin, *PE* 515) changed her personality for the worse, might have had something to do with a possible rivalry between Félicie and her sister, Jérôme's mother, over Jérôme's father. (Otherwise, it is odd that following the death of Jérôme's father his mother felt, according to Jérôme, that there was nothing keeping her in Le Havre [*PE* 495]: her only sister did after all live there.) If that possibility is valid, Alissa and Juliette could have been ever so subtly induced to comply with that model in their own love life.

But aside from arguable proclivities of a particular fictional French Protestant family, is there not also the painful past of the sisters? Already confined to inbred, hot-house circumstance, they would stand all the more susceptible to, and upsettable at, the perturbations created by their outsider mother's creole flamboyance (she was an orphan adopted by the Vautier family), by her sensuality, by her regular and highly dramatic "crises" (which, to judge from the reaction of Jérôme's mother, met with visible and virulent disapproval from the rest of the restricted community), and by her breath-taking repudiation of her children and their world by flight. How appealing then must have been the emotional security offered by the ever stolid, single-minded Jérôme, from childhood on eager to edit out of their common past anything inconsistent with his idealizing version/vision of Fongueusemare, ponderously set on making a glowing summer-time myth out of the fungous, stagnant reality implied by that name.

In brief, then, Jérôme the editor more than challenges Jérôme the narrator, editing not just for the convenience of his creator and not just in a variety of his story-telling ways, but also in a variety of psychological and inter-personal ways, almost as a way of being.

ii) *Editorial Unreliability*

There are further discoveries to be made in exploring the implications of Jérôme's editing, most readily by considering in further detail his unreliability as editor. Having lost confidence in his reliability as narrator but having seen how Alissa's diary is the main text, we are left, it would seem initially, at least with that tangible document and its companion pieces, her letters. Perversely enough, though, upon reflection we discover that even they slip away from us as they pass through Jérôme's hands. Let us start with the letters.

First of all, Jérôme admits that, while possessing all of them (*PE* 541), he has selected for inclusion only certain ones (*PE* 548, 551). Not only that, but starting with her very first letter (*PE* 512), his use of suspension points at the beginning of his citation gives rise to nagging concerns about what he has excised:

> Le lendemain, arriva mon oncle. Il me tendit une lettre de sa fille qui ne vint, avec ma tante Plantier, que le jour suivant.
> 
> ... Jérôme, mon ami, mon frère, y disait-elle ..., *combien je me désole de n'avoir pas pu lui dire avant sa mort les quelques mots qui lui eussent donné ce grand contentement qu'elle attendait. A présent, qu'elle me pardonne! et que Dieu seul nous guide tous deux désormais! Adieu, mon pauvre ami. Je suis, plus tendrement que jamais, ton Alissa.*
> 
> Qu'eût pu signifier cette lettre? Quels étaient donc ces mots qu'elle se désolait de n'avoir pas prononcés, sinon ceux par lesquels elle eût engagé notre avenir? (*PE* 512)

It is frustrating but attention-getting for readers when Jérôme, at the beginning of the process of quoting from Alissa's letters, offers just a part of an intriguing letter, only to throw back to them in their expectancy the very question clamoring for an answer: "Qu'eût pu signifier cette lettre?" Succinctly put! And how can we even begin to tell, or even know if we can tell, without seeing the whole document? (A not infrequent question for readers of *La Porte étroite*, one that we have already asked above, 104, about a decisive letter of his to her: "Qu'ajoutai-je qui pût la pousser à répondre ceci," *PE* 565.) In addition, Alissa's "adieu" seems to fly in the face of Jérôme's flat-footed optimism about what she would have said to his mother. Although attention throughout the rest of the text to the use of "adieu" among members of their community reveals that it is not necessarily for them a salutation anticipating permanent or long separation, its resonance for the outsiders' ears (that is, for most readers' ears) stirs up just that much more confusion about Jérôme's elliptical treatment of the letter.

What is, moreover, significant for our purposes here, grounds exist for wondering if the intention of the letter was not at all to hint at a desire for engagement, but the contrary. Whereas Jérôme assumes that his mother wanted him to marry Alissa, and that therefore Alissa's unpronounced words "qui lui eussent donné ce grand contentement qu'elle attendait" would necessarily have been words of engagement, the opposite assumption is made at least as valid by the tantalizing earlier scene (*PE* 511) between Jérôme and his mother where they talk about his feelings for Alissa. That the mother had been concerned, even Jérôme recognized: "Ma mère avait pu s'inquiéter d'abord d'un sentiment dont elle ne mesurait pas encore la profondeur . . ." (*PE* 511). Not at all certain is whether or not she came to feel as positively about it as her son convinced himself that she did. Facing, she senses, imminent death from another bout of her heart illness and "très oppressée," she responds to his declared intention to marry Alissa one day with the forthright and dramatic "Oui, c'est de cela que je voulais te parler, mon Jérôme." Unfortunately, after trying less than successfully to master her pain ("parlant péniblement") but managing only to make two equivocal pronouncements, ("Il faut laisser faire au Seigneur," "Que Dieu vous garde, mes enfants! Que Dieu vous garde tous les deux") that do not necessarily imply her approval – far from it – she suddenly dozes off. The combination of her dramatic improvement the next day and Jérôme's abrupt departure for school results in the conversation's not being pursued before her death shortly thereafter. But how reassured can one be by Jérôme's confidence that he would have had nothing more to learn from his mother's interrupted words ("qu'eussé-je appris davantage?")?[15]

---

[15] For a thorough treatment of the ambiguity surrounding Jérôme's mother, see Lévy 23-29.

Without that reassurance, his handling of this first, crucial letter weakens his credibility as an editor. We should note that, for those familiar with Gide's earlier *Les Cahiers d'André Walter*, the impression of an unreliable Jérôme is strengthened by a Gidean intertext, since the dying mother of the young Walter had asked him clearly and at length not to marry his orphaned cousin (Jérôme's cousin Alissa had been "orphaned" by the flight of her mother), which Walter agreed to do. Not only that, but he also viewed his renunciation as selecting "la route étroite" (*Walter* 19-21).

The problem grows, since throughout the rest of Jérôme's account the reader has to deal with other voids in Alissa's subsequent letters, voids of inestimable dimensions and consequences opened up by Jérôme's continuing use of suspension points. On a similar plane, one cannot dismiss the possibility that he is keeping his own letters out of his account for reasons that are not entirely clear.[16] While, then, there seems to be little reasonable ground for questioning the decision not to transcribe every single one of his and her letters in their entirety, given his unreliability and obtuseness, can anyone be sanguine about the wisdom of his choices? In spite of the initial impression of imminent verification created when the reader learns that Alissa's diary has been appended to Jérôme's text, no less concern is stirred by the decision that Jérôme makes (evidenced on *PE* 580, 583, 588) to include neither every entry, nor the entirety of those entries that he will include. Apropos of Jérôme's comments on page 580, Albert Sonnenfeld has asked astute questions:

> What proportion of the pages in the diary does Jérôme transcribe? What did the suppressed pages contain? What were the reflections those pages inspired in Jérôme as reader? Is not the choice of pages to transcribe itself the *commentaires* Jérôme denies making? (Sonnenfeld, *On Readers and Reading* 174)

A good example illustrating the soundness of such questions occurs on *PE* 588-90. We see that, whereas Alissa had made individual diary entries every day from July 1 to at least 24 September, Jérôme saw fit to include only nine of them, that is, no more than approximately ten percent. True, an argument could be made (but is only

---

[16] See Babcock, *Portraits* 43-44.

implied) for his rationale: "Suivait une sorte de 'pain quotidien', où la date de chaque jour, à partir du premier juillet, était accompagnée d'un verset. Je ne transcris ici que ceux qu'accompagnait aussi quelque commentaire" (*PE* 588). Presumably Jérôme would have us think that verses from the Bible, not being Alissa's own words, would not tell us much about her thinking – this in a context where two text-besotted personalities more often than not find and explain themselves by means of quotations from the Bible, Goethe, Baudelaire, Dante, etc.! (And where, of course, the very title of the book is a fragment from a quotation.) No wonder Jérôme gingerly works only on the level of implication. But even at that, he does not adhere strictly to his insinuation-based, barely justified agreement with the reader to pass along at least those verses that were accompanied by some commentary: in only two instances ("Vends tout ce que tu as . . .", *PE* 588 and "Regardez les lys des champs . . .", *PE* 589) does he not *exclude* the Biblical verse that presumably was an important part, and perhaps the very inspiration, of each comment. The result is that he creates new juxtapositions which can suggest developments and relationships that may not at all have existed in or may not even have been warranted by the original, and he may well have suppressed other relationships, not the least important of which would be intertextual ones. So, to put it mildly, it is arresting for those grappling with Jérôme's version of the diary that he considers it unnecessary to include most of the biblical verses chosen by Alissa for certain of her entries: since *his* entire text would read differently without the inclusion of the verses on the strait gate, uneasiness must stir regarding Alissa's "pain quotidien" entries that have been stripped of their relevant verses.

Not the least of the ironies of this book, of course, is that, as a matter of fact, Jérôme did not even get his own chief intertext right. Since it is profoundly askew that he presents the quoted basis of the meditation that he claims provides the single most important image for his life's goal and so for his story, the issue of his accuracy in other, less vital quotations arises *a fortiori*. In fact the issue is resolved unfavorably, doing nothing at all to dissipate malaise about his reliability as editor. For instance, in mentioning his aunt's constant state of agitation, he writes: "Belle apparence de l'amour, que devient ici ton reflet? . . . Car nous nous souvenions du mot de Goethe qui, parlant de Mme de Stein, écrivait: Il serait beau de voir se réfléchir le monde dans cette âme" (*PE* 515). Three pages later, he recalls that when he was waxing rhapsodic in his indirect statement of love to Alissa through Juliette, he declared: "Oh! si seulement nous pouvions, nous penchant sur l'âme qu'on aime, voir en elle, comme en un miroir, quelle image nous y posons!" Following so closely the allusion to Goethe, the trope of a reflection in a soul as in a mirror is too reminiscent of the German writer's not to suggest a very tight connection, indeed a loose quotation. How diametrically different, though, is the sense of the free quotation from that of its source![17] Whereas Goethe's interest lies in the other soul, to the point of yearning to see the world refracted through it, Jérôme's narcissistically rebounds immediately back to himself, taking in neither the other nor the world around them. (Much later, in one of her letters, Alissa indirectly recalls to attentive readers Jérôme's revealing misinterpretation: "O mon ami! je regarde à travers toi chaque chose" [*PE* 548]. In so doing of course, she makes more visible the chief difference between herself and Jérôme: unlike him, she is open to the other, both in love and in reading.) Close examination, then, of his handling and understanding of key quotations does nothing at all to dissipate malaise about his reliability as editor of Alissa's diary (her "quotations," so to speak), especially since it in turn is replete with biblical quotations, replete, that is, in the version that the reader never gets to see.

While misleading editing by means of juxtapositions distorts the verses on the narrow gate and the diary – key texts loosely bracketing Jérôme's principal account – it is hardly restricted to them:

> Théoriquement, à s'en tenir aux indications chronologiques que Gide nous donne, plus d'un an sépare la première et la dernière lettre [of the fifth chapter]; la première est probablement du mois d'août, la dernière de septembre ou d'octobre de l'année suivante. Et pourtant, à la lecture, toutes ces lettres semblent former un seul bloc, un ensemble où des contradictions se présentent, mais que Gide a justement tenu à présenter groupées, pour en accentuer, par le rapprochement, la dissonance. De plus, ce procédé donne l'illusion que les déplacements de Juliette, de Jérôme et d'Alissa ont eu lieu presque en même temps, qu'ils sont liés l'un à l'autre. . . . (Masson 27)

---

[17] As presented and translated by Jérôme, Goethe's original quotation is an accurate version of the original German, according to my gracious colleague Dr. Ilse Winter.

The emphasis on Gide's intentions notwithstanding, the illusion effected by Jérôme's handiwork is to the point here. He creates a misleading impression, not so much by distorting – although, like the *bouillons*, he necessarily does that, as must every narrator – but by combining selected, excised moments, as occlusive in the view he offers as the north and south walls of the Fongueusemare house that he chose to describe. Indeed, much the same issue arises for the memories that were "patched together" in the very opening paragraph of his first chapter: there was a deft slight of word, so to speak, in that, by drawing our attention to the fact that in putting down his memories he will resort to "aucune invention pour les rapiécer ou les joindre" (*PE* 495), he distracts us from an important point. Surely there must have been other, context-providing memories that he is passing over in silence, memories that would alter a little or a lot the impressions created by his selective recall. In the same vein, he surely did not record but rather created (at the very least) slightly new realities in quoting to us only partially from Alissa's letters to him. Similarly, in his later recollections he does not attend to activities in, e.g, Paris, Nancy, Athens, Palestine, that would lend (at a minimum) different shades to the impressions spun off by his sharply delimited and focussed recall. (Gide's own last-minute excision from the galley-proofs of the first edition [Gide, *La Porte étroite*, Editions Folio 184-86] of a passage dealing with Jérôme's debauchery "sous un nouveau ciel" gives a good idea of the possibilities.) Moreover, there would seem to be a connection here with his habit of selecting for Alissa's special attention passages from books. The effect of that habit of course is to create a specific impression of a book, and perhaps even to create the impression of one far from faithful to its fuller, more complicated source. We can say then that in editing Jérôme does for the would-be reader of Alissa's diary what he did for Alissa herself on many occasions: of a fuller book, he creates a special, more narrow one, one stripped down by being pressed through the gate of his self-serving, concocted interpretation. The richer text is barred, slipping away into inaccessibility.

### D) *Forme et Fond*

We can now move on to consider the question of *forme-fond* interrelationship in *La Porte étroite*. We saw in its *livre jumeau* that, because of the anonymous friend's letter, the framed quality of Michel's voice laid bare the nature of that text's central theme, authentic individualism, indeed we saw that it *was* that theme, exposed in its derived, dependent reality. In *La Porte étroite*, then, how is the "excessive" subject matter served by its basic narrative gambit? In the next few pages, I will spin out from what has preceded the argument that the *forme-fond* of *La Porte étroite* is the orchestrated frustration of erotico-religious and textual desire, frustration heightened by the illusion of a presence that would satisfy.

On the level of structure, from the opening paragraph we are induced to believe that *La Porte étroite* will be a straightforward first-person narrative, that Jérôme's voice and text are to be the main ones. We quickly see, however, their authority challenged first intrinsically by Jérôme's own shortcomings, then extrinsically by Alissa's progressively overpowering correspondence. We finally see his narration undermined completely by the main text, her diary. That the diary should impress so many scholars as the main text, in spite of its brevity, its bracketed position, and its editorial treatment at the hostile hands of Jérôme, bespeaks the mimetic power that Gide has managed to create in Alissa's illusory voice, a power evident, if less so, in the capacity of the flaccid Jérôme to aggravate knowledgeable readers. Illusion notwithstanding, the text undoes itself in splendid, *disponible* fashion. While the correspondence and then the diary initially beckon to readerly desire as a refuge ("main text") from the uncertainty spawned by Jérôme's account, they in their turn only recede tantalizingly beyond our grasp because of Jérôme's editing and because of the indeterminate mutual influence of his and her texts on each other.[18]

On the level of subject matter, the book deals with the erotically deluded search for/denial of/ the self in religious terms. The literally self-seeking Jérôme confuses spiritual elitism for his narcissistic rejection of an Alissa different from his projections onto her, whereas

---

[18] Working from the dynamics of quotation in *La Porte étroite*, Robert W. Greene writes of an impression quite compatible with this conclusion: "... Alissa's diary with *its* quotation replicates in miniature the *récit*'s larger narrative with *its* quotations. Moreover, the letters and conversations quoted by Jerome frequently contain their own quotations. One finally gets the impression from reading *La Porte étroite* that texts always enclose other texts, and that the act of quotation involves an infinite regression, an endless quest for an original, authenticating citation" (Greene 89).

Alissa, traumatized by her mother's flamboyant sexuality, confuses spiritual elitism for her anxious avoidance of her sexual self.

Where do the two levels intersect? The essential locus is the dynamic (and so non-locus) of the progressive cross-referencing of the four different kinds of discourse (Jérôme's account, his one letter, Alissa's letters, and her diary): it effectuates a serial passage from promises of diegetic accessibility that are broken, on to the fact of final inaccessibility of what had appeared, at last, to be the main text, the diary. That is, the narrative strategy orchestrates for the reader a deception and frustration of textual desire analogous to the deception and frustration of erotic and religious desire that comprise the story of Alissa and Jérôme. As Emily Apter has put it:

> Part of the reader's impetus to imagine a morbid, obsessive, even perverse sexual subtext when faced with censored [i.e., "edited"] pages and understated innuendos, derives from the fact that, as in *La Princesse de Clèves*, *La Porte étroite* contains one of the most protracted and frustrating accounts of sexual denial to be found in the history of literature. From the work's inception, the narrative, as a system of manipulative conventions, conspires against the fulfillment of reader expectations. (Apter 129)

It is, then, in the drama of illusion and thwarted desire that matter and manner meet. That intersection is of course as old as Quixote. Its true uniqueness in *La Porte étroite* – "novelty" would be more accurate – lies in Gide's orchestration of deception and frustration by means of a narrative structure that uses cross-referencing in a distinctive build-up. One can of course deconstruct almost any text to show the workings of illusion and thwarted desire. One would, however, be hard put to find another text like *La Porte étroite*, where those subjects are sustained and fore-fronted throughout, in such tight conjunction with the interplay of four sorts of discourse.

The consequent overriding sense of inaccessibility is aroused as well, although indirectly and more delicately, by considerations of story-telling itself. Once we realize that we cannot get any purchase on a solid position from which to evaluate the relationship of *histoire* to Jérôme's account, it becomes clear that, as in *L'Immoraliste*, a traditional story, which seems so insistently present, cannot be had outside the confines of the arbitrariness instigated by Jérôme's unreliable narrating and editing. Ultimately and in spite of beguiling appearances, we arrive at only a very meager tale that cannot derive from *histoire* but rather from what is left, just the playing out of Jérôme's account on its own terms and within its own frame of reference.

More specifically, what plot we observe has to do with the effect of a text on its writer during composition, a process that had fascinated Gide from at least the time of *La Tentative amoureuse*, (a story hinted at in the effect of Michel's retold story on its relayer). *La Tentative amoureuse* is essentially a story of desire expressed by a story-teller influenced by his story about the desire of a couple influenced by the telling of their story:

> J'ai voulu indiquer, dans cette *Tentative Amoureuse*, l'influence du livre sur celui qui l'écrit, et pendant cette écriture même. Car en sortant de nous, il nous change, il modifie la marche de notre vie; comme l'on voit en physique ces vases mobiles suspendus, pleins de liquide, recevoir une impulsion, lorsqu'ils se vident, dans le sens opposé à celui de l'écoulement du liquide qu'ils contiennent............................................................................
> Cette rétroaction du sujet sur lui-même, m'a toujours tenté. C'est le roman psychologique typique. Un homme en colère raconte une histoire; voilà le sujet d'un livre. Un homme racontant une histoire, ne suffit pas; il faut que ce soit un homme en colère, et qu'il y ait un constant rapport entre la colère de cet homme et l'histoire racontée. (*Journal* I, 40-41)

The plot available to us in *La Porte étroite* is that of an angry man, not coincidentally, given the manifest hostility of Michel toward Marceline and of the friend toward his brother in *le livre jumeau*, and even, as we shall see, of the Pastor in *La Symphonie pastorale*. That Jérôme started out his life irritable and stayed irritable is indisputable: "... repris-je un peu agacé" (*PE*, 528); "rien ne t'irrite, dans cette lettre, que de savoir qu'elle ne t'est pas adressée, me dit Abel" (*PE* 543); "Je fis un geste d'impatience [while speaking to Alissa]" (*PE* 569); "plein d'une haine vague ... [against 'vertu' and Alissa]" (*PE* 573); "je m'écriai presque hostilement [while speaking to Alissa]" (*PE* 577). We have already seen his eager mean-spiritedness in judging the "depoeticized" Alissa, but even his self-righteous, joyless attitude from childhood on would have more than sufficed for conveying his crabbiness, e.g.:

> l'idée même du rire, de la joie [on the part of his aunt Lucile] se faisait blessante, outrageuse, devenait comme l'odieuse exagération du péché. (*PE* 505)
>
> "*J'aime, que dis-je aimer – j'idolâtre Juliette!....*" Puis, riant et jouant [because of his feelings for Juliette], [Abel Vautier] m'embrassait à tour de bras et se roulait comme un enfant sur les coussins du wagon qui nous ramenait à Paris. J'étais tout suffoqué par son aveu, et quelque peu gêné par l'appoint de littérature que je sentais s'y mêler; mais le moyen de résister à tant de véhémence et de joie...? (*PE* 527-28)

On one occasion, by quoting his aunt Plantier's plea not to get angry, he himself draws attention to the sharp tone of voice with which he must have uttered certain words to her, words that could otherwise have been seen by the reader as just expressions of mild exasperation:

> C'est toujours avec Juliette que je t'avais vu jouer... j'avais pensé..., elle est si jolie, si gaie.
> –Oui, je joue encore volontiers avec elle; mais c'est Alissa que j'aime...
> –Très bien! très bien, libre à toi... moi, tu sais, autant te dire que je ne la connais pas; elle parle moins que sa soeur; je pense que, si tu l'as choisie, tu as eu quelque bonne raison pour cela.
> –Mais, ma tante, je n'ai pas choisi de l'aimer et je ne me suis jamais demandé quelles raisons j'avais de...
> –*Ne te fâche pas, Jérôme*; moi, je te parle sans malice... Tu m'as fait oublier ce que je voulais te dire. (*PE* 513; my emphasis)

One wonders with how much rancor many other seemingly innocuous expressions of his could be read.

But the distinctiveness of the plot in *La Porte étroite* is not so much that we watch an angry man write, but rather that we watch a *progressively* angry man write, one whose anger undermines his narrative responsibility. While Jérôme writes, trying narcissistically as we have seen to relive *his* vision of the past by retelling it in a way that would reassure him, more and more control is being exercised by Alissa's texts and past, upon which he grows increasingly dependent and at which, as we have seen, he grows increasingly irritated. It is worth repeating here what he wrote when describing her deceptive expressions of "depoeticization," in the words that could well characterize his feelings toward the final aggravation (the diary that counters his vision of the past and his controlled portrait of Alissa): "chacune des phrases d'Alissa, contre lesquelles je m'insurgeais d'abord, restait en moi vivante et triomphante après que mes protestations s'étaient tues" (*PE*, 573.) We divine the (barely conscious? barely acknowledged?) resistance that he puts up by means of his editorial inclinations, just as we divine the interplay between his anger and his narrative responsibilities. But we are forced to recognize the need for uncertain interpretation, having first been forced to give up any hope of satisfying our curiosity about the story, and now being left with no secure hold either on the story of the story-telling – all of which is not at all unlike Jérôme's uncertain understanding of himself as both story and teller. Gide brings the reader and Jérôme together in frustration.

Because of the narrative structure, the experience of the reader resonates in a special way with that of Alissa too. As we reach simultaneously the end of the diary and the moment of her final "éclaircissement" (a word stressed by her, perhaps ironically, in the original, *PE* 595), both we and she share some of the painful light shed by that illumination. In the distraught Alissa's case, of course, the light shows her the gulf between herself and what she thought she had been most eagerly seeking, God, a gulf reminiscent of the one appearing between readers *qua* readers and the main text. At the least, that readerly quandary is related allegorically to Alissa's, who feels abandoned by Jérôme as well as by God and whose last word (*PE* 595) is "seule": the strong hold on *histoire* seemingly promised by the book with its distinctive cross-referencing ultimately dissipates for the solitary reader into the loneliness of postmodernist *vertige* provoked by awareness of endless chains of elusive signifiers.

In addition, readers and Alissa share a sense of having been deceived. First readers who realize either dimly or acutely that the prestige and authority attributed to Jérôme's account (assumed up to the diary to be the main text) have suddenly been usurped by the power of the contradictory diary are not unlike Alissa who suddenly realizes that she may have been deceiving herself all along about the emotional and religious rationales behind her life. Even after the last line of the diary has been read, that sense of deception revives and surges into the fixity of a final impression when at the very end one guesses at Juliette's bitter tears and Jérôme's patent obliviousness to tragedy. His obliviousness is not unconnected with his narcissistic misunderstanding about what it is exactly that he wants. His frustration in many ways parallels Alissa's, except that he comes to no final understanding and so to no consequent despair. But because we as readers are fruitlessly stimulated to search for a reliable story, we appreciate better his feelings as his narrative communicates his growing testiness, attributable to erotic dissatisfaction as well as to Alissa's independence (both in the final analysis being closely tied together for him). In all three cases, desire is textbound: for the reader of course, for Jérôme who writes to recapture in his account his youthful self, and for Alissa in her mystical aspiration inspired by Jérôme's abusive interpretation of Matthew's and Luke's verses on the narrow gate. (In addition, this drawing of the reader's experience closer to that of both characters heightens mimetic confusion.)

Readers can as well come close to experiencing something of the excess undergone by Alissa when they read her final written wish that closes with an extreme word that she fears to use: "O Seigneur! puissé-je atteindre jusqu'au bout sans blasphème" (*PE* 595). For certain sensitivities, the reading proposed in the preceding paragraph may have indeed ventured into blasphemy by suggesting how religious, erotic, and textual desire can parallel and perhaps reveal each other. One can very easily imagine Gide wanting, or at a minimum being pleased at, the discomfiture resulting from some of the attendant reflections. How appropriate that Jérôme, the editor of these texts of converging desires, be named after the editor of the most sacred texts in the West, the Bible.

Although this interpretation of *forme-fond* interaction in *La Porte étroite* hinges on the reader's being lured along by deceptive impressions of textual accessibility, we can feel confident that the means of effecting that passage have been skillfully and overtly crafted by Gide, since there has been repeated critical testimony to the impact of Alissa's letters and to the coup of her diary relative to Jérôme's "flabby prose." Even for readers not attentive to the subtleties betraying Jérôme's unreliability as narrator and editor, or better yet (since Gide did not want readers who are inattentive to subtleties), even independently of such subtleties, the overall effect of the diary is the same: the obvious contradictions of the relationship between Alissa and Jérôme, their vacillation between desire and avoidance of each other, and her unexplained death all leave one wanting and needing further explanation, an additional text. The diary at first seems to be that text, only to ultimately disappoint, if for no other reason than Alissa's despair at the end. For purposes of the approach proposed in these pages, at least, this is critically reassuring, since attention to the theme of editing heightens awareness and understanding of how this obvious effect of the diary works, an effect in which textual inaccessibility and disappointment overlap. Therefore, the theme of editing stands validated as addressing what is a manifestly central feature of *La Porte étroite*.

It is also validated in this respect, that appreciation of the nature and consequences of Jérôme's editorship contributes to a sharpened understanding of the semantic openness commented on by more recent critics studying *La Porte étroite* and mention of which began this chapter:

> Fervent d'une disponibilité toujours plus esthétique qu'existentielle, André Gide était passionné, amoureux de l'ouverture de l'oeuvre. Personnification même de la volupté et de la cruauté des contradictions humaines, [in *La Porte étroite*] il a figé sur le papier une matière en ébullition permanente ............................ Par une démarche ironique qui fait penser à un mélange de délicatesse et d'hypocrisie à la fois, sa forme paradoxalement traditionnelle ou classique évite diaboliquement toute possibilité de précision, de définition et de certitude. (Kapetanoviç, m3-m4)

While the literature of the world is so rich, varied, and interdependent that claims of uniqueness for a single work are foolhardy, there must be few works that match the convergence in *La Porte étroite* of such features of its *forme* and its *fond*:[19] the skillful build-up and subsequent frustration of illusory narrative expectations by cross-referencing, the way that the ending puts characters and readers in several analogous situations of desire, and the equation of the kinds of readerly and character desire at work in the book. With those three features we have – after excursions down related byways of interest (it is hoped) to readers of *La Porte étroite* – reached an un-

---

[19] In an article entitled, "'Alissa Dans la Vallée': Intertextual Echoes of Balzac in Two Novels by Gide," Doris Y. Kadish has, however, made a persuasive case for the ways in which *La Porte étroite* and *La Tentative amoureuse* incorporate thematic and structural intertexts from Balzac's *Le Lys dans la vallée*, an earlier book about frustrated love.

derstanding of the excess of the *forme/fond* of that book. Perhaps Kapetanoviç had that excess in mind when he wrote, as just quoted, that *La Porte étroite* avoids any possibility of precision, definition, and certitude "diaboliquement."

## II. ONOMASTICS

We may corroborate some of the main points made above by taking an antithetical approach, to see if *La Porte étroite*, when viewed from a radically different perspective, appears compatible with the same conclusions. Reversing critical course, then, away from the priority of Jérôme's role as source of the text, we can attend to an area within the author's almost exclusive purview (and yet accessible to the reader), the text's use of names.[20] ("Almost," because Jérôme, who certainly is responsible neither for his and other characters' names nor for the book's place names, nonetheless "chose" whether or not to include names in his account, and he "chose" the context and manner in which to present them. Nonetheless, since he gives no sign of onomastic awareness other than including Alissa's diary entry about her curiosity over the names of plants and trees growing at Aigues-Vives, he can be excluded from consideration here.) The topic is not a peripheral one, for Pasco and Rollins have written convincingly of the importance of names in any of Gide's works. If, moreover, one is to judge both from the number of worthwhile articles and books dealing significantly with names in *La Porte étroite* (see for instance Bonheim, Cameron, Hunt, Perry) and from the number of times that critics of this *récit* invoke its names to corroborate their points, the subject is an especially rich and representative one for *La Porte étroite*. We will, however, see how opposed onomastic interpretations of *La Porte étroite* can be to each other. That opposition – and its single exception – will serve as a further argument for my position on an open, *disponible* reading of this *récit*.

---

[20] For a good theoretical overview of onomastics, see François Rigolot, *Poétique et Onomastique*, 9-14. No less useful is its succinct critical bibliography on onomastics, 248-53.

A) *Names of Secondary Characters*

We can begin by observing how an appreciation of the book is advanced by reflecting on the names of merely minor characters:

> ... Lucile is a creature of light. At the crucial point when Jerome sees Lucile in her room with the officer, he notes that "un rais de lumière sort de la chambre" and that "où les bougies de deux candélabres répandent une clarté joyeuse, ma tante est couchée sur une chaise longue." Even Lucile's name means light. (Bonheim, 488)

But in this opening, precipitating scene, what light is being cast? Is it the light of liberating illumination, as this creole child of sun-soaked Martinique prepares to bolt from the narrow, destructive path of self-repudiation too much in evidence in the Normandy in which *La Porte étroite* is primarily set, onto a life-affirming path of rejection not unlike that of Gide's Prodigal Son? (*Le Retour de l'enfant prodigue* was conceived and written during his struggles with the longer *récit*.)[21] Or are we to see the hellfire of selfishness, as Lucile, the rebellious daughter of Lucifer in spirit and name, prepares to abandon and damage husband and daughters? The question slips from awareness as the story progresses, only to be brought back to mind by nagging association just as the book concludes: Jérôme closes his account with the image of the maid bringing light – finally? too late? to no avail? – into another room, the darkened re-creation of the dead Alissa's room. Since light brackets this tale, one feels impelled to find in it special significance. But to date there appears to be no convincingly comprehensive and consistent reading of the book's use of that image. So one of its less disputable messages would appear to be only its contribution to Gide's onomastic irony: on the one hand the light of "Lucile" is an illumination that does not clarify, and on the other a hellfire with health-giving potential. Semantic "availability" gets forefronted again.

---

[21] "André Gide écrivit *Le Retour de l'Enfant prodigue* après une longue période de silence, à quoi l'insuccès de *L'Immoraliste*, après l'échec des *Nourritures terrestres*, n'était pas étranger. Venu d'un seul jet, ce traité interrompit la composition de *La Porte étroite*, sur laquelle Gide peinait beaucoup" (Gide, *Romans*, ed. Yvonne Davet and Jean-Jacques Thierry, 1539).

Jérôme's other aunt, Félicie Plantier, might at first seem to offer a "felicitous" alternative – indeed opposing double – to Lucile, having endured domesticity to stay put ("planted"?) instead of leaving. Her bustling breathlessness, her voice "sans mélodie," and her suffocating effusiveness certainly do stand in antithetical correlation to Lucile's indolence, singing, and seductive aloofness:

> Ma tante Félicie Plantier était la meilleure des femmes, mais ni mes cousines ni moi n'avions avec elle grande intimité. Un affairement continu l'essoufflait; ses gestes étaient sans douceur, sa voix était sans mélodie; elle nous bousculait de caresses, prises, à n'importe quel moment du jour, d'un besoin d'effusion où son affection pour nous débordait. (PE 512)

They do nothing, however, to make Lucile look less attractive to the reader (at least as portrayed by Jérôme who, for all his stated hostility to her, continued to keep a portrait of her with him), and so do nothing to resolve the reader's ambiguous understanding of Lucile and her light.

Considering next Edouard Teissières, we observe that his given name – very British (all those monarchs!) and so, because of centuries of bitter Franco-British history, very much alien – virtually tags him with what is his salient quality in Jérôme's eyes: "Plus grand, plus fort, plus coloré qu'aucun de nous, à peu près chauve, d'autre rang, d'autre milieu, d'autre race, il semblait se sentir étranger parmi nous . . ." (PE 538). Etymology ('rich guard') reinforces Jérôme's antipathetical view of him as merely a petty merchant having nothing in common with the refined Bucolin family. But as Lucile's apparent paramour makes us aware, "– Bucolin! Bucolin! . . . Si j'avais un mouton, sûrement je l'appellerais Bucolin" (PE 503), the bleating dependency of the aggrieved father and the sheep-like submission of the daughters to the ideals of their men adds a dull patina to the gloss of their presumed refinement. Conversely, Edouard the "mere" merchant is a purveyor of intoxicating wine, a contradictory role not wholly at odds with what is hinted at by his family name, strikingly similar to *tessère* (a Roman token used for sensible wheat-distribution or hard-nosed military communications on the one hand, but for entrance to the magic of the theater on the other.)

This semantic tension carries over to the name "Aigues-Vives" ('Living Waters'), to which Edouard takes Juliette (alleged by Alissa to be happy, *PE* 554). Christian Vandendriessche has expressed a fairly widespread interpretation of the impact of this name:

> Notons d'abord que [at the beginning of her diary] c'est la première fois qu'Alissa quitte la Normandie et sa chère terre de Fongueusemare – dont le nom est symbolique de toute une atmosphère d'humidité, de lourdeur, de couleur sans éclat, de lumière sans joie – et qu'elle se trouve brutalement sur une terre aride, sèche, brûlée par le soleil, où la vie sauvage et ardente d'une nature libre s'épanouit à son aise; le nom même d'Aigues-Vives semble avoir été choisi pour s'opposer radicalement à celui de Fongueusemare: D'un côté, la lourdeur de l'humidité (qui joue le même rôle que les paysages d'herbes mouillés dans l'*Immoraliste* ou dans *Paludes*); de l'autre côté, une nature riante, dionysiaque, offrant, avec la Garrigue, un paysage d'une brûlante nudité, qui n'est pas sans rappeler les heures chaudes de Biskra, dans l'*Immoraliste* ou du désert, dans les *Nourritures Terrestres*. (Vandendriessche 109)

Zvi Lévy, protesting against an allegedly facile view of Juliette's happiness, points out the inaccuracy of saying that the spring to which Aigues-Vives owes its name waters "une terre . . . où la vie sauvage et ardente d'une nature libre s'épanouit à son aise":

> La maison "à l'italienne et de plain-pied avec la cour sablée" (*PE*, 581) constitue un cadre agréable où Juliette somnolente peut "anesthésier" les cuisantes brûlures de l'épisode de ses fiançailles. Par son tempérament, elle aurait aisément pu s'identifier à l'image du ruisseau "que ne tarit aucun été" (*ibid.*) et qui féconde le jardin ainsi que le bosquet sauvage qui lui fait suite (féconde, Juliette l'est assurément avec ses cinq enfants). Cependant cette lecture, qui montre une Juliette "heureuse," n'épuise pas la signification du texte. En effet, le ruisseau est ensuite "resserré de plus en plus entre la garrigue sèche et les vignobles, et bientôt complètement étranglé." (Lévy 52)

Life and fecundity, then, eventually dribble out into barrenness and death.

Nor is "Aigues-Vives" the only place name touched by ambivalence. Le Havre, as it functions in the boyhood memories of

Jérôme, might at first glance seem to be a "haven" for, e.g., Easter vacation (*PE* 502), but upon inspection appears no less a site of instability and tragedy. It is a haven to be fled:

> Le Havre tient dans ce récit le rôle d'une plaque tournante, d'un véritable carrefour. C'est le point de convergence de la plupart des personnages.... C'est donc un point d'arrivée et de départ, mais bien peu y demeurent.... [U]ne ville portuaire, c'est le symbole du large, du départ, des rêves de pays lointains, et Jérôme souvent en parle (*PE*, 502, 533, 534).... Le Havre, c'est un peu l'invitation au voyage, une source de mouvement ainsi qu'un facteur d'instabilité, et rien ne peut s'y créer de bien durable: le ménage Bucolin, l'installation des Palissier, les amours d'Abel et de Juliette, de Jérôme et d'Alissa; tout s'y noue et s'y dénoue presqu'en même temps, et presque toutes les scènes tragiques du livre s'y déroulent, que ce soit la découverte par Jérôme d'Alissa en pleurs, la fuite de Lucile, la dramatique soirée de Noël ou les retrouvailles manquées de Jérôme et d'Alissa. De ce lieu de sables mouvants, le plus sûr est donc de fuir, comme le fait, après Lucile, Abel.... (Masson 10-11)

Moving closer to the center of the book in order to consider the name "Juliette," one moves no farther from uncertainty. On the one hand, some critics find in it corroboration of the positive way in which they see that character:

> ...Juliette... is as her name indicates the embodiment of love, fecundity and July. She will later get married to a Provençal wine-grower, will go to live in the South of France at Aigues-Vives (live waters), leaving Alissa to pine at her Normandy estate of Fongueusemare (the name suggests fungus and marshy ponds). The time of hope and happiness in *Strait is the Gate* is summer.... (Sonnenfeld, "Byroads in Gide's Labyrinth" 121)

But one can hear in her name additional, less positive echoes:

> And the book closes with Juliette weeping – weeping, it would appear, for a life that can no longer be hers. Like her Shakespearian namesake, she herself destroys, with one tragic error, all chances of happiness with the man she loves. (Bonheim 492)

B) *"Alissa" and "Jérôme"*

In addressing finally the name of the main character (so considered because she is the source of the "main text") we find that Gide's "Alissa" is extraordinarily rich in meaning and so not surprisingly awash in indeterminacy. On the one hand, it fairly bursts with etymological possibilities that are consistent with the lofty way in which Alissa endeavored to define herself. Her name has been taken by the Bonheims to suggest "winged" in its Romance connotations. To add weight to this possibility, the Bonheims continue: "We note that Jerome, when he sees Alissa put aside all the things he had helped teach her to live, cries out: 'Alissa! Pourquoi t'arraches-tu les ailes?'," (Bonheim, 490). Or it can be taken to evoke "consecrated to God" (Perry, 154) if read for Hebrew etymons. Similarly, one could maintain that it derives from the Old French "Aliz," in turn coming from the Germanic "Adahleidis," 'noble kind.' All three possibilities converge appropriately on the religious idealism that helps to motivate Alissa. Furthermore, given Gide's fancy for the piquant desert colocynth,[22] it is hard not to speculate whether, when the author chose "Alissa," *alise* ('sorb') was not making itself heard ("alisier – ses fruits ont à la maturité un saveur acidulé assez agréable," *Dictionnaire Robert*), because it can evoke the bitter-sweet self-denial of religious idealism.

In one of its intertextual echoes (for another, see Kadish, "'Alissa Dans la Vallée'"), the name pulls in much the same direction. Keith Cameron speculates persuasively that Gide had had occasion to read the relatively popular *Lettres choisies de Saint Jérôme* of Mgr. Lagrange (four editions between 1870 and the turn of the century). Cameron then highlights, among the many parallels between the *Lettres* and *La Porte étroite*, the profound ones between Jérôme and his most famous namesake:

> Saint Jérôme était un expert notoire dans l'art épistolaire, et on a conservé la plus grande partie de sa correspondance, datée des

---

[22] "Je donne ce livre pour ce qu'il vaut. C'est un fruit plein de cendre amère; il est pareil aux coloquintes du désert qui croissent aux endroits calcinés et ne présentent à la soif qu'une plus atroce brûlure, mais sur le sable d'or ne sont pas sans beauté" (Gide, "Préface" à *L'Immoraliste*, *Romans* 367).

> IVe et Ve siècles de notre ère. Il correspondait, entre autres, avec des jeunes filles et des veuves de la société romaine et, tout en célébrant les louanges de la vie monastique et de la chasteté, il leur écrivait pour les encourager à conserver une vertu inébranlable. (Cameron 58)

Even some of the less striking parallels perceived by Cameron bear repetition:

> Est-ce pure coïncidence que, d'une part, Jérôme, comme Saint Jérôme, ait exercé une grande influence sur le choix des lectures de son amie; que, d'autre part, Alissa ait suivi le conseil de Saint Jérôme en renonçant à la littérature mondaine au bénéfice d'ouvrages de piété (*Lettres*, p. 88); et qu'enfin Jérôme ait voyagé en Orient ainsi que l'avait fait Saint Jérôme (*La Porte étroite*, p. 574, et *Lettres*, p. 89; voir aussi lettre XIV, *A Asella*)? Ne pouvons-nous voir une analogie certaine entre l'apparente candeur de Jérôme et les revendications d'innocence de Saint Jérôme lorsqu'il répondait, tout à la fois, aux critiques suscitées par sa lettre à Eustochium et aux attaques scandaleuses de ses adversaires, dans la lettre XIV à l'adresse d'Asella? (Cameron 65)

Cameron also notes that, as Mgr. Lagrange puts it, the letters reveal "des âmes d'élite, grandes et fortes, allant résolument à la perfection, aspirant aux sommets. Rien là de médiocre; le goût, non seulement de la vertu, mais de la vertu héroïque . . ." (Cameron 60).

All this more than warrants serious consideration of Cameron's postulating a connection between "Alissa" and the name of one of Saint Jerome's more important correspondents, the above mentioned Asella:

> Le nom même d'*Alissa* rappelle celui d'une des jeunes femmes à qui Saint Jérôme écrivait: *Asella*. Bien qu'Alissa puisse être un nom hébreu signifiant "consacré à Dieu", il représente aussi la forme invertie de *Asella* en phonétique. Ce ne serait pas la première incursion de Gide chez les auteurs anciens et classiques pour y chercher le nom d'un personnage, et ce prénom serait aussi en harmonie avec le symbolisme de *La Porte étroite*. (Cameron 62-63)

But when another critic, Tony Hunt, delineates the common elements between Gide's book and the story of Abélard and Héloïse, the name "Alissa" takes on a radically different sonority, emitting notes of eroticism and troublesome pride, even as it rings louder with spiritual heroism:

> ... we can quickly establish the following elements as common to both *La Porte étroite* and the story of the medieval lovers. First, there is the obvious similarity of the names Alissa and Eloissa. Second, these two women shared academic or literary studies with the men with whom they are in love. Third, they are eventually sacrificed to these men. Like Heloise, Alissa is really passionately involved with the man she loves but is denied (in her case from the very beginning) the love which she desires and needs and, rather than interfere with his life, she seeks consolation in religious sublimation. In this escape she discovers pride. Fourth, her story is dominated by the theme of renunciation, a renunciation which has its roots in resignation. Fifth, she reveals her torments in a series of letters. These similarities all concern the role of Alissa, since it is obvious that Jérôme is no Abelard. There thus seems to be a strong link between the two stories and although the situations differ in various respects, the essential concerns remain the same. Indeed, Bowman [in "Notes Toward the Definition of the Romantic Theater," *L'Esprit Créateur* 5 (1965), 125] describes [Charles de] Rémusat's play [about Abélard, which Gide had read with "emotion and passion" as a student and which he had occasion to recollect in the year before he started to think about *La Porte étroite*] as "a pamphlet in favour of free intellectual inquiry and the sane, full life, against all restraints on freedom," a description which has obvious appropriateness to Gide's purpose in his early writings. (Hunt 185)

The new notes take on added resonance as Hunt goes on to point out the flaw in the heroic renunciation of both Alissa and Héloïse:

> The common peculiarity of the theme of renunciation in both the story of Abelard and Heloise and that of *La Porte étroite* is, of course, impurity of motive, which itself promotes the presence of illusion and delusion. (Hunt, "Alissa-Eloissa" 189)

As with all the other names discussed above, then, "Alissa" lends itself to an equivocation: its etymological and historical reverberations of heroic spirituality notwithstanding, the name also bears within itself the threat of pride and delusion, along with disastrous eroticism. It threatens, then, tragedy. The tragic potential conjured up by the name is heightened ever so subtly because in addition "Alissa ['Elissa' in Latin] is . . . another name for Dido, who committed suicide because Aeneas deserted her" (Bonheim 490).

That equivocation is of course most appropriate and in a sense necessary in light of Gide's informed use of names throughout his work, since it reflects a central question of the book, the degree to which Alissa's spiritual self-sacrifice is due to unrecognized sexual self-repression. Critical near-unanimity about the sterility of her spiritual efforts notwithstanding, there is however no reason not to note that Alissa's last words, ones of despair ("Je voudrais mourir à présent, vite, avant d'avoir compris de nouveau que je suis seule" 595) are only her last *written* words. What St. John of the Cross has called the "dark night of the soul," the stripping away of attachment to anything that is not a sincere love of God, is often painfully experienced by spiritual idealists such as Alissa but *can* end in hope and joy. After all, Gide was well aware that Christ himself, as portrayed by the severe Matthew (and by the nearly identical – for this incident – Mark), suffered no less from the final written emotions of Alissa – anguish, fear, solitude, abandonment, and perhaps even something close to despair.[23] Jérôme may not have profited from Alissa's sacrifice as she intended, but an air-tight conclusion about her final disposition (not her final words) is simply not possible. It is as well hard to imagine that Gide could lend so allegedly discernable an air of certainty to the decisive spiritual moment of his main character – so discernable, that is, only if we postulate that her spiritual life ended when her diary did. Even if it did, her final lines offer a portrait no more anguished than that of Christ as the Bible-reading Gide surely knew.[24]

Most significantly, Jérôme's name is more straightforward and less rich in imparting its intrinsic message (as seems only right for a

---

[23] See Matthew, XXVI, 36-40, XXVII, 46, XXVII, 50, and also Luke XXII, 40-45.

[24] Interestingly enough, the expression of despair in Matthew XXVII, 46 and Mark XV, 34 is, as is suggested by the presence of Hebrew words within the Greek of the Gospel, a quotation (from Psalms XXII 2). Christians who do not accept a despairing Christ would probably argue that the learned, scripture-conscious Christ quoted his forebear David to make a point, one hardly congruent with despair alone. One wonders if Gide was aware of the issue and, if so, what he thought of it.

flabby character who claims that language works simply). As just indicated by the quotations from Cameron, the salient features of Jérôme's life and relationship with Alissa create tight correspondences between him and – who else? – his patron saint. Consider the aptness in light of the following qualities culled from a portrait of Saint Jerome drawn from learned opinions prevalent during the period of Gide's youth and early manhood: "son extrême irritabilité, son manque de tact,... l'ascétisme exalté qu'il propageait et qui le singularisait"; "manque de générosité, de courage et de droiture"; "penseur médiocre," etc. ("Jérôme," *La Grande Encyclopédie*). One should, however, add to the similarities noted by Cameron and suggested by a reading of *La Grande Encyclopédie* the most important achievement for both Jeromes and the similarity that ties in with all the earlier comments about the centrality of Jérôme's editing: the primary role of both men was to edit a text far more valuable than what they themselves could write. Too, Jérôme's family name, "Palissier," appears to suit him squarely with a dull aptness: the *palis* ("stake," "paling-fence made of stakes") would be an emblem worthy of a character bent on preserving self-centered memories of a lamentable past against a damning present.

But the distinctive accessibility of the meanings of his name is not completely untouched by irony. On a minor scale, there is first the etymology of "Jerome," originally "hieronymus," 'holy name.' Unlike Alissa, Jérôme would surely find few defenders of his sanctity. Second, with his family name, there may be another, somewhat strained, ironic note: the image of the stake could connect him in a far from holy way with Alissa's virtual martyrdom to ideals that he encouraged for the wrong reasons. But on a more significant scale, just as Jérôme is no Romeo to his cousin Juliette, no Abelard to his cousin Alissa, he is in the stature, quantity, and quality of his correspondence no Jerome (only a fragment of one indistinctive letter reaches us, by his choice), nor is he a Jerome in the reliability and impact of his editing. That is to say (and to recapitulate this chapter), in his onomastic as well as narrative relationships, Jérôme the relaying voice, reduced from narrator to editor to producer of a text orchestrating frustrated desire, is a void. The excisor becomes excision, and in that sense stands as the least accessible of all. But how grating his flabby voice, how haunting and present the voice that fell victim to his excisions!

CHAPTER THREE

## *LA SYMPHONIE PASTORALE*[1]

I. HOW DO WE READ A LYING NARRATOR?

How does one read a work of fiction in which there is a strong possibility that the only narrator is lying to his readers? In spite of traditionally uncritical acceptance of the Pastor's basic narrative integrity, that is the tricky question with which we will be dealing in studying Gide's last major *récit*, *La Symphonie pastorale*. The intent is to demonstrate that the "forme de mensonge à soi-même" (Gide, *Oeuvres Complètes*, XIII 439-40) which Gide himself considered to be at the heart of this book, draws in its wake many, many things, among which is a conscious dishonesty on the part of the narrating Pastor vis-à-vis his readers, resulting in radical textual inaccessibility much like that of *L'Immoraliste* and *La Porte étroite*.

But the demonstration will first be set within the context of the Pastor's self-righteous obliviousness to his own motivation, errors, and faults. In and of itself, such mindlessness will be seen to distort *histoire* outrageously, independently of the question of conscious deception. His consequent narrative unreliability is so pronounced and sweeping that the misrepresentations which he deceptively offers about his feelings for Gertrude, the blind aphasic that he had brought into his family, will appear not as jarring narrative anomalies, but as part of a comprehensive delusional stance. The narrator

---

[1] Parts of this chapter appeared previously in articles in *The French Review* ("Verbal-Erotic Anarchy in Gide's *La Symphonie pastorale*" 60.2 [October, 1986], 20-29) and in *Literary Onomastics Studies* ("Onomastics and Narrative Convention in Gide's *La Symphonie pastorale*" 14 [1987], 81-110). *The French Review* and the American Name Society have kindly granted me permission to reproduce here material from those articles.

will not be found to be a bald-faced liar unworthy of any trust. Rather, he will be seen to be lying in the service *both* of an attempt at higher truth and of hypocritical self-interest. That is only appropriate, since heavy-handed, one-sided deceit would have made the text less beguiling, less teasingly pulled between the poles of sincerity and insincerity, and so, less Gidean.

A) *The Critical Dawning*

The reception accorded to *La Symphonie pastorale* shortly after its appearance in late 1919 tended to focus on Gide's style and his ideas, often viewing the book as a slight, elegant *roman à thèse* and characteristically confusing Gide with his narrator (C. Martin, cxx-cxlii). This tendency toward critical simplicity, still lamented by Jean Hytier in his 1945 book on Gide (Hytier 159-60), was slow to disappear. It took until the 1950s for the scattered comments on the complexities of *La Symphonie pastorale*'s irony and narrative structure to enter the critical mainstream in close analyses increasingly worthy of the name. In two articles dating from 1954 and 1957, John Cruickshank, building on books by Albert Thibaudet, (*Réflexions sur le roman*, 1938) and A. Guérard (*André Gide* 1951), studied the three levels of time in *La Symphonie pastorale* (the narrator's past, his present, and the reader's present), and thus helped take formal considerations beyond belle-lettristic pronouncements on "style," and helped move critical analysis beyond the misguided discussion of the work's alleged ideas alone:

> Because of the way Gide handles time in *La Symphonie pastorale*, it seems very short-sighted to assess the book's merits purely on the basis of its ideas. Indeed, this purely ideological approach has led to the ridiculous situation where one critic denies it value because he sees it as a caricature of the Protestant conscience, while another admires it precisely because he believes that the pastor offers a solemn warning to his co-religionists concerning the intellectual perils implicit in their faith. (Cruickshank, "Gide's Treatment of Time" 142)

Rare had been such insights at the time of publication of *La Symphonie pastorale*. Those few whose worth Thibaudet, Hytier,

Guérard, and Cruickshank recalled came from Charles Du Bos and Thibaudet himself. Du Bos had drawn attention to "[l]e trouble du fond transparaissant sous la limpidité de la forme" (Du Bos 7). Thibaudet for his part had eschewed the biographical approach in vogue at the time, setting the tenor of his 1920 review in his opening paragraph: "Les livres d'André Gide, qui sont des livres d'intelligence, de réflexion et de critique sollicitent l'intelligence, la réflexion, la critique, parfois avec eux, parfois contre eux, y trouvent leur milieu et leur prolongement naturels" (Thibaudet 124). Consistent with his awareness of the wiles of this text, he stressed the theme of the illusion and lies of love, associated with blindness which, he made clear, applied to the Pastor as well as to Gertrude. (Although he himself was not the first to make the point, subsequent critics have with growing regularity noted that the original title, *L'Aveugle*, in its indeterminate gender, described no less the morally blind Pastor than the physically blind Gertrude.) In a sense, making explicit Thibaudet's implicit connection between the demands of this text on the reader and the presence of those themes has been ever since the most pronounced undercurrent in the best criticism of *La Symphonie pastorale*. His repeated emphasis on the Pastor's blindness was, however, going to have more direct and obvious impact, becoming from the 1950s on progressively the single most frequent critical commonplace concerning this book.[2]

Rightly so, since the Pastor's self-righteous obtuseness has few equals in literature. Examples of it are as easy to find as they are shameless. On the one hand, he protests the reworking of Virgil's quotation by his friend Dr. Martins (from "O fortunatos nimium sua si *bona* norint/Agricolas!" into "Combien heureux les hommes, s'ils pouvaient ignorer *le mal*," my underlining, 28-30 in Gide, *La Symphonie pastorale*, ed. C. Martin, the critical edition from which all further quotations will come). He equally deplores Dickens's story of the happiness resulting from cultivating a blind girl's igno-

---

[2] See for example Moore, "André Gide's *Symphonie Pastorale*"; Parnell, "André Gide and his *Symphonie Pastorale*"; Lafille, *André Gide Romancier*; Freedman, "Imagination and Form in André Gide: 'La Porte étroite' and 'La Symphonie pastorale'"; Harvey, "The Utopia of Blindness in Gide's *Symphonie Pastorale*"; Décaudin, "Sur trois récits d'André Gide"; Strauss, "Cécité et aveuglement"; Kingcaid, "Retreat from Discovery: Symbol and Sign in *La Symphonie pastorale*"; Martens, *The Diary Novel*; and Booker, "The Generic Ambiguity of Gide's *La Symphonie Pastorale*: Reading the Pastor's First *Cahier*."

rance. On the other hand, he educates Gertrude – indeed, he makes a moral and spiritual crusade of educating her – in thoroughgoing ignorance of evil, for the sake of an allegedly higher happiness. David H. Walker formulates nicely another blatant example of hypocrisy writ large, indicting the Pastor's "extraordinary bad faith in drawing up such a flagrantly one-sided set of comparisons" between the household run by his wife Amélie and Louise de La M's, where Gertrude had been residing (Walker, 'Les Nourritures terrestres' and 'La Symphonie pastorale', 57-58). Professor Walker later sums up the growing critical sense of the Pastor when he writes that the Pastor is "so obtuse as to defy belief" (Walker 71).

Intended or not, the two senses of Walker's "defy belief" (not believable as a fictional creation, and not reliable enough within the fiction to be trusted to tell the truth) provide a nice bridge to approach the question of whether the Pastor's obtuseness is so egregious as to justify the conviction that he is lying. While critics have indeed been right to stress that the Pastor deceives himself, it is likely that he does not do just that, and there is cause to challenge the widespread, lingering implication that he deludes his readers only because, and to the same extent that, he deludes himself. One of the causes for that skepticism sketches itself when we pore over the interplay between *le temps du récit* and *le temps de l'histoire*, and get a firm grasp on what signal events had transpired in the thirty months *before* the Pastor started writing. (See the diagram at the end of this chapter.) A comparison of the two kinds of time shows, among other things, that from his opening sentences the Pastor postpones telling far too many crucial details to his reader. Only when we are well into his account do we discover that before picking up his pen, he had already had what he recognized to be intense and profoundly disturbing disputes with his wife Amélie and son Jacques over Gertrude (e.g., the incident of the harmonium when Jacques's helping Gertrude in secret had stirred up violent emotions in him; his virtual banning of Jacques when the young man expressed a desire to marry Gertrude; and Amélie's "mysterious" comments about what her husband was failing to see). He is tardy in telling us that Gertrude had already told him both that she is in love with him and that in her opinion he loves her more than Jacques does (*SP* 82). In addition, about four months before starting his account he had arranged for her to move from his house to

Louise de La M.'s, where he has been seeing her daily, away from Amélie and the rest of his family.

This initial lack of forthrightness is of a piece with the misleading way he deals with his reasons for beginning to write in the first place. He starts off disingenuously, claiming he is going to chronicle "*tout* ce qui concerne la formation et le développement" (*SP* 4) of Gertrude (my emphasis). But in spite of the comprehensiveness suggested by the "tout," only pages later does he tell us that he has no notes (*SP* 30), nor any systematic memories (*SP* 34) to go on. In fact, at no earlier point in the time between the moment when he discovered her orphaned and beast-like, and the moment when he started to write, had he shown any interest whatsoever in pursuing the recommendation of his friend Dr. Martins that he keep a record of Gertrude's development, precisely in order to write such an account. Indeed, he subsequently mentions that he *still* has no interest in "*tous* les échelons de cette *instruction* qui, sans doute, se retrouvent dans l'*instruction* de tous les aveugles" (*SP* 40, my emphasis). While there may be some grounds for a quibble about the distinction I am suggesting between the later use of '*instruction*' and the earlier '*la formation et le développement*,' his cavalier disregard for the spirit of his previously stated objective of comprehensiveness nonetheless makes us wonder about the real reason why he started writing.

In addition, he begins as if he need not make clear from the outset his very close relationship with a young girl who turns out to be very attractive. And yet, such a relationship is surely socially charged for any married man with five children, and an absolutely flabbergasting one for a devout Reformed minister in a small Swiss village. He is quite aware, moreover, both of the possibilities in their relationship and of what others might think: "Et elle répéta très haut: non, je n'avais pas besoin de toucher vos joues – ce qui me fit rougir, parce que nous étions encore dans la ville et que des passants retournèrent" (*SP* 46). Likewise, although he claims not to pay attention to gossip ordinairement, in the case of his rapport with Gertrude, he realizes that his situation is out of the ordinary:

> Et je la quittais d'autant plus volontiers que la chapelle ne me paraissait guère un lieu décent pour m'y enfermer seul avec elle, autant par respect pour le saint lieu, que par crainte des racontars – encore qu'à l'ordinaire je m'efforce de n'en point tenir compte.... (*SP* 58)

Finally, when it serves his purpose (e.g., when portraying his wife in an unflattering light), he himself recognizes the obvious, that passing over significant details in silence is incompatible with the truth ("J'ai trop souci de la vérité pour taire le fâcheux accueil que je dus essuyer à mon retour au foyer," *SP* 12).

This dodge – discoverable of course only in retrospect by the dutiful, reflective reader – stands out less than it might because of the way the slow, piecemeal, and seemingly incidental unfolding of details slips into reader awareness among the series of highly interesting – and so distracting – vignettes of Gertrude's remarkable traits, achievements, and insights. Another reason for the success of the Pastor's ploy is that in spite of his visible bad faith, he manages to create an idealistic vision that is no less seductive for the reader than it is for Gertrude. (And we might add that like many a reader, Gertrude nonetheless understands that the Pastor is conjuring up a distorted even if appealing vision.) Just as he characteristically shields Gertrude from any knowledge of evil, sin, death (*SP* 46), of her beauty (*SP* 48-50), or of the letters of Saint Paul, so too he keeps his readers from troublesome issues no less important. But for all its being deluded and self-serving, idealism does contribute something – and perhaps a lot – to what drives the Pastor's restriction of our and Gertrude's range of knowledge, idealism that makes it difficult to condemn his experiential editing immediately and out of hand. That difficulty doubtless helps to explain why the outrageously tendentious beginning – the true nature of which, to repeat, becomes visible only piecemeal in the later pages within the context of the Pastor's utopian education of Gertrude – has not been criticized as frequently as it could be.

For all that, having assembled the scattered details, we must judge his narrative insincerity harshly: it is simply too sweeping. Since he broached with Gertrude troublesome subjects only under pressure from her, and since we can exert no pressure on him, how can we know all that he may have kept from us? Because of his truly outstanding bad faith as a narrator, the answer is that we cannot know, that we cannot trust him to have given us all the relevant details. So in *La Symphonie pastorale*, any text understood in a traditional sense, e.g., one communicating a dependable account of *histoire*, remains inaccessible, if for no other reason than the Pastor's blatant lack of narrative forthrightness. But *so* glaring is the Pastor's bad faith that critics have started to take the unusual step of wondering whether he simply must be suspected of lying to his readers.

## B) *Accusing The Pastor*

In his 1971 book *André Gide: 'La Symphonie pastorale,'* W. D. Wilson drew together three complaints voiced in the 50s by Albert Guérard, Germaine Brée, and S. Ullman, according to all of whom, in Wilson's terms, "the irony [created by the Pastor's insincerity] is obvious to the point that it is not quite credible that the Pastor himself should have been capable of writing as he does while remaining unconscious of what was happening to him" (Wilson 22-23). The three critics, instead of at least considering the possibility that the Pastor may indeed have been conscious of his feelings from the start of his document and so deliberately deceptive toward his reader, reacted understandably enough, taking the path most easily open to logocentric analysis that requires fundamental narrative integrity: they charged Gide with a lack of verisimilitude, instead of the Pastor with bad faith.

But in Pierre Lafille's book of 1954, *André Gide Romancier*, the issue had already been more tightly pressed, and the charge of lying had come close to momentary articulation in the form of a discretely couched "hypothesis" provoked by the Pastor's narrative inconsistencies (see Maillet's summary of them, below, 169):

> Légères bavures qu'une mise au point méticuleuse eût pu facilement éviter. Ou encore, autre jugement possible, faut-il penser qu'il n'y a pas là inconséquence d'auteur, mais calcul très subtil? Serait-ce fine psychologie et refoulement à demi-conscient? Celle de l'insincérité envers soi-même, celle d'une demi-hypocrisie qui ferait le pasteur moins innocent d'intentions qu'il ne peut paraître? L'hypothèse est possible. (Lafille 175)

While the words "demi-conscient" and "demi-hypocrisie" betray Lafille's effort to deny critical *droit de cité* to the notion of a lie, it was prowling around the walls, ready to breach, thanks to the expression "moins innocent d'intentions qu'il ne peut paraître." Lafille ended his ground-breaking paragraph on the same note of indecision. On the one hand, the possibility of a lie was kept at arms length by the suggestion that it would "gauchir la personnalité du pasteur" as Lafille understood it. On the other hand: "Mais

Gide aime assez l'incertitude et la diversité des interprétations possibles" (Lafille 175). But overall, this moment of indecision does not undo the impression left by Lafille's many assertions that the Pastor should be taken at his naive word ("l'innocence des intentions," "Lorsque . . . il entreprend la rédaction des événements . . ., il est encore sans aucun trouble" 163, "il [s']exprime sans masque" 172, "C'est un homme non éclairé sur ses sentiments, dupe de lui, dupe de ses paraboles, qui rédige de modestes mémoires" 174, etc.).

So it is Wilson who apparently should get the credit of at least being the first to address explicitly the issue of the consequences for the reader of the Pastor's lying. He goes on, though, to deny the possibility that we can reject the Pastor's account:

> Although we know that the Pastor's narrative is not an objective one, we cannot go so far as to assume that there is no truth in his portrait of his wife and son, nor indeed that his opinions of them are invalid. A certain amount of convention enters into our reading of a first-person narrative such as *La Symphonie pastorale*, for the story would have no meaning if we could not accept that the account given of events in the past, both physical actions and dialogue as well as thoughts, was an accurate one. The reader accepts that the narrator tells the truth, that his memory does not deceive him; what the reader is required to 'restituer', are the gaps in the narrative. He can question the validity of the narrator's reflections and opinions, but not their reality. (W. Wilson 62-63)

For one thing, without appropriate definitions, it is too restrictive to assert that there can be "no truth," "no meaning" within the fiction if one questions the honesty of the Pastor's account, i.e., diegetic accuracy. For another, there *are* textual inconsistencies that suggest lying. A good presentation of them can be found in Henri Maillet's book of 1975, *'La Symphonie pastorale' d'André Gide*, which built on the observations of Lafille, Herbert Greenberg, and C. Martin. Summing them up, he points out four proleptic sentences – written by the Pastor in March claiming that he *will* discover he is in love – that cannot be squared with the first entry of the second notebook, written in April, in which he declares that he realizes *for the first time* that he is in love: one cannot identify what one *will* know unless it is *already* known.³ The conclusion to be drawn, one completely consistent with the Pastor's exceptionally bad faith, is that he appears to be lying.

One could, of course, dismiss the textual inconsistencies which lead to that conclusion as a slip-up on Gide's part ("even Homer nods") and not on his narrator's. That is plausible in light of several inconsistencies that seem imputable exclusively to Gide.⁴ In fact,

---

³ "Et pour que personne ne s'y trompe, le narrateur insiste et détaille: [. . .] *Ce soir même où elle en parlait comme j'ai rapporté* – c'est-à-dire un soir d'août dernier – *je me méprenais encore, et encore en transcrivant ces propos* – c'est-à-dire le 12 mars; et plus loin, dans le journal de ce même 25 avril, au sujet des conversations avec Gertrude relatées dans le premier cahier: [. . .] *Ce n'est qu'en les relisant cette nuit-ci que j'ai compris*. Apparemment donc tout est simple: le Pasteur a compris dans la nuit du 24 au 25 avril, en relisant le récit du premier cahier. Cependant quatre passages au moins de ce premier cahier jettent le doute sur l'affirmation initiale du deuxième cahier, à moins qu'ils ne mettent en cause l'écriture elle-même de l'ensemble du récit:

–le 8 mars, après avoir raconté la scène entre Jacques et Gertrude à la chapelle (un des premiers jours d'août), le Pasteur ajoute: *J'en étais plus étonné, plus peiné que je n'aurais voulu me l'avouer à moi-même*;

–le 8 mars encore, analysant l'insatisfaction dans laquelle l'avait laissé la conversation consécutive qu'il eut avec son fils, le Pasteur écrit: *C'est ce qui ne devait s'éclairer pour moi qu'un peu plus tard*;

–le 10 mars, à propos d'une réponse de son épouse, faite le même jour d'août, le Pasteur écrit encore: *Que signifiait cette insinuation? C'est ce que je ne savais, ni ne voulais chercher à savoir*;

–le 10 mars encore, à propos de la même scène : *Ces phrases d'Amélie, qui me paraissaient alors mystérieuses, s'éclairèrent pour moi peu ensuite*.

Comment, dans le premier cahier, le 8 et 10 mars, le Pasteur peut-il savoir que ces faits, datant du mois d'août précédent, s'éclairèrent *plus tard* ou *ensuite*, si, comme il le reconnaît au début du deuxième cahier, il n'a *compris* que dans la nuit du 24 au 25 avril, en relisant précisément ce qu'il avait écrit dans le premier cahier? Comment le 8 mars peut-il dire qu'il n'aurait pas voulu s'avouer quelque chose à lui-même si, au moment où il l'écrit, il ne se l'est pas déjà avoué? Comment aussi, le 10 mars, peut-il dire qu'il ne voulait pas *chercher à savoir*, s'il ne savait pas déjà qu'il y avait quelque chose à savoir? Bref, comment des réflexions qui paraissent bien devoir nécessiter l'éclairage du 25 avril peuvent-elles avoir été faites antérieurement à ce jour?" (Maillet 44-45).

⁴ For example, the word *hier* is used in the opening paragraph of the Pastor's second entry, dated February 27, to refer to the day that he wrote the previous entry, dated February 10, not February 26. And the same entry, written as were all the others in "189.," quotes Dr. Martins referring to the historic Laura Bridgeman of the nineteenth century as having lived "vers le milieu du siècle dernier" (887). But Arthur Babcock (see below, 172) has proposed a fascinating explanation for the apparent misuse of *hier*. As for "le milieu du siècle dernier," we ought not to forget that neither Gide nor the Pastor has direct responsibility for the expression, since the Pastor is quoting (or at least recreating) the language of his friend Dr. Martins. The latter, as will be shown in section G.i, gets easily muddled, witness the relative clause preceding the culpable expression: ". . . elle était aveugle et sourde-muette,

Herbert Greenberg has explained the inconsistency between the April opening of the second *cahier* and the proleptic March comments in this simple, direct way. Basing himself on Gide's abundant comments about his haste and unease in writing the second *cahier*, which Gide claimed disappointed even himself, Greenberg ends his observations with apparent logic:

> A conclusion which seems unavoidable is that at the time he wrote the March entries Gide could not have had the present method of enlightening his pastor in mind [i.e., having him suddenly realize on April 25, at the beginning of a second notebook, that he is in love]. It is difficult to resist the conjecture that some other method, more time-consuming and, perhaps, more difficult of execution was at first planned, but that Gide was willing to sacrifice it (and, along with it, some amount of psychological probability among other things) for the ease and speed of execution which the method he adopted allowed. In this view the time inconsistencies which *Symphonie Pastorale* displays are remains of the earlier plan, overlooked by Gide when impatience caused him to abandon it. (Greenberg 106)

But we have already seen Michel admit to lying, we have already seen the consequences of Jérôme's excluding editing. We have seen, in other words, a developing pattern of narration that need not be restricted to conventions applied traditionally, that yields fruit when approached more consistently and rigorously than is usually done, leading, not to what Wilson asserts is "no meaning," but to more and richer meaning, to a subtler Gidean meaning. So in the interests of what, it is hoped, will be shown to be a more inclusive reading, I will assume that the Pastor is responsible for the document we read, inconsistencies included. I will disagree with Greenberg's faulting of Gide. I will also disagree with the letter of Wilson's reading strategy, coming back to its more productive spirit later. Unlike Wilson, I *will* question the reality of this narrator's reflections and opinions, in the hope of coming to a fuller understanding of what they are.

---

qu'un docteur de je ne sais plus quel comté d'Angleterre recueillit, vers le milieu du siècle dernier" (*SP* 26).
  But critics have not yet found justifications for all such discrepancies. For an argument that says they will not, and for the latest comprehensive survey of the discrepancies, see Pierre van den Heuvel's article, "Révélations d'un discours mensonger: Les Déictiques temporels dans 'La Symphonie pastorale' d'André Gide."

In a 1978 article entitled "*La Symphonie pastorale* as Self-Conscious Fiction," Arthur Babcock took a "novel" approach to the Pastor's narrative inconsistencies, arguing that the inconsistencies of *La Symphonie pastorale* "are resolvable only if one sees the pastor not as a diarist but as a novelist" (Babcock 65). For instance, when in his second entry, dated February 27, the Pastor refers to the first entry, dated February 10, as "ce récit que je commençai *hier*" (emphasis added), Babcock sees in the confusion a tell-tale slip by the Pastor. For Babcock, Gide would have us understand that the Pastor's inadvertence betrays a divorce for him between writing and living (Babcock, "*La Symphonie*" 65). As a fabulist, the Pastor finds writing more real than reality, such that the vivid experience of writing the first entry, while occurring over two weeks earlier, took precedence in his sense of time over all the calendar yesterdays of the life endured between entries. The only real time being time spent writing, the Pastor's earlier entry necessarily becomes "yesterday."

Seeing the Pastor as a "creator of fictions," an "artificer," Babcock concluded that Gide's narrator wrote falsely:

> On the thematic level, the pastor's dishonesty is to have performed a false reading of the New Testament. It has been argued here that he writes falsely as well, and that his attempt to pass off fiction as truth is another "forme de mensonge" [as Gide himself had observed in his *journal*]. (Babcock, "*La Symphonie*" 65)

But performing "a false reading of the New Testament" and passing off "fiction as truth" is more benign and less confrontational than putting it as crudely as I propose, "the Pastor lies to the reader." If the Pastor "reads falsely," if he passes off "fiction as truth," is he *not* a liar in what he tells his readers? If he is lying in some things, how then do we identify those things where he is not lying? We ask again how we are to pick out the *histoire* from the misleading *énonciation*? Babcock did not dwell on the implications of his finding, not even later in a 1982 book, one of the chapters of which was essentially a reprise of his article. (Nor does Sheng-Tai Chang, building on Babcock in a 1990 article, dwell on lying, content merely to acknowledge in passing that the possibility exits: "If the pastor is not willfully lying . . .," Chang 72). Significantly, at one point in his book Babcock puts quotation marks around the word 'lying.' That suggests that he saw the Pastor's insincerity as something not reducible to simple lying: "To be sure, 'lying' through language is a trait shared by the pastor with Michel and Jérôme [. . .]" (Babcock, *Portraits of Artists*, 71).

Is it or is it not lying?

C) *Justifying a Consideration of Narrative Lying*

Lafille's, Babcock's, and Chang's hesitancy is surely understandable: a fictional text becomes wildly unstable if we insist on the consequences of the narrator's being a liar. No one has ever so insisted apropos of *La Symphonie pastorale*, and very rarely about other fictional *récits*.[5] Let me now justify my insistence.

i) *External Justifications*

By way of external authorization, we can recall that among Gide's *récits*, the issue of lying is not unique to *La Symphonie pastorale*. In the preceding chapter on *La Porte étroite* we could do no more than wonder if Jérôme's general editing and specific, notable misquotation of the Gospel's verses on the narrow gate had anything of the lie to them (a question not vitiated by speculation regarding the effects on him of Alissa's lying about her feelings for him). But the problem of lying had already arisen foursquare regarding Michel in *L'Immoraliste*, when we saw that he admitted that he was making up ex post facto his alleged first thoughts about his "rebirth," and that he had become practiced in deceit. But the example occurred embedded within another problem, that of the frame and its voice, and so lost an appreciable amount of its critical immediacy, ultimately becoming subsumed under the issue of individualism. There will however be no loss of the issue's immediacy in *La Symphonie pastorale*: we have direct contact only with the Pastor's words, and if doubt arises about the integrity of his intent, we need to establish how we can read and understand his text.

---

[5] For an interesting exception, see *Le Bavard* by Louis-René des Forêts, the narrator of which forces the issue of his lying.

Another external reason is that the same issue arises in much the same terms for an entire sub-genre of first-person fictional narration, the picaresque novel, which has had considerable impact of course on many of the best first-person narratives, among which, I submit, are Gide's. In Claudio Guillen's authoritative book *Literature as System*, the hispanist has characterized the picaresque model as the "fictional confession of a liar" (Guillen 120). Ulrich Wicks, in his no less authoritative book *Picaresque Narrative, Picaresque Fictions*, points out the obvious: "Even in the narrative act, the picaro is still up to his old tricks. He assumes yet another role and becomes a trickster of narration, a verbally manipulative rogue" (58). And yet, when I read the rest of Wicks's book and even his benchmark bibliography on the picaresque, I find nothing to indicate that any sustained, consistent effort has been made to explore what would seem to be the logical status of a trickster's alleged *histoire*, to wit, and again, radical inaccessibility.

Which is not to say that the status of the picaro's story has not been identified. Barbara Babcock, for one, in her contribution to a collection of essays on symbolic inversion and the picaresque, put it this way:

> [the narrator] who tells the reader to trust the credibility of his tale then describes himself (protagonist) as the master of deception and deceit............................................................................
> The liar's assertion that 'this is not an *un*true story' establishes a paradoxical frame comparable to Epimenides' 'Liar' paradox: 'All Cretans are liars. I am a Cretan' (Colie 1966:6). Like all paradoxes, the paradox of the picaresque is both a direct criticism of itself as narrative statement and an oblique criticism of absolute judgment or absolute convention in general. Ultimately, of course, the reader, like the picaro himself and his other victims, is taken in, caught in the vertigo of infinite reflection and the play with human understanding. (Barbara A. Babcock 108)

Yet, for all that and characteristically of our profession, Babcock will still go on to treat the events narrated by a picaro as reliably known, accepting, for just one example of her inconsistency, that in "*El Buscón* Don Pablos' career culminates in the profession of actor and playwright . . ." (B. Babcock, "'Liberty's a Whore'" 109), as if readers can be sure that the profession alleged by the admitted narrator/con man is a given. So, even savvy critics read as if the wily, prevaricating rogue will not simply lie to *them* about his story, just because . . ., well, . . . and that is the problem – just because.

As we saw regarding *L'Immoraliste*, it might be argued that questioning a position such as Barbara Babcock's is disingenuous, since there can be no literary text to "read" without arbitrary convention. Since logic and convention need not be consistent with each other, one could presuppose – and examining the scholarship suggests that critics have indeed presupposed – that, by convention, a lying narrator lies to everyone except the special reader, the perceptive reader. But apropos of *L'Immoraliste*, we also saw that Bakhtin, in keeping with the name of "novel," that is, in viewing it as "the genre of becoming," the genre of "new," "novel" things, (Bakhtin, "Epic and Novel," in *The Dialogic Imagination* 22), positioned himself to argue persuasively that in fact and contrary to traditional practice "one of the most basic tasks for the novel [,broadly defined, is] the laying bare of any sort of conventionality" (Bakhtin, "Forms of Time and Chronotope in the Novel," in *The Dialogic Imagination* 162). As a consequence, Bakhtin viewed the novel-writer of genius as one who teases out the hidden implications of a genre's conventions, and I in turn saw Gide's text teasing out the implications of its own narrative gambit, the frame. I maintain that *La Symphonie pastorale* does the same with the gambit of the lying narrator.

One of the results of being a stickler about the lying picaro in general, and about the lying Pastor in particular, is to show that for even the most informed reader mimesis and the challenging of mimesis can *in some cases* co-exist in the same text unreconciled, unarticulated, and – to what should be our discomfort – glossed over by our profession. I say "in some cases" because the real-seeming and its contrary are of course articulated and, if not reconciled, at least addressed in highly self-conscious fiction, such as *Don Quixote*, where verisimilitude and literary illusion explicitly play off and illuminate each other. But the other cases that I have in mind are *un*-self-conscious narratives that are booby-trapped, such that careful reflection reveals them to be riven by an inner contradiction that is no more reconciled than it is flaunted. On the one hand, scrupulous and sometimes pain-staking reading can wind up showing that the narrator's deceit undermines any possibility of relying on the story as told. On the other hand, the history of criticism and our own experience show that, narrative deceit notwithstanding, we are unfailingly inclined to believe in the voice that we hear. Attribute that inclination to the alchemy of verbal symbol-making at its best, attribute it to our desire to be seduced by our own symbols, attribute it to our fear of recognizing the all-encompassing arbitrariness of the symbolic systems running our lives – attribute it to what we will, we just believe the story. It has even been argued that literature and the stories that it tells are essentially hallucinatory, because the medium, language, is essentially hallucinatory:

> ... I shall say with Lacan that as "subjects" – and the concept will have to be defined very carefully – we speak because we are separated, cut off from the world. By definition, the notion of subject implies an incompleteness, which can also be read as division within the individual; between subject and object, the difference cannot be reduced, and between the two the distance is insuperable, which is simply to say that from my particular place and point of view I shall never be an object, except for others. Hence the need to imagine, invent, create a link with objects. But the link is an illusion, although an illusion we cannot recognize as such (except theoretically) since confronted by the *real* it is all we have; it has the value of a hallucination, and what characterizes a hallucination is that one believes in it. Language is effective because of this suspension of disbelief, and so is art. Even though theory keeps repeating to us that the word is not the thing, we stop being conscious of this when we speak (or read or write), and this forgetting constitutes one of the necessary conditions of the production of language. (Silhol 6-7)

ii) *Internal Justifications*

Which leaves us with an intriguing question and one that leads to an articulation of internal justifications for insisting on the narrative implications of the Pastor's lies: what is the result when one insists on taking into account not only the compelling illusion of the story (as criticism heretofore has done), but also the fact of its being logically undermined by the deceit of the story-teller, which criticism has not addressed systematically? Leaving for others the application of that question to the picaresque novel, we can say that Gide wrote *La Symphonie pastorale* in a way that gives every appearance of soliciting and even requiring the sort of conventional, mimetic reading that its own subtleties can be seen to go on to undermine. Why would his book do that? (We should recall that Gide did in fact write highly self-conscious fiction, such as the parody-driven *les Caves du Vatican* and his notorious novel about itself, *les Faux-Monnayeurs*. Clearly, then, it was *en toute connaissance de cause* that in his *récits*, he chose not to use the self-conscious mode, but rather what could be called the self-contradictory mode.)

Among several possible answers, there is one that is fairly abstract. I propose that the tension between a text's unreconciled narrative opposites of verisimilitude and its debunking, whether overt as in *Quixote* or more concealed as in *La Symphonie pastorale*, is an inevitable consequence deriving necessarily from the medium of all of literature: words. For as Brian Stonehill reminds us in his book, *The Self-Conscious Novel: Artifice in Fiction from Joyce to Pynchon*:

> ... in the word, the unit of language itself, we find in elementary form that same duality of creation and disruption of illusion which the ... [novel can enact] ... on a macrocosmic scale. A written word is an arbitrary sign; a spoken word is an arbitrary sound. We have merely *agreed* to let these arbitrary sounds and signs 'stand in for' or 'represent' the objects around us and the thoughts and feelings within.... (Stonehill 15)

Ultimately, then, the question is not whether the tension exists in literature, but rather, whether and how a text deals with it. The more satisfying ones do deal with it, I think. Gide's *La Symphonie pastorale* does, and in a way that, while subverting diegetic realism, takes us to other levels of realism, those of the story-teller and of users of symbols. For not only do we have a convincing if inadvertent self-portrait of an overly self-assured story-teller whose inseparable moral and verbal arrogance leads to the death of the no less separable Gertrude and story. We have as well an accurate illustration of an all too common failure, that of not taking into adequate account the arbitrariness of our illusory symbolic systems, systems that we prefer to the way things are.

Among other answers to the question of why Gide made this narrative strain with self-contradiction, there is the heightening of the poignancy of this tragedy of certainty. Catching the Pastor, an apostle of certainty, in his lies increases the reader's revulsion at defenders of certitude. But if we ourselves as readers are caught in the uncertain tension between mimesis and its subversion, it becomes less easy to dismiss either certitude or its undoing, as a result of which the death of Gertrude seems less facile and all the more tragic. Another answer is that the Pastor's lies paradoxically dupe the reader into lending the text more verisimilitude than it would otherwise have, a reader-generated *effet de réel* à la Barthes. Lulled by the magic of the story, we stumble on the lies and are immediately inclined to think: "Oh, no you don't – what really happened must have been that . . .," as if there were a real anything in the story to begin with. By having us conjure up "what really happened," the author tricks us into supplying his text with an imagined situation that seems more real precisely because we each craft an explanation according to our own most persuasive imaginative criteria. Or, for still another answer, if we are deprived of diegetic story, we are left with the story of the fictional writing as it unfolds before our eyes, the story of the imagined personality producing and in turn *being influenced by* his uncertain mix of self-revelation and distortion. That kind of story, as we have already seen, was of enormous and continuing interest to Gide, and it is a story yet to be appreciated in *La Symphonie pastorale*. We are not left – *pace* Wilson – with no meaning, but with the meaning of story-telling, and if we accept the troubling epistemological and ontological thrust of post-Kantian, postmodernist questioning of the relationship among mind, reality, and language, that may be the only meaning that will lead us to literature as it is, and to ourselves as we are. Another, obvious answer develops if we again take cognizance of the inherent qualities of *disponibilité* itself. In this scheme, Gide's narrative derives distinctive life from the polar pull exerted on it by conventional mimetic illusion and by the countervailing undermining of convention and illusion.

In fact, to end this section with a tangent, the text subtly corroborates the need for *disponibilité* as one reads it. It turns out that in the Pastor's and his son's arguments about how to apply a reading of the Bible to Gertrude's situation, there exists an allegory of precisely such a Gidean reading. Alain Goulet, in still another of his superb articles, "La figuration du procès littéraire dans l'écriture de *La Symphonie pastorale*," highlighting the confluence of the theme of writing and the book's use of water images (snow, the lake, running water, tears, the water sprite, and ice), has already shown "la manière dont le procès littéraire – c'est-à-dire le couple écriture/lecture – s'implique dans les textes de Gide, se signifie dans et par la fiction" (Goulet 27). Enlarging upon his point, I would like to argue that the reason why *La Symphonie pastorale* readily lends itself to an allegory of reading is that in large part the subject around which the whole book turns is how one reads *the* text of Western culture, the book whose name means 'book' in its Greek etymon. I refer of course to the Bible, a subject discussed from one end of *La Symphonie pastorale* to the other.

Both the Pastor and his divinity-school son are heavily determined as readers: for them, reading the Bible stands not only as their professional activity par excellence, but also, given their religious devotion, as their most personal activity, their supreme value, indeed and quite literally as for many believers, the key to their very *raison d'être*. The hostility that arises in the first of the two *cahiers*, when they both try to help the blind Gertrude read braille, prefigures the overriding subject of the second *cahier*, their argument over how to read the language of Christ and apply it to their and Gertrude's life. The Pastor is, of course, a free reader impatient with convention, following his *élans* where they take him, looking for an affirmation of joy and love, standing in opposition, of course, to Jacques who is a constrained reader, one highly respectful of law and tradition, convention's offspring. In keeping with Gide's hostile views on a reader such as Jacques, it is expected that the latter be identified with *le livre*, the one that Nathaniel of *les Nourritures terrestres* should presumably throw away. Jacques admits to preferring "le livre à l'alpenstock" (*PE* 62) – in a context where the Alps are portrayed as achingly beautiful – and Jacques "parle posément comme on lit un livre" (*PE* 62). We note in passing that a Derridian or Lacanian appraisal of him would see him laid bare as reader and thinker by his putative "extraordinaire possession de soi" (*PE* 62).

Interestingly enough, Saint Paul, as author of guiding texts about texts and so as ultimate source of Jacques's conventions for reading the texts about Christ, has an originary story that eerily parallels what sounds like a convincing parable on the origin of convention itself. An expert on law, he derives his authority arbitrarily from nothing more than his own assertion of authority. He maintains that his vision of Christ – a blinding vision, no less! – on the road to Damascus allows him to explain Christ's teachings, even though Paul had not known Christ who said he came to kill the law, and even though he had persecuted and killed Christ's followers. The unsophisticated Pastor might even claim that Paul, having started by killing Christians out of conservative concern over law, went on to kill with arbitrary law the essence of Christ's message of love.

The Pastor, as the one who presumably pens our text, is of course also a writer as well as a reader, as Babcock has argued. It does not take a great leap of the imagination to see that this writer produces not one, but two, kinds of tightly intertwined texts, his document and "Gertrude herself." Since we do not have direct contact with "Gertrude," but only with the Pastor's textual representation of "her," and since presumably there would be no story without that textual representation, each text is a dependency of the other, an impossibility without the other. Her status as a work, a product, a text, is underscored by the plainly developed Pygmalion-Galatea archetype at work in the relationship between the Pastor, the verbal sculptor, and the blind, aphasic "être incertain" (*SP* 878), "masse involontaire" (*SP* 879), and "paquet de chair sans âme" (*SP* 880) whom he brings to language, to understanding, and to sexuality.

Gertrude, a "text," then, that is blind to reality but capable of great verbal beauty, is fought over by the two "readers," each of whom in his excluding tendencies contributes to her death. One might suspect that, of the two (catastrophic) readings, Gide would favor the Pastor's more liberating one. In this line of thinking, were "Gertrude" to have been "written" from Jacques's point of view, she would probably sound too much like the pinch-lipped "Réprimande du frère ainé" of Gide's *Le Retour de l'enfant prodigue*, leaving the Pastor's "Gertrude" the preferable one. (To strain the point, Jacques's broken arm, which prevents him from writing, suggests how he is not a *lecteur scriptible*.) But such a line of thinking would fail to take into account the dynamics of *disponibilité*, which refuses to abandon the live-giving tension between unreconciled opposites. Gertrude dies precisely because she is forced into a choice between the Pastor's illusions and Jacques's destruction of those illusions.

## D) Reading the Lie

Given then the Pastor's grossly misleading opening pages, recent readings such as Babcock's, and both internal and external justification for pursuing the narrative consequences of the Pastor's lies, we can confidently move beyond Lafille's hesitancy to pursue his own ground-breaking insight, and we can affirm without reservation that the Pastor is indeed "moins innocent d'intentions qu'il ne peut paraître." How, then, can we read the text of a liar? There are two ways, one based on theoretical considerations, the other on concrete ones.

First, to the extent that we accept the Pastor as a simulation of a real person, we accept that when he lies, he believes something else:

> Si nous acceptions les termes de la théorie des actes langagiers, il faudrait postuler chez des personnages littéraires, quoiqu'un personnage ne soit nullement un être humain, un ensemble de croyances et d'intentions, telles qu'*un personnage qui ment croit le contraire de ce qu'il dit*. (Wall 268; emphasis in the original)

So we accept the mimetic illusion that there *is* a "truth" that we can look for or that at least "exists." If then we believe that in lying he is hiding "the truth" from us, we assume emotions, thoughts, intentions, and deeds that "really exist" and are "hidden behind" his misrepresentations. That assumption points to an area of inquiry that is as vast as it is conjectural, as fascinating as it is difficult to work with. But "difficult" is not "impossible." Let us not then hastily extrapolate from the Pastor's lie that the mimetic game is up, that one cannot "make believe" if there is no determining reliably what exactly one is to pretend is true. (As we saw above, 178, it could even be argued that his lying envelops the Pastor even more thickly in our impressions of verisimilitude, because to the extent that we believe he is lying, we *both* believe in the "reality" of his lies *and* presuppose the possible "events" covered up by the lies.)

Furthermore, the Pastor's deception does not pollute irremediably what in semantics is called "the rule of sincerity" (the assumption of an effort on the part of every communicator to communicate at least something true – see, e.g., Gabriel, "Fiction – a Semantic Approach" 249), and does not leave the reader so mired in the constitutive arbitrariness of fiction that there are no longer any rules whatsoever whereby to suspend disbelief. So even if we suppose that Gide wrote this mimetic text such that we could play by (and Gide being Gide, *with*) the usual rules of fiction, we can accept – we indeed want to accept – that, while the Pastor is lying in some and – just for the sake of argument – perhaps even in most particulars, he is nonetheless writing to communicate, if not *the* truth, the whole truth, and nothing but the truth, at the very least *a* truth. Against the void left by the diegetic corrosiveness of lies, we have a voice that succeeds in stimulating belief because of our own tendency to cling tenaciously to the "rule of sincerity."

Granted, an extreme position could be staked out here, reminding us again that Gide acknowledged and would have his readers acknowledge the imperium of the game in literature. But that position would minimize the claims of *disponibilité*, claims buttressed by Gide's repeated attempts *not* to dismiss mimesis, *not* to allow the arbitrariness of literary conventions to prevail completely. In *disponibilité* we have our second, more concrete means of reading the text of a liar. Suspending complete adherence to an unyielding posture, we can even wilfully choose not to disregard the claims of (and pleasures offered by) so many rich studies of *La Symphonie pastorale* that assume easy and reliable access to narrated events. At the very least, those studies took it as a given that, the Pastor's bad faith notwithstanding, he tells his story with a rudimentary narrative integrity, with a discernable desire to give a representative account at least of events of central importance to him. Somehow, it has been sensed, the integrity and desire are not incompatible with his flaws.

That sense can indeed be argued for from within the text. The Pastor's document will of course always be subject to a limiting caveat (once we catch him in insincerity and deceptive inconsistencies, how can we know for sure when he is being sincere and when he is telling the truth?) and so, as with *L'Immoraliste* and *La Porte étroite*, one is reduced necessarily to being very speculative and even arbitrary in approaching Gide's text. Let us grant ourselves, then, an admittedly arbitrary hold on the events recounted in this inaccessible text. That done, if we continue with the fictional convention that the Pastor wrote what we read, we have to recognize that, even in his eyes, the tragedy of the concluding events that he set down on paper clearly repudiates him and his understanding of

Christianity. He goes so far as to record what is incontrovertibly Gertrude's indictment of him at the end, where she explicitly repudiates "notre faute, notre péché" (*SP* 929), insists that "il ne faut pas qu'il reste aucun mensonge" between them (*SP* 929), and in her very last words to him says: "Je ne supporte plus de vous voir" (*SP* 930). Finally, he notes that he is left with a "coeur plus aride que le désert." So while he may have misrepresented much of his story, especially its earlier pages, he was nonetheless prepared finally to show himself in the worst light possible, pursuing his account to its bitter end. (The question of exactly why and in what spirit he wrote down the last entry has of course no simple, obvious answer. Did he do it out of guilt? out of a writer's compulsion to complete a story? because reality had lost its presence for him until it became textual? because he still felt somehow justified? etc. Even assuming that he was less devastated than driven by other compunctions, it would reduce him to insignificance to maintain that he was fully blind to the implications for him of the final events.) Continuing to push vigorously the limits of narrative convention, we could also maintain that as the author of the text, the Pastor was probably the one who had it published, which would argue even more strongly for his final narrative integrity. (If Gide wants us to see the Pastor as the agent of writing, why not as the agent of publication?) However one views the "publication" of "the Pastor's" text, the forthright nature of "his" final entries bespeaks a fundamental narrative honesty not easily squared with insistence on the negative implications of all his examples of bad faith.

Nor should we underestimate the power of much of what the Pastor has to say. His message about a gospel of ideal love is too beautiful for us not to want to give credence to the story conveying it (Harvey). It seems virtually certain that Gide intended this, and that he too found the Pastor's message of Christian love attractive, for the simplest of reasons: it is straight out of his own heartfelt, private book of meditations, Numquid et tu . . .? (*Journal* I, 587-606), written in the heat of conviction in 1916 but published in a very limited edition only in 1922, and from which he cribbed many of the passages he attributed to the Pastor in the 1919 *récit* (C. Martin lxix-lxxviii). Moreover, Wilson has observed that "the Beethoven symphony serves as a symbol in Gide's *récit* because it is, like any work of art, an imaginative idealization of reality" (Wilson 53). Not unlike the symphony, the high beauty of the Pastor's ideal can make us want to consider the question of its "factual" accuracy appear secondary. Wilson goes on to attribute to Gide a response that is probably shared by many readers:

> ... unmistakably Gide retains a nostalgia for the vision of a truer, superior reality underlying this one. In practice he must condemn the Pastor's errors, but one must suspect that he has considerable sympathy with his attempt to see the world in more optimistic terms, to discount the existence of sin and recover the blindness of total innocence. (W. Wilson 58)

In a different but harmonious register, Alain Goulet makes a similar point. Drawing on the variety of the Pastor's voices in order to argue for the complex way Gide used the writing of *La Symphonie pastorale* to work through his own tangled feelings of guilt and liberation at leaving his wife Madeleine for Marc Allégret, Goulet reminds us of the positive effects of many key passages:

> En fait, le statut de la voix narrative est éminemment variable, ambigu, oscillant de la ferveur à l'ironie. Tantôt nous nous trouvons dans le régime du lyrisme et de l'émotion, comme dans ce passage initial de la redécouverte du 'petit lac mystérieux' et de la contemplation émue du paysage environnant, au soleil couchant, qui présente bien des traits d'une anamnèse; ou encore à quelques moments de vraie rencontre, de communion entre le Pasteur et sa pupille, comme lors des larmes de Gertrude. L'adhésion qui se produit alors entre l'auteur, le narrateur, le personnage et le lecteur laisse supposer une charge d'investissement particulière de Gide, une participation inconsciente et/ou libidinale qui confère au texte sa dimension d'auto-analyse. Tantôt se déploient divers registres de l'ironie, qui retourne les propos du Pasteur en autant d'actes d'accusation dressés contre lui, ou qui caractérise certaines remarques d'Amélie ou de Jacques que notre Pasteur s'obstine à retranscrire en se refusant de les comprendre. (Goulet, "L'Ironie pastorale en jeu" 43-44)

At the moments of lyricism and emotion, so remote are any signs of bad faith that we are impelled to identify with and applaud the Pastor.

So we loop back to the beginning of this chapter, to join in the spirit if not in the letter of Wilson's argument about the Pastor's lack of sincerity, that we should, finally, believe that there is some sort of truth in the Pastor's account. In lying the Pastor hides something, and we can look for what he has hidden; the "rule of sincerity" prevails even against the lies; *disponibilité* warrants an openness to the potential truth-telling dimensions of the Pastor's document; the severe condemnation of the Pastor represented by his own final pages suggests a fundamental if tardy good faith; and the beauty of much of his message remains: all those factors would make it foolhardy to write the Pastor off as only insincere, only a liar. Those same factors, moreover and to the point of my larger argument, add particular body to the voice countering the void of diegetic indeterminacy.

E) *Lying or Evangelizing?*

The acceptance of the Pastor's basic integrity leads to the question of when he first decided he might communicate a truth, if not the truth, to the public. The question has a certain complexity, since it refers to the relationship of the decision both to the time (and nature) of the writing and to the time of the events narrated. Regarding the first, he clearly took up the pen to address the public at large, the apparent diary format notwithstanding. On one occasion, in his second entry, he anticipates that Amélie may one day read his document:

> Il m'est pénible d'avoir à dire que ces reproches me venaient d'Amélie; et du reste, si j'en parle ici, c'est que je n'en ai conservé nulle animosité, nulle aigreur – je l'atteste solennellement pour le cas où plus tard ces feuilles seraient lues par elle. (*SP* 30)

One could maintain that this proves no more than that he assumes she may one day stumble across his diary-notebook at home, in its handwritten form. The argument would have to be admitted, were it not for a sentence in his third entry. There, he anticipates a reader not at all acquainted with any of the events, that is, a general reader outside the circle of his family and acquaintances: ". . . celui qui par aventure lirait ces pages s'étonnera sans doute de l'entendre s'exprimer aussitôt avec tant de justesse et raisonner si judicieusement" (*SP* 54). That expectation makes it possible to interpret his other comments about his writing as statements, not to a diary, but to a reading public (e.g., "J'ai projeté d'écrire ici tout ce qui concerne la formation et le développement de cette âme pieuse . . .," *SP* 4, "J'ai trop souci de la vérité pour taire le fâcheux accueil que je dus essuyer à mon retour au foyer," *SP* 12).

But it is possible even to offer reasonable speculations about exactly when, vis-à-vis the events, he first decided to write for publication, timing that sheds light on his motivation and the nature of his document. He tells us that heavy snows kept him blocked in his home from February 12 until some point after March 12 but before April 25. And after reading through the text carefully, we know that at the time he started the text, Gertrude had already told him she loved him, and that he had been in the habit of seeing her every day, away from his wife and family. If we postulate that part of the reason for his writing was to re-present to himself the beautiful young woman whom he most certainly missed, at least one textual puzzle makes more sense, namely, why so many novelistic details cram an account written by an obscure Reformed minister (still assuming that we should push the fictional convention of the narrator's authorship as far as possible). It is true that Dr. Martins's earlier recommendation that the Pastor record the details of Gertrude's coming to language served as a retrospective excuse to communicate those steps. But as the chronological table at the end of this chapter shows, he had ignored that recommendation for thirty months, as a result of which he had no detailed notes to consult, and no especially accurate memories of all the pertinent details to go on. So he apparently wanted to revisit novelistically the more personal details of their encounters and conversations because, missing Gertrude, he could by writing re-present her and relive their experiences together.[6] David Walker speaks of the snowbound Pastor's writing as "compensation" for being deprived of Gertrude's company. It is that, naturally, but I am arguing that it is also and significantly and literally re-presentation, which is more indicative of what he really wants from Gertrude, even when they are together. It is less herself than *his* idealized vision of what she could become. Not surprisingly, it smacks of narcissism. The liter-

---

[6] Babcock notes the connection between the Pastor's writing and his confinement, but oddly enough posits an intention to "speak privately," an intention not in keeping with Babcock's thesis that the Pastor is something of a novelist: "The pastor, prevented from speaking publicly (he cannot preach the Word), will in effect speak privately, in his own words, to his diary" (Babcock, *Portraits* 63). A private purpose also seems inconsistent with the Pastor's asides to readers.

ary, ideal quality of his re-presentation comes through distinctly in the Pastor's consistent use of the literary tense, the *passé simple*, the preferred tense for those of his passages where Gertrude is the focus (Maisani-Léonard 138-44), which is in contrast to his use of the *passé composé*, the tense, as Maisani-Léonard points out, which is used more for his family. That is especially appropriate because of that tense's mix of present auxiliary and past participle: his wife and children are present when he writes, and their past claims on him engage his responsibility in the unpleasant present (separated from the woman he desires, trapped with the very people whose presence condemns his adulterous yearnings). In those verbs' mix of present and past realities for him, his family members are also "other" than the purer writing of the literary tense used to summon up the absent Gertrude.

So, à la Babcock, he is something of a novelist, but a novelist-minister, which makes an important difference. That difference suggests a second reason for writing: being snowbound had made him miss something else, namely, his preaching. Postulating that lack too as part of the reason for writing for this compulsive moralizer, we see that the first notebook could well have been written partly out of a sermonistic impulse, in this case, to exhort spontaneous charity of the heart over the mind that allows one to respond Christ-like (according to the Pastor) to an alleged "lost sheep." Once we get to the second notebook where the Pastor finally (and in the timing, misleadingly) acknowledges his illicit love, i.e., a love that violates biblical law, he is forced to refocus the argument onto the superiority of Christ's message of love over Paul's message of law. Arguably, he concluded and published his document in spite of its condemnation of him, for the same reason he had planned to publish it in the first place, for its value as a spiritual text, as something of a sermon based on personal experience.

Preaching as an incitement to writing and publishing appears even more credible when we keep in mind that at the time pastors such as our narrator could be expected to publish their collected sermons. Gide apparently started out assuming such an expectation, as the original manuscript shows. The next to last paragraph of the first entry reads (with deletions in the brackets): "travaillant jusqu'au matin, lisant ou préparant [le recueil de] [mon] mon sermons[s] [que j'ai promis à Fishbacher]" (C. Martin, "Introduction" 21). Moreover, as Maisani-Léonard points out, there is an ambiguity in the opening paragraph that lends an especially pastoral cast to the narrator's document:

> J'ai projeté ici d'écrire tout ce qui concerne la formation et le développement de cette âme pieuse, qu'il me semble que je n'ai fait sortir de la nuit que pour l'adoration et l'amour. Béni soit le Seigneur pour m'avoir confié cette tâche. (*SP* 4)

Maisani-Léonard observes:

> Les derniers mots sont ambigus, car 'cette tâche', c'est évidemment l'éducation de Gertrude, mais aussi la relation qu'il va en faire et qu'il ne dissocie pas de sa tâche pastorale: le récit du pasteur se trouve donc pour ainsi dire intégré à sa fonction religieuse; c'est d'ailleurs uniquement à titre de pasteur que le narrateur se présente à nous, et le fait que nous ne lui connaissions pas de nom est significatif. (Maisani-Léonard 59)

Consequently, we can nuance Babcock's findings: the Pastor did not so much intend to write fiction, as he set out to prepare a devotional story based on his experiences with Gertrude, which take on a novelistic cast because of his desire to re-present her in as much detail as possible. The Evangelists' example, which he had been pondering day in and day out for much if not all of his reflective life, illustrates admirably the devotional approach to narrative most present to his mind. The four gospels, written (like so much of the Bible) to nourish faith and not to satisfy modern criteria of historiography, assume a very free approach to the facts of Christ's life. Even the three synoptic or similar gospels of Matthew, Mark, and Luke, when compared to each other can be seen to rearrange and alter events and sayings, both major and minor, suppressing some and dramatizing others, in accordance with their different goals and intended audiences. John's gospel, of course, presents a Christ even more strikingly different from each of the synoptic portraits. Much like the Evangelists, the Pastor would have felt free to manipulate the order of events, to dramatize and even alter telling details, in brief, to craft the story in order to highlight important religious truths, the chief of which for him was the beauty of a gospel of love.

The beauty of his vision notwithstanding, the Pastor characteristically started his account in the flush of an *élan*, in this case one provoked by Gertrude's absence, without thinking through completely what he was embarking on and why, without the grain of common sense Gide felt he lacked. Once started, he got distracted by the call back to pastoral duties, and then no doubt by the surging erotic drives that he felt upon seeing Gertrude after their long separation. By that time, he felt himself caught up in new circumstances, as his starting a second notebook indicates. But his muddled motivation at the start would help explain, among other things, how he could with breathtaking aplomb simply abrogate after a few pages the initial intention to write "tout ce qui concerne la formation and le développment" of Gertrude:

> C'est l'histoire du développement intellectuel et moral de Gertrude que j'ai entrepris de tracer ici. J'y reviens.
>
> J'espérais pouvoir suivre ici ce développement pas à pas, et j'avais commencé d'en raconter le détail. Mais outre que le temps me manque pour en noter minutieusement toutes les phases, il m'est extrêmement difficile aujourd'hui d'en retrouver l'enchaînement exact. (SP 54)

In his own befuddled way, then, the Pastor is working on three main agendas:[7] first, foremost, and least explicitly, he is endeavoring to re-present Gertrude, which explains the novelistic elements emphasized by Babcock. The second agenda – a dodge that allows him to indulge the first one – is to comply with the recommendation of his friend, Dr. Martins, to record in detail the steps of Gertrude's progress. That he is complying after considerable delay, and that he usually skips blithely over the very details that would be of most interest to someone like Martins, expose his confusion about his purposes. The rest of his expression of intentions from the first page, starting with the words '*cette âme pieuse*,' then suggests strongly the impact of a third agenda, to make of his "record" a sermon-like parable on a Gospel of love (v. his opening lines,

---

[7] Alain Goulet makes a good case for muddled intentions on Gide's part, brought on by the erotic firestorm ignited at the chance to love Marc Allégret spiritually *and* physically, free to be true to his full homosexual self, instead of furtively satisfying himself carnally with anonymous boys and only spiritually with his wife. For Goulet, Gide set out to explore one of his "possible selves," a blind "counterfeiter" seeking spiritual/erotic fulfillment outside of a constricting marriage. But his exploration got detoured from the start by the compulsion to repudiate his wife and her values (Goulet, "Ironie"). This muddled intention presumably got echoed in the muddled narrative intentions of the Pastor.

quoted above, 188). If he expected to publish his account, the dated, diary-like form was used, then, not because he intended to write to and for himself alone (an explanation not compatible with the asides about and to his readers), but because it was consistent with the record-keeping he purported to present.[8] That he did in (fictional) fact intend to publish the account would seem to be explainable in terms of both the second and third agendas, but mostly the third. His irrepressible moralizing proclivities would certainly have made it difficult for him to keep his pages to himself.

Given, then, the moralizing intentions of a devotional story in which, like the gospels, historiographic accuracy is secondary to the movements of faith, should we conclude that 'lying' is too harsh a term for the Pastor's narrative inconsistencies? Not necessarily, first and most obviously because, when all is written and done, Gertrude died and the Pastor's family was devastated. The incongruity between the intention and the consequences bespeaks a more complicated, more sordid etiology.

## F) *The Hidden Agendas*

If the Pastor sought to reveal a superior truth, need he be held to the exigencies of a documentary account? Yes, for several reasons. First of all, what he writes raises troubling questions of self-serving subjectivity, which is not surprising in light of the fact that the story is, unlike many devotional tracts, more about its author than about God or about anyone else. For one thing, he is much too concerned about *les qu'en-dira-t-on*, nearly to the point of pathology. At the moment when Gertrude, struggling on death's threshold to explain how they have sinned, admits that she had tried to kill herself because of the sadness she and the Pastor had caused, the Pastor mentions his distraction and discomfort at the thought that someone might hear her: "Elle parlait dans un état d'exaltation extrême, à voix très haute et cria presque ces derniers

---

[8] See Booker and Chang for other answers to the productive question of why the Pastor started with a diary format (i.e., dated entries) for what at first seems essentially a memoir. The memoir-diary becomes a true diary only with the *deuxième cahier*, when contemporaneous events start impinging more and more forcefully on, and become the consistent topic of, the narration (starting with the Pastor's rereading of the *premier cahier*).

mots, de sorte que je fus gêné à l'idée qu'on la pourrait entendre du dehors . . ." (*SP* 128).

Such shallow embarrassment, coupled with the comparative chronology of events and writing, authorizes even more retrospective suspicions about how self-serving his presentation of his gospel of love had been from its beginning (being truly read of course only in retrospect.) Before he had started writing, he had already been sensitized to how outsiders could "misconstrue" his relationship with Gertrude: he saw that the passers-by in Neuchatel had not understood the "innocence" of Gertrude's talking aloud about touching the Pastor's cheek, and he understood that his parishioners would not appreciate how his spending time alone with Gertrude in the chapel was "special" enough to obviate scandal. So it appears entirely too possible that he postponed the telling details to his readers until he could first preach his way into the reader's good graces, establishing his apparent charity in bringing the "lost sheep" into his home, and thereby implying first the spiritual and so innocent nature of their initial bond, and then the specialness and so acceptability of their companionship. The reader, having first been informed of the seeming beauty of the origins of the Pastor's and Gertrude's feelings for each other, without knowing all that had transpired between them before the Pastor took up the pen, could avoid a worldly, "misconstrued" interpretation. That interpretation, however, as the ending implies, would have been the more accurate, comprehensive one.

So, crafting a "superior truth" when writing an account involving one's own extra-marital love offers too much scope to the mundane inclination toward self-justification. Ordinary prudence militates against it. The heightened prudence expected of a person professing to cultivate awareness in the life of the spirit almost forbids it. The Pastor's *im*prudence suggests such bad faith that, his evangelistic narrative impulses and the attractiveness of his message of innocent love notwithstanding, we see him drawn back under the shadow of hypocritical deceit that his narrative inconsistencies first cast for us.

Apropos of the Pastor's apparently charitable *élan* that initiated the whole chain of events by leading him to take Gertrude into his home, we have to be careful. While it is true that "[c]ertainly there was no physical attraction in the beginning," that does not mean that "[t]he action must be considered as emanating from pure *cari-*

*tas*" (Henry 18). There is a case to made for considering it as emanating from pure orneriness compounded with hostility toward his wife Amélie.

The chain of events leading up to his decision to take Gertrude in is a complicated, complicating one. At the request of the young servant girl who intercepted him on his way home that first evening, the Pastor did indeed go on an errand of mercy to the *chaumière*, where he would first see Gertrude. But once there, before making his decision (or as he characteristically views it, after he had prayed and suddenly understood "God's" will), he gave signs of a quickness to annoyance out of keeping with the urgings of charity:

> Comme souvent déjà, dans ce pays perdu, il me fallait tout décider. J'étais quelque peu gêné, je l'avoue, de laisser cette maison, si pauvre que fût son apparence, à la seule garde ce cette voisine et de cette servante enfant. (*SP* 6-8)

An apparent habit of aggravation ("Comme souvent déjà") at feeling obliged to make every decision for people, and perhaps a habit of feeling aggrieved at finding himself in "ce pays perdu" (where – what? – his preaching talents go unappreciated?) are too likely compatible with his admitted annoyance ("J'étais quelque peu gêné, je l'avoue") at having to leave in charge of the house the servant girl and a woman neighbor who had attended Gertrude's dying aunt. In light of what we will learn about later events, we have to wonder if the annoyance extends to all the presumably benighted residents of "ce pays perdu," or whether it was provoked just by a resemblance between the couple comprised by the two women and the one comprised by his wife and teenaged daughter Sarah, for whom he will later betray signs of considerable antagonism.

Next, he moves from annoyance to anger at the woman. Not knowing that Gertrude, an "être incertain" (*SP* 8) at this point, could not understand anything said in her presence, he took umbrage at what he deemed the brutal way in which the woman said what would have to happen to Gertrude: "Il faudra la mettre à l'hospice; sinon je ne sais pas ce qu'elle pourra devenir" (*SP* 8). Ready aggravation, annoyance, and anger suggest a troubled, barely contained personality at odds with a charitable cast of mind.

That suggestion is confirmed by a curious eruption of apparently unrelated resentment at the limits that the Pastor – in sweeping imprecision – reports "les hommes" place on him. We find an abrupt, superficially unconnected tirade interlarded between his telling the neighbor about his intention to take Gertrude home and his description of how Gertrude responded when he finally led her away. In the quotation below, the lack of overt verbal transition at the beginning ("Et ce fut tout") or end ("L'aveugle s'est laissé . . .") betrays something occasionally irrepressible, which is, I propose, a hidden ire whose fruit promises to be fearsome. But once we have taken notice of the earlier clues to his bristling personality, we see how all the details are connected by that ire, bubbling up from, among other things, his hostile frustration at his circumstances and at the people around him (not the least of whom is his family):

> Puis me retournant du côté de l'aveugle, je fis part à la voisine de mon intention.
> –Mieux vaut qu'elle ne soit point là demain, quand on viendra lever le corps, dit-elle. Et ce fut tout.
> Bien des choses se feraient facilement, sans les chimériques objections que parfois les hommes se plaisent à inventer. Dès l'enfance, combien de fois sommes-nous empêchés de faire ceci ou cela que nous voudrions faire, simplement parce que nous entendons répéter autour de nous: il ne pourra pas le faire.
> L'aveugle s'est laissé emmener comme une masse involontaire. Les traits de son visage étaient réguliers, assez beaux, mais parfaitement inexpressifs. (*SP* 10)

The strange, only apparently misplaced paragraph in the middle, evokes thoughts of anything but charity.

But for those who, rereading the text, realize all that had transpired *before* the Pastor started setting down his version of remembered events, the paragraph and indeed the entire scene do evoke his hostile attitude toward his wife. Keeping in mind his resentment of Amélie at work perhaps at the beginning of the events and most assuredly at the time of writing,[9] and given his certain sense that

---

[9] "So acute is Gide's grasp of human psychology that he makes it impossible to decide which reaction comes first in the Pastor, whether he turns to Gertrude as a relief from his family or whether he turns against his family as a pretext for devoting himself to Gertrude" (Wilson, *André Gide* 38).

Amélie is a barrier between him and Gertrude, the reader surely finds it hard not to feel that the three female figures surrounding Gertrude in the beginning have taken on, in his retrospective narration, Amélie's emotional coloration in their differences to Gertrude: the uncommunicative girl who cannot or will not converse with him (like Amélie or "her" daughter Sarah) as Gertrude so wondrously will, the woman (probably more or less of Amélie's age and condition) who advises him that Gertrude should be cast aside by being placed in a home, and the dead woman who pursed lips seem uncomfortably like the pinch-lipped Amélie who came perilously close to being emotionally and spiritually dead for him. (The image of the ungiving, miserly purse-like lips is also curiously evocative of the Pastor's view of his wife as instinctively ungenerous and too often attentive to material needs.)

The ire and hostility threaten anarchy, and it is the barely repressed anarchic impulses of the Pastor that provide the hidden agenda explaining the unreliability of his gospel of ideal love.

G) *Verbal and Erotic Anarchy*

As we observed at the beginning of this chapter, Gide declared that *La Symphonie pastorale* criticizes ironically "une forme de mensonge à soi-même."[10] He did not of course say exactly what he

---

[10] We have already mentioned that Gide's deception of his wife vis-à-vis Marc Allégret, the youth who was the homosexual love of his life, had a major impact on the inception of *La Symphonie pastorale*. One can go so far as to maintain that Gertrude represented Marc Allégret for Gide: "it appears fairly evident that the *Symphonie pastorale* is, at least in part, a confession of this love, and that Gide, like Proust for his Albertine, has made a transposition of sexes, so that the blind girl Gertrude is the literary counterpart of the adolescent Michel" [the name used by Gide in his *Journal* for Allégret] (Parnell, 65). (See also C. Martin lxxix- xcviii, and Adam.) But one has to wonder as well if World War I, this century's first great exercise in propaganda and distortion on national and international scales, did not also play a part in the genesis of *La Symphonie pastorale*, this book about "une forme de mensonge." Even though Gide made an effort at the time to keep politics and the Great War out of his diary (see, for example, 13 décembre 1917), they still burst through, and often in terms of deception and lies, as evidenced in the following entries from just before (1917) and during (1918) the composition of *La Symphonie pastorale*: "Et parfois m'envahit une tristesse sans nom, à contempler ce clair miroir de vérité qu'*était* la France se ternir" (7 janvier 1917; my emphasis); "Les journaux, suivant leur criminelle habitude, n'ont cherché qu'à chloroformer le pays" (10 mai 1918); "Autour de nous je ne vois que désordre, désorganisation, négligence et

meant, leaving that to the text itself and its readers. As we have seen and as befits a case of deceit presented by Gide, the Pastor's deception is a wily, subtle thing of far-ranging consequences. It ought not to be limited, I have argued, to the horizons of the critical perspective at any given moment. It most emphatically should not be identified just with the Pastor's self-deception, or his obvious misrepresentation of his feelings for Gertrude, or even his intentional misleading of the reader. Among what are no doubt numerous other things, his lie can be shown to take in an assault upon traditional linguistic and sexual values. This contention evolves out of a peculiar feature of the beginning of the Pastor's text.

i) *Narrative Disorder*

A close scrutiny of the Pastor's first diary entry reveals that it includes – but does not reflect upon – an impressive number of errors and of details underscoring narrative (i. e., verbal) unreliability and uncertainty (unreliability for the Pastor as narrator and uncertainty for the him and us as readers of his diary). Pressing again the conventions of the *récit*, one must wonder about the significance of the "Pastor's" including such material in abundance, since it has no immediate relevance to events recounted in his first entry and since he makes no attempt to explain it.

Let us consider the very opening page. In what is clearly an inaugural trope, the Pastor writes suggestively that when called to minister to a dying woman, he observed that he was mistaken in thinking that he knew his little world thoroughly: "Je croyais connaître admirablement tous les entours de la commune; mais passé la ferme de la Saudraie, l'enfant me fit prendre une route où jusqu'alors je ne m'étais jamais aventuré" (*SP* 6). The rest of the paragraph chronicles with no comment or even apparent awareness complementary confusion on his part. In spite of his sense of unfamiliarity he recognizes a mysterious lake in such a way that even his certainty about remembering it loses, dream-like, its authority:

> Je reconnus pourtant, à deux kilomètres de là, sur la gauche, un petit lac mystérieux où jeune homme j'avais été quelquefois

---

gaspillage des vertus les plus radieuses – que mensonge, que politique, qu'absurdité" (2 juin, 1918).

> patiner. Depuis quinze ans je ne l'avais plus revu, car aucun devoir pastoral ne m'appelle de ce côté; je n'aurais plus su dire où il était et j'avais à ce point cessé d'y penser qu'il me sembla, lorsque tout à coup, dans l'enchantement rose et doré du soir, je le reconnus, ne l'avoir d'abord vu qu'en rêve. (*SP* 6)

The disruptive placement of the disjointed last temporal clause ("lorsque tout à coup, dans l'enchantement rose et doré du soir, je le reconnus") between "il me sembla" and its complement "ne l'avoir d'abord vu qu'en rêve" makes for difficult reading, highlighting the Pastor's sense of disorientation and confusion. His opening reference to the lake as "mystérieux," and his closing words, "qu'en rêve," frame and mist it over with even more uncertainty.

Next, the use of a pluperfect subjunctive gives reason to believe that he initially if only momentarily erred in believing that the cottage to which he was being led was not the right one, for he describes it as "une chaumière qu'on eût pu croire inhabitée, sans un mince filet de fumée qui s'en échappait, bleuissant dans l'ombre, puis blondissant dans l'or du soir" (*SP* 6). The Pastor's mindfulness of the shifting colors of the insubstantial smoke, while anticipating for example the theme of metamorphosis, certainly does nothing to detract from the sense of far from solid perceptions. At the very least, an atmosphere propitious to error is reinforced in the reader's mind, all the more so when in the very next sentence it is learned that the woman the Pastor was called to visit is not – as reported – dying, but is actually dead.

The mistakes go on in the next paragraph: he had presumed that his young guide was the grand-daughter of the deceased and that the woman waiting by the bedside was also a relative, whereas the former was merely a servant and the latter a neighbor; he took offense at the pain that the neighbor's inconsiderate words cause the "être incertain" (a perfect description for Gertrude in the context that I propose), only to be told that she cannot understand anything that is said (which was true) because she was an idiot (which was not). Thus, the Pastor goes beyond being just another unreliable narrator, to open seemingly unawares his account in such a way as to involve it lavishly and almost systematically in unreliability/uncertainty that bodes ill for efforts to grasp *l'histoire*.

Skipping for the sake of economy to another key moment several pages later (just before beginning the crux of his account when Gertrude comes to language and to the awareness it brings), we find the Pastor again effectively if unreflectively weaving into his tale imposing threads that reinforce the issue of verbal disorder. For instance he reports Dr. Martins's words (*SP* 26-30) about the historical figure Laura Bridgeman. His editing of his friend's words produces a confused *récit* within a *récit* whose plot parallels that of what will be the Pastor's own story: both deal with the efforts of an older man to teach a young blind girl without language how to communicate. In this three-paragraph companion piece that invites and perhaps requires comparison, the narrator Martins betrays considerable befuddlement in trying to sort out facts from his fancies, dramatizing appropriately the tricks of memory to which all narrators must fall prey:

> Ne t'en souviens-tu pas? du temps que nous faisions ensemble notre philosophie, nos professeurs, à propos de Condillac et de sa statue animée, nous entretenaient déjà d'un cas analogue à celui-ci.... A moins, fit-il en se reprenant, que je n'aie lu cela plus tard, dans une revue de psychologie. (*SP* 26)

And again:

> A partir [d'un certain] jour elle fit attention; ses progrès furent rapides; elle s'instruisit bientôt elle-même, et par la suite devint directrice d'un institut d'aveugles – à moins que ce ne fût une autre.... (*SP* 28)

Characteristically, he got even her nationality wrong, describing her as English instead of American.[11]

It is worth remarking in passing that the Pastor records Dr. Martins's mention of Dickens's *The Cricket on the Hearth*, which the Pastor tells us he went on to read. We may wonder how well he read it, since to say as he does that *l'histoire* of *Cricket* is that of the blind Bertha and her father is to misrepresent it. While the reference to the father's lie highlights indirectly the issue of narrative unreliability/uncertainty, Dickens's Christmas story has other ramifica-

---

[11] See C. Martin, "Introduction," li, note 47.

tions that pertain more directly to the present analysis: the conclusion of his story could stand as a model for self-reflexive *récits* that raise the fundamental question of the narrative problems with which their readers must deal. On the final pages of Dickens's work, the narrator depicts his characters having a rousing dance in the home of the central couple, Dot and the Carrier (interestingly enough, a young woman and an elderly man who is jealous of a younger man). As the following paragraph shows, the book ends in a void:

> But what is this? Even as I listen to them, blithely, and turn towards Dot, for one last glimpse of a little figure very pleasant to me, she and the rest have vanished into air, and I am left alone. A Cricket sings upon the Hearth; a broken child's-toy lies upon the ground; and nothing remains. (Dickens 311)

In brief, the entire prelude to the body of the *La Symphonie pastorale* is charged with elements, the logical consequence of which is a clear warning about the reliability of narrative.

No less importantly, those elements, while chosen in abundance for inclusion *by the Pastor*, go unexamined by him. In that regard we should recall he started writing after his mix of idealism and bad faith had ample time to flourish and take deeper and more devious root under the nurture of developing passion. One can maintain, therefore, that his raising repeatedly but indirectly the issue of unreliability/uncertainty fits the larger pattern manifest and multifarious by that point: as with his adulterous feelings, the Pastor parries full self-revelation and comprehensive self-criticism by being sure to give an account of drives which he senses are incompatible with his view of himself, but only while passing over them in silence or disguising them by attributing them superficially to other, usually noble causes. In the case at hand, the presence of all the details related to unreliability/uncertainty bespeaks the thoroughness and authenticity expected of a sincere account, so many *effets de réel*, although of course the Pastor forgoes a forthright, probing explanation that might uncover troublesome concerns behind the nature of those details. The *unaddressed* presence of those details also suggests that there is at work something more ominous than thoroughness and authenticity.

ii) *Limping Comparisons:* Parabole>parole>parler

Looking for a way to explain what the Pastor will not, we do well to reflect on a further peculiarity of his document, the unusual extent to which he lingers over his difficulties with his famous sound/color comparison, difficulties to which he himself draws considerable attention. On the one hand, for approximately the first half of the account of his now unconscious now disingenuous seduction of Gertrude, the Pastor has no problems in using and accepting metaphorical thought. He readily makes comparisons to justify and gloss over his conduct, as well as to help explain without exploring some of the mysteries he felt and feels going on in and around him. Most obvious in this respect is his comparing the bringing of Gertrude into his family to the parable of the lost sheep. Less central examples abound, to such an extent that it is safe to say that the Pastor has an analogical cast of mind [12] that makes itself felt at virtually every point of his narrative, as one would expect from a Bible-oriented clergyman who deals with life by constantly comparing it to sacred writ, itself crammed with comparisons. But on the other hand the uncritical Pastor is inevitably caught up short by the limits of comparison, in spite of himself. In the passage that is much commented because of the prominence that the Pastor lends it, his attempt to explain colors to the blind Gertrude by comparing them to the sounds of musical instruments only adds to her confusion. Because of her enduring difficulties in understanding the comparison and his in clarifying it, the Pastor is forced to recognize the inherent shortcomings of his simile: "Ainsi j'expérimentais sans cesse à travers elle combien le monde visuel diffère du monde des sons et à quel point toute comparaison que l'on cherche à tirer de l'un pour l'autre est boiteuse" (*SP* 44).

---

[12] Raymond Mahieu, arguing cleverly for a reading of *La Symphonie pastorale* centered around "la lutte des tropes" (metaphor vs. metonymy), claims that Gertrude is more gifted and seductive in the use of poetic metaphor than her teacher the Pastor. Because of such language practices, allegedly foreign to the world as it is, in the end she is destroyed, so the "realism" of the metonymy-practicing Amélie can prevail. While it could be objected that Mahieu does not give enough credit to the metaphor-and parable-spouting Pygmalion who fashioned (very nearly literally) the vision of this verbally enticing Galatea, Mahieu's article certainly establishes the pervasive importance of metaphor in *La Symphonie pastorale*.

But he does not get beyond the qualifying phrase "de l'un" (the visual world) "pour l'autre" (the world of sounds), to address the more general implications of his observation that beg to be made: he will not acknowledge how *all* analogies limp. And for good reason. Were he to do so, he would of course have to scrutinize, for example, his comparison of the parable's lost sheep to Gertrude which, in his eyes, justified bringing her into his life. Much more, however, is at stake here than the faultiness of individual comparisons used by the Pastor. Reflecting on comparisons could leave him open to an insight troublesome indeed for literal-minded believers such as he would be. Although Christ's parables are rather typically invested by the Pastor with a givenness and a sanctity that discourages the demystification of routine analysis, they remain comparisons (the Greek *parabolé* means no more, after all). As such, they can limp as badly as any comparison, especially when reapplied to new situations by a self-serving believer. Moreover, the stress he puts upon the problems with his sound/color comparison suggests that on the verge of his awareness there prowls a sense of this, as well as of a much larger related issue. Language itself (*la parole*) remains basically an exercise in comparison, as the etymological chain *parabolé>parabole>parole>parler* testifies.[13]

The Pastor has the potential to appreciate such an insight since he is doubly a man of the Word. He is of course a minister/preacher practiced in poring over texts word by word. But in addition, we have already seen that there is reason to view the Pastor not so much as the naive documentary diarist that one of his impulses would have him appear and maybe want his reader – that is, himself primarily – to believe him to be, but rather as something of a writer/preacher seeking effect through language, that is, as someone growing in active use of *la parole* in all its complexity.[14] One could even argue that the Pastor has the capacity to deduce the above etymological chain since he has the background necessary for etymological musings: as a Reformed minister he is a biblical exegete doubtless trained in at least Greek and because of his schooling he knows at a minimum profane Latin – v. the allusion to Virgil [*SP* 28-30] – and apparently acquired some English – v. his use of the

---

[13] For another reading of *parole* in *La Symphonie pastorale*, see Spacagna.

[14] See also Elaine D. Cancalon, "Création et Destruction" 81-90; and C. Martin, "Introduction" ci-cvii.

words "pin" and "pen" [*SP* 26] and the reference to Dickens, perhaps read in the original language.

In his own oblique, repressed way, moreover, the Pastor does indeed acknowledge the shortcomings of *la parole*. For instance, in preparing to confront Amélie about the reasons why their son Jacques must not consider marrying Gertrude, the Pastor acknowledges that *la parole* can be a woefully inadequate device for communicating:

> J'éprouvais aussi, devant que de parler, à quel point deux êtres, vivant somme toute de la même vie, et qui s'aiment, peuvent rester (ou devenir) l'un pour l'autre énigmatiques et emmurés; les paroles, dans ce cas soit celles que nous adressons à l'autre, soit celles que l'autre nous adresse, sonnent plaintivement comme des coups de sonde pour nous avertir de la résistance de cette cloison séparatrice et qui, si l'on n'y veille, risque d'aller s'épaississant. (*SP* 70)

In reviewing the sentence, one surmises that "devant que de parler" the Pastor senses *la parole* as one of the agents – and perhaps *the* agent – threatening to thicken the barriers of separation.

In a similar vein, he writes of his reluctance during their duel over *la parole divine* to mention a Pauline verse to Jacques. Having hesitated for fear of his son's misconstruing his father's intent because of the verse's missing antecedent, the Pastor remarks:

> Evidemment il s'agit ici d'aliments; mais à combien d'autres passages de l'Ecriture n'est-on pas appelé à prêter double et triple sens? ("Si ton oeil . . ."; multiplication des pains; miracle aux noces de Cana, etc. . . .) Il ne s'agit pas ici d'ergoter; la signification de ce verset est large et profonde. . . . (*SP* 98)

While his verbs *être appelé* and *ergoter* do create the impression that the repressive side of the Pastor would prefer the security of a more stable, unitary text, he concedes again – if ever so discreetely – inherent verbal multivalence, the sort of multivalence that the text of his creation serves so well from its opening lines.

It is precisely the overall impact of his text that argues most visibly for viewing the idealistic Pastor as also a verbal and moral or religious hypocrite. While one side of the amorous Pastor-diarist-novelist seeks to serve *la parole* as an illuminating, creative force, his use of language turns it into an obfuscating tool of anarchic confusion. We see this clearly in his lying and in his obvious narrative unreliability about the main incidents and their motivation, which results in an ironic text that has been aptly called a "riot of . . . plural and unstable meanings" (Renée Kingcaid 40). But attentiveness to the Pastor's uneasiness with comparisons and *la parole* has the merit of sensitizing us to a stylistic tendency of the Pastor's which highlights that "riot" and helps to situate it as the very fruit of language. While, as already noted, the Pastor makes abundant use of similes and metaphors, he does not limit himself to the simple *être comme* and parallel expressions to make his analogies, instead relying often on the more indirect, interesting *dire* in either the conditional or pluperfect subjunctive. For instance, in describing Gertrude's "birth" (i. e. her coming to a sense of language), he says:

> Tout à coup ses traits *s'animèrent*; ce fut comme un éclairement subit, pareil à cette lueur purpurine dans les hautes Alpes qui, précédant l'aurore, fait vibrer le sommet neigeux qu'elle désigne et sort de la nuit; on eût dit une coloration mystique; et je songeai également à la piscine de Bethesda au moment que l'ange descend et vient réveiller l'eau dormante. (*SP* 34; emphasis in the original)

Of the four similes ("fut comme," "pareil à," "on eût dit," "Je songeai à") the last two show a turning away from the simplicity and assertiveness of the first two which, of themselves, deceptively imply certainty of near metaphysical as well as epistemological weight, focusing on what seems more real, the physical. The point of the sentence, however, is not physical, but rather what is more important to him (and presumably to most readers), the spiritual. To communicate that quality with any verisimilitude, the Pastor must resort to analogical language more expressive of approximation and mystery, and so after the would-be objective similes he switches to a clearly less objective one with a form of *dire* and from there goes on to the purely subjective and cerebral "je songeai à." At the moment of that switch, we are removed from the realm of the apparently more real but in fact less important, back again to the realm of language, that is, from limping comparisons of what seemingly is, to what is perceived and uttered. Considering that the subject is Gertrude's birth to language, we can only admire the appropriateness of the switch.

While one finds similar uses of *dire* with similar implications (*SP* 12, 80), of more interest are the four instances of the same verb in which the Pastor relinquishes comparisons of nouns to use the more subtle implied comparison of a clause. Let us look at the first example, where the Pastor compares Gertrude's intellectual progress to the triumph of the Spring over Winter:

> C'est tout de même ainsi . . . que la tiédeur de l'air et l'insistance du printemps triomphent peu à peu de l'hiver. Que de fois n'ai-je pas admiré la manière dont fond la neige: on dirait que le manteau s'use par en dessous, et son aspect reste le même. (*SP* 34-36)

"On dirait que": like a fiat, it assigns a meaning where none or a different (correct) one had been, while magically its appealing creation crowds in on awareness, distracting us from our impressions of contact with what is not language. One senses in this usage that the Pastor's language, like all language, has an imperialistic capacity to absorb apparently independent experience and perception back into itself.

In much the same way, other examples of this kind of use of *dire* show the Pastor's language creating out of itself, revealing his *parole* as a step away from what is: "on dirait qu'elle [Amélie] répugne à tout ce qui n'est pas coutumier" (*SP* 52). In this example, it is open to discussion whether or not Amélie feels an aversion for the unusual. But with "on dirait qu'elle répugne" as opposed to a simple "elle répugne," *la parole*, even while seemingly softening its own assertion, gently pushes Amélie aside, creating out of itself a possible Amélie to vie with the actual one who is already only dimly grasped by the reader. Gertrude herself, ever an adept student for the Pastor, picks up early this possibility in language to create of itself, independently of what is. Speaking of the now non-existent lilies of the fields mentioned in the biblical verses that the Pastor chooses to read to her, she says: "Moi, quand j'écoute cette parole, je vous assure que je les vois" (*SP* 80), even though she knows that they are not there. Indeed, she proves herself to be a better practitioner of *la parole* than the Pastor himself when she reduces the elements of a vast, sweeping Alpine scene to a poetic series of similes and metaphors that invoke one of the privileged arenas of *la parole*, the classroom:

> A nos pieds, comme un livre ouvert, incliné sur le pupitre de la montagne, la grande prairie verte et diaprée, que bleuit l'ombre, que dore le soleil, et dont les mots distincts sont des fleurs – des gentianes, des pulsatilles, des renoncules, et les beaux lys de Salomon – que les vaches viennent épeler avec leurs cloches, et que les anges viennent lire, puisque vous dites que les yeux des hommes sont clos. (*SP* 80-82)

But in subsequent examples of *dire*, we see the word turned on her: "on eût dit qu'elle [Gertrude] n'entendait rien ou qu'elle avait résolu de se taire" (*SP* 122); "on eût dit qu'elle [Gertrude] avait découvert un secret. . . ." (*SP* 122). In these examples it is quite likely that Gertrude was indeed keeping her thoughts from the Pastor, but to introduce a statement about her with *on eût dit* (as opposed to letting the statement stand by itself) has two effects. First it makes less of her too by imparting both subjectivity (that of *on*) and distance (another layer of *la parole*) to our perception of her state of mind. Second, even while communicating the Pastor's anxiety as he tries to understand what is happening, it serves as a reminder that in *all* his efforts to articulate the story (and not just in crisis), he has only the matrix of the "riot" of meanings, *parabole> parole*, a limping comparison, a poor approximation to what is. Indeed, we have here at work in these uses of *dire* an inversion of the luminous Word, source of being in the Pastor's frequently cited Gospel, for while the words in the Pastor's account do create, their perverse creations distance from what is, absorbing what is into themselves and into the darkness of their own anarchic unreliability/uncertainty. Significantly (in this reading which emphasizes the Pastor's role as author), the Pastor chose to include all the indications and clues about his and language's uncertainty.

iii) *The Erotic* Parole

But the anarchy found in *La Symphonie pastorale* has a field of activity other than just *la parole*, namely, eroticism. Or differently put, the field of activity for *la parole* appears as erotic as it is linguistic, a not terribly surprising congruence, especially in a work the title of which harkens back in one of its senses to love verse, a source and component of the pastoral. As used by the Pastor *la parole* becomes a seduction, most obviously in the case of Gertrude. (Similarly, the Pastor needs only to be allowed to speak to bend his wife and his family to his wishes – v. *SP* 16-18, 18-20, a power that helps to explain the reluctance of those close to him to argue with him – v. *SP* 22, 50, 68, etc.)

We glimpse anarchy in the Pastor's eroticism because not only does his adultery threaten the well-being of his family, but his appealing theological rationalizations about love threaten his very religion as well by turning Christ's teachings into destructive erotic license.[15] Indeed, the Pastor's eroticism goes to the extreme of encompassing even incest, which stunningly menaces the order of his severe Calvinist world.

The first inkling that incestuous desires too may be stirring beneath the barely contained surface of the Pastor's account arises when one notices that the Pastor identifies his daughter Sarah with Amélie and Gertrude, both women that he engages carnally. Sarah, probably a little older than 15 (the erroneous supposition about Gertrude's age, *SP* 8, at first links her age with Sarah's, *SP* 22), may be supposed to be maturing into her sexuality and so of more than passing notice libidinally to her father. Furthermore, early in his first *cahier* the Pastor notes during one of his only two comments on clothes that, after delousing, Gertrude is – and presumably remains – dressed in Sarah's hand-me-downs. Sarah's name as well fosters identification with Gertrude, since "Sarah" is a substitute name as is "Gertrude." (Sarah the wife of Abraham was so renamed to mark her "second womanhood" since she conceived in her nineties, whereas Gertrude got her second name as she came into her "second existence" following her removal from her dead aunt's home.) No less thought-provoking is the degree to which the Pastor tends to see Gertrude as one of his children, a view that makes itself felt when he compares her to them (e. g., *SP* 56), and when in molding her perceptions and values he makes of her his intellectual and moral offspring. Gertrude herself gives evidence of sensitivity to the Pastor's feelings of kinship between her and his children, as her calling Amélie "tante" suggests (*SP* 46). But as the Pastor becomes more and more involved with Gertrude and less and less with his family, his daughter Sarah becomes more closely tied in his mind

---

[15] For a schematized, different view of anarchy – "la destruction" – see Cancalon.

with the repudiated – but still sexually familiar – Amélie, as is indicated by his growing awareness of the adolescent's mothering of the teething Claude and of her alleged similarity of character with her mother (*SP*, 102). Finally, this inkling of incestuous tendencies takes on added substance in the reader's mind because Sarah's name recalls the incestuous marriage of the biblical Sarah and Abraham, while Amélie's name evokes the same passion treated in another famous *récit*, Chateaubriand's *René*.

This inkling of incestuous stirrings, ever so fragile in the case of the Pastor's attitude toward Sarah, blossoms elsewhere into a full-blown suspicion. In dealing with a narrative where to speak is to seduce, we must come to terms with the realization that it is Jacques that the Pastor feels compelled to try most frequently and strongly to persuade. Also, Jacques alone of all those mentioned in the narrative draws from his repressed father's pen comments of considerable physical appeal, comments that would not be out of place in a lover's portrait:

> . . . Gertrude ne laisserait pas d'admirer ce grand corps svelte, à la fois si droit et si souple, ce beau front sans rides, ce regard franc, ce visage enfantin encore, mais que semblait ombrer une certaine gravité. Il était nu-tête et ses cheveux cendrés, qu'il portait alors assez longs, bouclaient légèrement à ses tempes et cachaient ses oreilles à demi. (*SP* 68)

There are other intimations of the hidden sexual nature of his feelings toward Jacques, for example that we see the Pastor kissing him (*SP* 68) on the brow in the same way (*SP* 34) that he kissed the woman to whom he will make love, Gertrude, and that these are the only people that he chooses to show himself kissing and perhaps that he does kiss during the time of the narrated events. (Knowledge of Gide's affair with Marc Allégret – his ward and so in a sense son – makes it hard not to suspect that Gertrude and Jacques conflated in Gide's mind. Gertrude has been found to be the fictional emotional substitute for Marc vis-à-vis Amélie/Madeleine in Gide's attempt at narrative self-exploration, while Jacques clearly evokes Marc physically. The conflation helps explain how both the apparent outsider Gertrude and the Pastor's son get equally absorbed in the generalized nimbus of incestuousness. See note 10).

Furthermore, since both the evocation of Narcissus in the Pastor's recollection of skating on the "petit lac mystérieux" and the narcissistic quality of the Pastor's account itself have appeared transparent enough to critics, there is no reason not to insist upon the fact that Narcissus turns from Echo to yearn for his own masculine reflection. "Il [Jacques] avait exactement votre visage," remarks the perceptive Gertrude to the Pastor, "je veux dire celui que j'imaginais que vous aviez . . ." (*SP* 128). So this discovery by Gertrude upon becoming sighted that the face she imagined on the Pastor belonged to Jacques appears a bit less contrived and melodramatic than it does otherwise. While the Pastor erotically drew this blind yet insightful woman to himself in an unconscious but poorly concealed effort to form her in his own image, he brought to the effort an even deeper but not totally hidden desire to make Jacques and himself one. Gertrude, having sensed that desire, incarnated it for herself by imagining a facial substitution.[16]

We have on the Pastor's part, then, an indiscriminate erotic drive to absorb others – Amélie, Gertrude, Sarah, Jacques – into a

---

[16] Looking at the Pastor's sexual confusion in the larger context of the three *récits*, we sense an easy affinity with the sexual disorientation of the two earlier characters, Michel's repressed, unrecognized pederasty and Alissa's mistaking sexual anxieties for a call to religious elitism. Does their drive to examine themselves in narration owe something to that confusion? Valérie Raoul's study of fictional diary writers would lead us to think so: "La femme qui écrit, donc, ne serait-ce qu'un journal intime, abandonne son rôle assigné de reproduction physique pour entreprendre la re-production de sa vie, de son moi, à travers l'écriture. Faut-il en conclure qu'elle n'est plus féminine, qu'adoptant le rôle de sujet réservé à l'homme elle devient phallique ou exerce du moins sa bisexualité fondamentale? La femme intimiste, par son dédoublement, s'imagine dans des rôles actifs et passifs, masculins et féminins, mais il en est aussi de même pour l'homme intimiste. Tout intimiste se conçoit comme la matière à fouiller et l'instrument (speculum) qui sert à fouiller. D'où les questions posées par tout intimiste plus ou moins consciemment, sur sa propre identité sexuelle" (Raoul, "Discours du 'je' féminin imaginaire: les femmes intimistes dans le roman français" 71).

Lest there be a quibble that Michel is not properly speaking a diary-writer, David Keypour orchestrated the observations of *Gidiens* on the role of the diary in *all* of Gide's work: "S'agissant de Gide, Alain Girard remarque que l' 'oeuvre de Gide s'organise autour du journal, [et que ses récits] sont le journal du personnage central.' Enfin, il conclut :

'En définitive, il ne semble pas exagéré d'avancer que sans le procédé du journal, et sans le journal, l'oeuvre de Gide, sinon sa personnalité même, sont inconcevable.' [*Le Journal intime*, PUF, 91]

Et Daniel Moutote nuance avec raison que 'toute oeuvre de Gide affecte plus ou moins la force du journal' [*Le Journal de Gide et les problèmes du moi*, PUF, 1969, 44]" (Keypour, "Le Journal fictif dans l'oeuvre d'André Gide," 217).

boundless self-involvement that denies them their subjectivity. (This situation cannot fail to call to mind that around the time of composition, anarchy reared its head in Gide's sexual conduct by moving beyond his already cataclysmic realignment from Madeleine to Allégret, to encompass his other intellectual ward Elisabeth Van Rysselberghe who bore him his daughter.[17]) In pondering the Pastor's eroticism we realize that the only adequate measure of its anarchy is to be found in its other side, the Pastor's seductive language that absorbs everything that it touches into its unreliable/uncertain self.

iv) *The Destructive* Parole

But then what motivation lurks behind the Pastor's (as opposed to Gide's) spinning a tale so many of the threads of which sketch a vague anarchy? If we reckon with what seems to be the Pastor's unconscious inclination to create verbal-erotic chaos and if we do not overlook the fact that the result of his taking up the pen has been to create a text that remains a monument to *la parole* at its destabilizing best, it becomes possible to maintain that he may have unconsciously started to write in his notebooks to destroy control and certainty. In starting his tale, which stops only after death and desolation have triumphed, he satisfies the anarchic side of himself that he dares not contemplate, a side the suppression of which would explain the development of the tyrannic, hostile *persona* so visible to the reader (see section I.F. above, 190) and so at odds with his conscious values of openness, spontaneity, and love. The side that he so doggedly persists in not seeing would be Narcissus' mirror image that we divine skating reversed but locked – because totally unacceptable – under the opaque ice of the "petit lac mystérieux" of the opening pages. Not coincidentally, from the beginning of Gide's literary career, his Narcissus/Adam had a bent for destruction: "Et puis, tant pis! cette harmonie m'agace, et son accord toujours parfait. Un geste! un petit geste, pour savoir, – une dissonance, que diable!" (*Traité de Narcisse*, in *Romans*, 6). So the *mensonge à soi-même* mentioned by Gide apropos of *La Symphonie pastorale* transcends adultery and narrative misrepresentation, taking

---

[17] See Parnell, Adam, and C. Martin, lxxix- xcviii.

in as well the Pastor's refusal to acknowledge the deep, dim, fearsome traits of his personality. Indeed, one can wonder whether the Pastor's patent, grating obtuseness is not itself an exquisite part of the larger lie, since it creates so compelling a locus of attention that it misdirects questioning readers.

We should note that this conflict-fraught slide to anarchy parallels the much commented "hasty" quality of the end of *La Symphonie pastorale*. As the Pastor's *parole* generates a progressively more disordered verbal-erotic situation that he has more and more difficulty controlling consciously, it generates a parallel narrative rhythm more Balzacian than Balzac, leading to a precipitous conclusion of breathless sketchiness that clashes violently with the magnitude and number of events related. (In the last few pages the Pastor finally makes love to Gertrude, the operation is planned and performed, Jacques converts to Catholicism and persuades Gertrude to do likewise, after which Gertrude returns from the hospital to reject the Pastor, to attempt suicide, and to die). The confusion and problems created by this rhythm reflect its source, *la parole* as used by the Pastor, that increasingly loses control over, and contact with, what is not itself.

### H) *Semiosis and the Drama of Substitution*

Finally, to take a global view of all that we have seen thus far, *La Symphonie pastorale* can be read as a drama of would-be substitution: of a self-serving but attractive *récit* not without redeeming values substituting for a more damning *histoire*, of the rebellious Pastor substituting for the Good Shepherd, of a gospel of love for a gospel of law, of Gertrude for Amélie, of father for son, of tabooed relationships for authorized love, of anarchy for order. But viewed in a certain light, substitution takes the text back to, and anchors it in, *parole*, for it takes it back to, and anchors it in, semiosis: "A sign is everything which can be taken as significantly substituting for something else" (Umberto Eco, *A Theory of Semiotics* 7, in Culler 114). In consequence, the Gertrude of the text is (just within the fiction) doubly a sign, one operative on the semantic and the emotional level. The narrated "Gertrude" of course is for the Pastor's reader a mere substitution for the "real" Gertrude of the Pastor's "experience," but too, as suggested above in Section E, the whole narrative derives in large part from the Pastor's desire to re-present to himself the woman with whom he has fallen in love but from whom he has been blocked by the snow. This doubly semiotic genesis of "his" narrative act helps us to appreciate the aptness of the drama of substitution on all the other levels.

But to tie the text so tightly to the principle of semiosis is to tie it to lies, for, Eco's definition continues: "[s]emiotics is in principle the discipline studying everything which can be used in order to lie. If something cannot be used to tell a lie, conversely it cannot be used to tell the truth" (Eco, in Culler 114). The lying, the substitutions, and the anarchy run together, then, into a troublesome unity, for *la parole* is a deceptive attempt to re-present, an attempt that does the simplifying violence of metaphor to the reality of what would be re-presented. *La parole* would usurp the very universe. Gidean reflexivity is, therefore, once again well served, for in being about "une forme de mensonge à soi-même," *La Symphonie pastorale* is ultimately about itself, about all verbal art, about language.

Furthermore, seen in its relationship to semiosis and seen as still another Derridean *supplément*, the Pastor's lying, at first apparently outside the diegesis itself, comprises the center of the text's events, both their motivation and outcomes, it comprises the principle of their narrative being. But the margin-become-center "within the fiction" is the center-become-margin in real life, since there is every reason to believe that the story, evolving slowly after being conceived a quarter of a century earlier, (C. Martin, "Introduction" xxx-lv), was born only when Gide could use it as a substitute for his love affair with his own Gertrude-Jacques, the young, malleable Marc Allégret whom he wanted to teach to "see," and who challenged Gide's wife Madeleine by offering him for the first time the possibility of combining spiritual and physical love in one relationship. So *La Symphonie pastorale*'s process of substitution that extends to the gliding back and forth between center and margin, between Gide's art and his life, is itself an admirable representation/substitute for the dynamic of fiction that shows language's lie – which we so much want to marginalize, to make a *supplément* – to be the center of its life.

On that note of substitution/lying, we will turn our attention to onomastics, since naming too is a form of substitution/lying.

## II. ONOMASTICS

Basing their position on an analysis of the names of characters in *Les Caves du Vatican, Les Faux-Monnayeurs,* and *L'Immoraliste,* Allan H. Pasco and Wilfred J. Rollman have argued that "Gide tended to pick names which through historical or literary antecedent, etymology or phonetic similarity support the themes or images of his works" (Pasco and Rollman, 524). They close their discussion by saying that Gide's choice of names reflects his demanding sense of aesthetic integrity, indeed his drive for artistic perfection (Pasco and Rollman, 531). The following pages will show that their conclusions apply as well to *La Symphonie pastorale,* the most widely read of his works (C. Martin, cxlii-cxlv). But in their study Pasco and Rollman do not distinguish between the way in which onomastics works in *Les Caves du Vatican* and *Les Faux-Monnayeurs,* which are novels, and in *L'Immoraliste,* which is of course a first-person narrative. So the rest of this chapter proposes to show also how fruitfully a study of personal names too can be applied to *La Symphonie pastorale* qua *récit*[18] "written by the Pastor."

### A) *Onomastics in Gide's Text*

i) *Names and the* Fatum *of Writing*

Let us look first for the contributions of onomastics to *La Symphonie pastorale* viewed *more* as a work of fiction written by André Gide than as an account by the Pastor. ("More," because of the difficulty of not taking the Pastor into consideration: Gide's text is meant to be seen, not as his, but the Pastor's. But the logical, if not textual, distinction will help make a useful emphasis.) We can observe that when the etymologies of the names of its main characters are taken together, they carry a virtual summary of the plot: the

---

[18] While *La Symphonie pastorale* starts out narrating its events retrospectively from a distance of thirty months, it slowly narrows the temporal gap between narrated events and the act of narrating, so that toward its end, the text recounts events contemporaneous with the act of writing. While part of the text thus becomes properly speaking a diary, making *La Symphonie pastorale* a narrative hybrid, it does remain an entirely first-person account. On this point, see C. Martin, ci-cii.

Protestant *Pasteur* 'Pastor' (Latin, "shepherd" of course) confronts his long-suffering, house-wife spouse Amélie (Teutonic, "industrious") with an alleged lost-sheep of an orphan – whom one of the children will unwittingly recognize as a source of marital strife by naming her "Gertrude" (Germanic, "spear-maiden"); Gertrude's potential for sowing discord will be enhanced greatly through the advice of Doctor Martins (from Mars, the Latin god of war) regarding her education and operation, and through the help of a neighbor, Louise (from *Louis* < *Chlodovisius* < *Hluodowig*, Teutonic for "famous war"); although the Pastor will fall in love with and seduce Gertrude, he will lose her heart to his son-rival Jacques (from 'Jacob,' Hebrew, 'he supplants'). Furthermore, independently of etymology but consistently with Gide's perfectionist attention to details, the name of Dr. Roux carries subtle menace for Gertrude that is amply realized for her in his disastrously successful operation on her eyes. Just as peasant tradition has it that a springtime *lune rousse* freezes and withers plants (and so reddens them), so too Gertrude, closely associated with flowers and a water plant,[19] is frozen and withered in the aftermath of the light brought to her in the Spring by Roux.

To the extent that the names encapsulate the plot, they predict it and make it necessary or fated (*fatum* 'what is said'), thereby laying bare again the power of *la parole*, this time the extent to which the text's language – of which names are a key part since they are "princes des signifiants" (Roland Barthes, "Analyse textuelle d'un conte d'Edgar Poe" 34) – not only takes control of the story but even becomes the story. It is a commonplace that what takes form in a verbal account can never be even close to the stuff of experience, nor will it be exactly what one remembers, and rarely is it exactly what one anticipated telling. In part, this occurs because in recounting events, one quickly finds that one's very narration starts

---

[19] Privileged by faith and blindness to see alone the absent lilies of the field admired by Christ (*PE* 78-80), perhaps the most memorable scene in the book, Gertrude is crowned with flowers from the Pastor both before and after her operation (*PE* 108, 124), receives them as gifts from the children (*PE* 118), used the pretext of gathering them to deny initially her suicide attempt in the frozen waters (*PE* 122, 124), and asked for them on her death bed (*PE* 124). Moreover, her wet hair evoked for the Pastor the small plants that grow on water, algae (*PE* 122-24). This connection with the vegetal is just one of the many parallels between Gertrude and her predecessors, Marceline and Alissa.

exerting an influence on its own rendering: once they are given expression, facets of story-telling such as diction, plot pacing, sentence rhythm, images, etc. assume a momentum, a life of their own, and so can have an impact on the teller. We have already seen (regarding the parallel between *La Tentative amoureuse* and *La Porte étroite*) Gide's expression of abiding interest in that phenomenon, which he termed narrative "retroaction." The Pastor's experience as author is of a piece, since he himself apologizes on several occasions, recognizing how his text keeps getting away from him. As early as his third entry, dated 28 February, he writes regarding his second entry ("hier"): "Je reviens en arrière; car hier je m'étais laissé entraîner" (*SP* 38) and in his fourth, dated simply "29," he writes concerning the third: "Tout occupé par mes comparaisons, je n'ai point dit encore l'immense plaisir que Gertrude avait pris à ce concert de Neuchâtel" (*SP* 44). Similarly, he has to reorient the next entry, of March 8: "C'est l'histoire du développement intellectuel et moral de Gertrude que j'ai entrepris de tracer ici. J'y reviens" (*SP* 54). Thereafter, his account essentially abandons that subject, taking its own direction, to deal more and more with the development and justification of his adulterous love for Gertrude. Apropos, David Walker, in his sleuth-like reading of the chronology of *La Symphonie pastorale*, underscores how the present of the Pastor's marital difficulties keep intruding into his retrospective account (Walker, *André Gide* 60, ff.), and how, as the diarist writes in the breathless second notebook, "he is under great pressure from events which are advancing outside his control" (Walker, *André Gide*, 76).

Moreover, toward the end of the second notebook, as the account catches up with the events recounted, the Pastor notes: "J'écris pour user cette attente" (*SP* 120, where he is waiting for Gertrude to return after the operation that has given her sight). The writing, then, has fulfilled its self-actualizing potential to the point of finally becoming the event narrated. The destiny of writing in *La Symphonie pastorale*, as elsewhere in Gide and so many writers, is to become its own independent subject, with its own destiny.

ii) *Names and Subversion*

Names resonate on the level of other themes as well. On the one hand the analogy-minded Pastor cleverly formulates comparisons justifying his conduct (e.g., his equating Gertrude with the lost sheep of the parable enables him to bring her into his home). Like all the narrators of Gide's *récits*, he usually exhibits confidence that narration can lay bare truth simply and rather completely. On the other hand, we saw that when discussing his color/sound comparison, he recognizes that some comparisons limp (*SP* 40-44), and that, regarding his problem in talking freely with his wife, he states that language itself sometimes communicates imperfectly, indeed counterproductively (*SP* 70). We suggested above that, had he explored the consequences of his concessions, he would have eventually confronted the old logical saw that *omnis comparatio claudicat* 'all comparisons limp' (and perhaps approached the semantic implications). But in spite of the Pastor's failure to pursue his concessions, Gide's text offers an ironic, onomastic hint of the inadvisability of his confidence in analogy and language. His infant son is named "Claude," the Latin source of which (*claudus* 'lame') shares a common root with the verb of the above Latin dictum. Claude appears in the text, moreover, only when howling (*SP* 16, 102), compounding ever so subtly the message hinted at by his name: analogies and language itself can limp even more than usual when human utterances fail to rise much above a childish level of self-involved emotion innocent of thought. That observation is not without application to how one reads the Pastor's account.

In the same vein, the story shows that in approaching and evaluating people, the Pastor would have them be as he would consciously have language be, that is, univalent and accessible to ready understanding. For instance, caught up in his own agenda when he brings the blind and mute Gertrude home, he expects her to slip effortlessly into the simplistic role of "saved sheep" that he assumed obvious. But the real Gertrude genuinely and frequently surprised him. She did it before he succeeded in communicating with her: "Il me faut avouer ici la profonde déception où je me sentis sombrer les premiers jours. Certainement je m'étais fait tout un roman de l'éducation de Gertrude, et la réalité me forçait d'en rabattre" (*SP* 24). After acquiring language, she continued to elude his control and to cause him discomfort, as when she preferred Jacques to him for her experiments with the harmonium (*SP* 56 ff.), and when she confronted their love openly, indicated in his entries of March 12 and May 18. His wife and children likewise resisted his view of them.

It is therefore interesting to observe that so many of the names occurring in the narrative are in several senses doubles, thus echoing the reality of the people to whom they belong, people who much like language and the story itself have far more than one facet and indeed evolve, thereby evading facile comprehension. As mentioned above, the names of his older daughter and son, Sarah and Jacques, come from biblical characters, ones given new names to mark momentous new developments: Sarai-Sarah, Abraham's wife, who became pregnant with Isaac in her nineties; Jacob-Israel who, from supplanting second-born, rose to strive with God himself.[20] Similarly, "Gertrude" designates the person whom the Pastor was obliged, initially at least, to call an "être incertain" (*SP*, 8), and who lost at the beginning of the story her first name along with her apparently futile first life when they slipped into oblivion upon the death of her aunt and upon her being subsequently renamed and given a new life. "Gaspard," the name of Amélie's and the Pastor's middle son who has no visible function in the story except to exist as a name and as a chore for Amélie, on the one hand basks in the comfortable, homey Christian tradition associated with the first of the three Magi, and on the other evokes the tortured Romantic fantasy of A. Bertrand's *Gaspard de la nuit*, much appreciated by symbolists such as the young Gide (and perhaps by devotees of poetry like the Pastor, *SP* 104-06). Charlotte, the second youngest offspring, introduces ambivalence on a different but at least equally important register, the sexual one so unsuccessfully muted by the Pastor, in that "Charlotte," coming from "Charles" or "man," means "little (female) man." We can say, therefore, that, on their own and independently of the Pastor, in their subtle doubleness the names – and through them *la parole* – work slyly at cross purposes to the simple views and values prevalent on the surface of the Pastor's account.

---

[20] "Israel" means "strive with God," the name given to Jacob by the angel with whom he wrestled. In passing let us note that in the Christian Testament "Jacques" has several diverse antecedents. Not the least appropriate of them for the Protestant-Catholic conflict between the Pastor and his son is the name of the author of an epistle traditionally called the "catholic epistle" because of its universal appeal. See also Freeman G. Henry, "*La Symphonie pastorale* Revisited." On pp. 17-18 of his article Henry sees hagiographic significance in the names "Jacques" and "Gertrude," in that Saint Jacques, the first bishop of Jerusalem, and Sainte Gertrude La Grande, a German cloistress, represent for him two opposing interpretations of the Holy Scriptures, interpretations germane to the differing views of the Pastor and Jacques on the New Testament.

## B) *Onomastics in the Pastor's Text*

But let us now try to recast Pasco's and Rollman's basic question, pushing the conventions of a first-person narrative back toward the Pastor's role as exclusive narrator. In addition to asking why Gide chose those names, we can also ask why Gide had the Pastor, the fictional author of the text, choose the ones that *he* did. Let us look, then, upon the names in *La Symphonie pastorale* as "a problem of point of view."[21]

### i) *Naming and Point of View*

In a first-person narrative, naming always occurs in the choices made by the narrator when referring to the other characters (even if there is a steadfast adherence to pronouns) and it occurs (quite rarely but as with the work under discussion) in the names chosen by a parent-narrator for offspring. Concerning the first possibility, illustrative for *La Symphonie pastorale* are the names for the woman who generously agrees to take in Gertrude after the Pastor determines that his ward should no longer live with his family (in particular, with Jacques, his son and rival in Gertrude's affections). What are we to make of the Pastor's electing to call that generous woman variously "Mlle de la M . . ." (*SP* 56, 74 twice, 104 twice, 120 twice, 122, 130 twice), "Louise de la M . . ." (*SP* 56, 74, 104 twice, 106 twice), "Mlle Louise" (*SP* 88, 106, 124 twice) and "Louise" (*SP* 106)?[22] First of all, one could see in the shifts and timing of his use of those names a tendency to growing familiarity (occasioned doubtless by his visits to her guest, Gertrude) which finally withers under the duress of the tragic ending. Accordingly, the distant "Mlle de la M . . ." opens and closes the series, while the less distant "Louise de la M . . ." and "Mlle Louise" prepare and accompany (with the latter also reappearing twice after) the sharp peak of the

---

[21] For names as a problem of point of view, see Uspenski 20-32.

[22] An invaluable resource for the study of names in *La Symphonie pastorale* is the work by Joyce I. Cunningham and W. D. Wilson, *A Concordance of André Gide's "La Symphonie pastorale"* (New York and London: Garland Publishers, 1978).

single example of the very close "Louise." (The peak occurs about four-fifths of the way through the narrative, just before the precipitous conclusion generated by Gertrude's final seduction, operation, and suicide.)

But the tensions among the various names for this one person suggest a complexity not totally compatible with a perhaps too glib progression. At the one extreme stands the remote Mlle de la M . . .: remote experientially as an elderly spinster (indicated by "Mlle") foreign to the life led by the Pastor the cleric, spouse, and five-fold parent; remote socially as well as economically because of her aristocratic (v. the nobiliary particle *de*) and moneyed (*SP* 104) origins. As a result, she stands remote personally, a state effectively communicated by the incomplete patronymic, "de la M. . . ." Given the Pastor's general lack of warmth with people, we surmise that, even though he certainly never so addressed her, we have in "Mlle de la M . . ." – his text's most frequent name for her – the "natural," longstanding tone of their contacts with each other. Such a tone is completely in keeping with the Pastor's innate reserve. After all, even on those occasions when he mentions his presumed best friend, Martins, whom he had known since at least their *lycée* days together (*SP* 26), he avoids using his friend's given name, writing instead "Martins" twelve times and "le docteur Martins" twice. This inclination to reserve makes the use of the rather intimate "Louise" at the other extreme to "Mlle de la M . . ." stand out all the more egregiously.

There is, furthermore, an anomaly, the exploration of which offers an explanation of the tension between the two kinds of names introduced by the Pastor for the same person: why does the Pastor not name her completely, using instead the ellipsis in "Mlle de la M . . ." and "Louise de la M . . ."? If the distancing effect discussed above is alone advanced to explain it, how is the reader to deal with "de la M . . ."'s being combined with the familiar "Louise"? Nor can it be argued convincingly that conventional discretion in protecting last names explains away this curiosity, since the Pastor uses Martins's last name and since the scene of events (readily situated in the canton of Neuchâtel thanks to the mention of Le Brévin and la Chaux-de-Fond by the Pastor, *SP* 4) would allow identification of those involved. A solution is to recognize that the ellipsis bespeaks not only a distancing but at least as much an absence – indeed a refusal – in the Pastor's identification of her, creating a deliberate void that he can more easily fill to his own purposes. The anomaly and the very multiplicity in his names for her suggest the fits and starts of an unstable perception of her, unstable because he is forcing onto her an identity that is not hers.

That identity comes cleanly to the fore once when, late in his narrative, the intimate "Louise" appears by itself in a sentence for the first and last time. The circumstances under which he writes imply a great deal:

> Chaque dimanche [Gertrude] vient déjeuner chez nous; mes enfants la revoient avec plaisir, malgré que leurs goûts et les siens diffèrent de plus en plus. Amélie ne marque pas trop de nervosité et le repas s'achève sans accroc. Toute la famille ensuite ramène Gertrude et prend le goûter à la *Grange* [the home of Mlle de la M . . ., where Gertrude is by that time staying]. C'est une fête pour mes enfants que Louise prend plaisir à gâter et combler de friandises. (*SP* 106)

We see here Mlle de la M . . . cast almost explicitly in a maternal role rivaling Amélie's, whose alleged nervousness and proclivity to cause *accrocs* makes her value as mother wane as Louise's waxes.

Moreover, this scene captures in one revealing moment how the Pastor transforms in the course of his account an otherwise secondary figure into a foil against which to contrast his wife. (For the reader apprised of the etymology of "Louise" mentioned above, 212, the hostile overtones of the Pastor's language become that much more audible.) In an ever so typical prelude to emotional repudiation, he establishes between the two individuals contrasts so increasingly numerous and stark that they finally appear artificial: in the Pastor's eyes Amélie is slow to take in Gertrude, Mlle de la M . . . quick; Amélie feels indifferent to music (and perhaps even averse to it, *SP* 52), Mlle de la M . . . loves, plays, and teaches it; his wife has no taste for reading, poetry, and intellectually stimulating conversation (*SP* 102-04), whereas his neighbor enjoys and fosters them (*SP* 106); according to him, Amélie's household offers a morose focus of tension, discord, recrimination and petty concern for the material, while Mlle de la M . . .'s fairly glows with gaiety, harmony, permissiveness, and a strong spirituality free from every day concerns; etc. This dubious antithesis stands even farther removed from "reality" in that it glosses over Mlle de la M . . .'s power and wealth (treated above apropos of the particle of nobility and echoed by "Louise" which, through its masculine counterpart, evokes the mightiest kings of France and the gold louis). Reinforced reminders of her power and wealth need to be reconciled with her alleged spirituality. Surely Mlle de la M . . . -Louise is less a person (within the conventions of the text) than a device created by the Pastor. On the level of his narrative as justification, he tends to leave her devoid of her personal identity because he makes of her a rhetorical figure to reject Amélie's conjugal rights, thereby facilitating his emotional involvement with Gertrude.

On the level of his narrative as personal revelation, the exaggerated polarity (as opposed to incidental differences) between the two women suggests that his portraits of them result from the extremes of his emotional response to one person with whom he is most closely involved, his complex and more "real" wife, a woman the reader only barely glimpses between the unrealistic visions of the earthbound harridan Amélie on the one hand and the indulgent saintly Louise on the other. The Pastor lays the groundwork for recognizing his bi-polar way of seeing the woman he married, but characteristically he fails to explore and so profit from a near insight:

> Sarah ressemble à sa mère, ce qui fait que j'aurais voulu la mettre en pension. Elle ressemble non point, hélas! à ce que sa mère était à son âge, quand nous nous sommes fiancés, mais bien à ce qui l'ont fait devenir les soucis de la vie matérielle, et j'allais dire la culture des soucis de la vie (car certainement Amélie les cultive). Certes j'ai bien du mal à reconnaître en elle aujourd'hui, l'ange qui souriait naguère à chaque noble élan de mon coeur, que je rêvais d'associer indistinctement à ma vie, et qui me paraissait me précéder et me guider vers la lumière – ou l'amour en ce temps-là me blousait-il? . . . (*SP* 102)

The overlap between the young Amélie viewed as an angel and Louise viewed as a saint calls out for cautious reflection, but the call goes unheeded by the Pastor. Had it been otherwise, the Pastor might have sensed that his perception of Mlle de la M . . . -Louise did not spring *ex nihilo*, but rather derived from the callow way that he as a young man in love had first viewed Amélie. Idealized, simplistic memories can be an insidious weapon in repudiating the reality of a loved one. They become all the more damaging when, as with the Pastor, one can force their reincarnation onto an acquaintance handy for invidious comparisons.

Attention, then, to the *Pastor's* (as opposed to Gide's) choices in naming Mlle de la M . . . helps bring out the main goal of the *récit* for Gide, namely, making as many of its elements as possible contribute to the nuanced richness of his depiction of the Pastor's actions, the chief of which for us readers is his narration. Before we leave this point, however, lest there arise an oversimplified impression of the distinction between Gide's and the Pastor's picking names, we should highlight at least one example of their interplay. Since it is difficult not to surmise that Amélie-Louise reflects Gide's own relationship with his wife-cousin Madeleine, the sense of distance/absence imparted by the incomplete patronymic M . . . reflects the distance/absence of M(adeleine) to so much of Gide's work, emotion, and sexuality.

ii) *Naming as Assault*

In *La Symphonie pastorale* there is a second, more fundamental way in which our narrator chooses names. Consideration of the Pastor's attitude and conduct toward his family allows us to presume that this literate, authoritative, and – one could argue – tyrannical figure had more of a voice in choosing the children's names than did his too frequently deferential wife. In this regard, within the narrative there appears to be no immediate explanation of what the Pastor means when he refers to his *élans inconsidérés* that he tells us have contributed to Amélie's weariness (*SP* 16). In the absence of an explanation from him, is it not permissible to apply Occam's razor, seeing those fatigue-producing drives and Amélie's complaints about being harried by too many children as addressing essentially the same point, namely, his getting her repeatedly pregnant in spite of their restricted circumstances? Apropos, we note that when the Pastor kisses Gertrude for the first time, the act results from what he calls an *élan* (*SP* 34). The next time he has such an impulse he will make love to her. So the Pastor in his *élans* with the reluctant Amélie would have been that much more inclined to view the children as "his" and to view himself as the one responsible for naming them. Assuming then that the Pastor was largely responsible for choosing the names of the children, we can glean from a precious indication of his childhood attitudes an intimation about a reason at work behind his choices:

> –Mieux vaut qu'elle ne soit point là demain, quand on viendra lever le corps, dit-elle [the neighbor present at the death of Gertrude's aunt]. Et ce fut tout.
> Bien des choses se feraient facilement, sans les chimériques objections que parfois les hommes se plaisent à inventer. Dès l'enfance, combien de fois sommes-nous empêchés de faire ceci ou cela que nous voudrions faire, simplement parce que nous entendons répéter autour de nous: il ne pourra pas le faire . . .
> L'aveugle s'est laissé emmener comme une masse involontaire. Les traits de son visage étaient réguliers, assez beaux, mais parfaitement inexpressifs. [Etc.] (*SP* 10)

As already mentioned, the most striking feature of this passage is the jarring, unexplained middle paragraph. While as a non-sequitur it offers another example of how our narrator either ignores or overlooks some of his critical thought-processes, the abrupt transition has the added value of encouraging us to linger over the paragraph in an effort to situate it better. As a result, we note the tone of annoyance and the use of the specific pronouns *nous* and *il* instead of, for instance, the more general *on* which would be perfectly suitable here. They reinforce the impression that the Pastor of course is the one whose inclinations since childhood on have been squelched constantly by his nay-saying community (now represented primarily by Amélie, at least in his eyes). Furthermore, the sudden, unexplained, unexplored annoyance suggests the possibility of depths of hidden frustration and antagonism on the part of the Pastor toward his society and its values that we have already seen. In that light, the doubleness (mentioned above, 215) of the names he chose for his children corroborates the hint made by the quotation immediately above that he had been living an equivocation: he accepted general conformity to what he felt was a repressively uniform society, even while he harbored a long-standing but unexplored resistance to it. That doubleness and resistance burst out expressively and tragically when the Pastor takes the opportunity to mold the malleable Gertrude into a devout Christian and yet a compliant fornicator.

One senses further corroboration of his unarticulated conflict in his failure to reveal his own name. Given the etymology shared by *nom* 'name; and *connaître* 'to know', it becomes highly suggestive for the Pastor to veil his name behind the title *Pasteur* and familiar designations *mon ami*, etc. when he quotes in his narrative others addressing him. (It may be that he in fact has those near to him avoid his name in addressing him, so that his text merely records the use of the titles and designations. If so, the suggestion would remain essentially the same, only more damning.) He can be seen to be skirting and to have his readers skirt knowledge of that deeply personal part of himself at odds with what the title and designations represent, the part at the source of his antagonistic, devious drives. Ironically, however, his title itself winds up betraying him, as it proves to be as unstable and revealing as the other names. While he would of course have *Pasteur* recall only his function as spiritual shepherd to his flock, his mention (*SP* 28-30) of Virgil the author of eclogues and bucolics actualizes the potential of his title to call to mind also a love-sick shepherd spinning out amatoria, a persona woefully out of place in the Alpine fastnesses of a Calvinist community, but one played out nonetheless in the Pastor's own repressed way.

Looking back on all the Pastor's naming practices, we spot the common thread of devious antagonism. While directed most immediately against his wife, it has too fertile a potential for violence to affect only Amélie: his younger children withdraw from him at a tender age (by his own admission, *SP* 20) and too become a target of hostility (*SP* 20, 56, 102-04); victimized by his father, Jacques finally repudiates him formally and emotionally when he abjures the Pastor's Protestant faith (*SP* 130); and Gertrude kills herself. While it would surely be reductive to try to explain such violence in terms only of naming, let us recall that names – "les princes des signifiants" – carry an impressive charge of literariness and all that goes with it. Consequently, Jacques Derrida's observations on the connection between *l'écriture*, naming, and violence ring true in the case of the Pastor (who of course produces the *écriture* that is *La Symphonie pastorale*):

> Le concept de nom propre [revealing a proper name was forbidden among the Nambikwara], tel que Lévi-Strauss l'utilise sans le problématiser dans *Tristes Tropiques*, est donc loin d'être

simple et maniable. Il en va de même, par conséquent, des concepts de violence, de ruse, de perfide ou d'oppression qui ponctueront un peu plus loin la "Leçon d'écriture." On a déjà pu constater que la violence, ici, ne survient pas d'un seul coup, à partir d'une innocence originelle dont la nudité serait *surprise*, au moment où le secret des noms *soi-disant* propres est violé. La structure de la violence est complexe et sa possibilité – l'écriture – ne l'est pas moins.

Il y avait en effet une première violence à nommer. Nommer, donner les noms qu'il sera éventuellement interdit de prononcer, telle est la violence originaire du langage qui consiste à inscrire dans une différence, à classer, à suspendre le vocatif absolu. Penser l'unique *dans* le système, l'y inscrire, tel est le geste de l'archi-écriture: archi-violence, perte du propre, de la proximité absolue, de la présence à soi, perte en vérité de ce qui n'a jamais eu lieu, d'une présence à soi qui n'a jamais été donnée mais rêvée et toujours déjà dédoublée, répétée, incapable de s'apparaître autrement que dans sa propre disparition. A partir de cette archi-violence, interdite et donc confirmée par une deuxième violence réparatrice, protectrice, instituant la "morale," prescrivant de cacher l'écriture, d'effacer et d'oblitérer le soi-disant nom propre qui déjà divisait le propre, une troisième violence peut *éventuellement* surgir ou ne pas surgir (possibilité empirique) dans ce qu'on appelle couramment le mal, la guerre, l'indiscrétion, le viol: qui consistent à révéler par effraction le nom soi-disant propre, c'est-à-dire la violence originaire qui a sevré le propre de sa propriété et de sa propreté. (Derrida, *De la grammatologie* 164-65)

The extrapolation from Derrida's triadic insight to *La Symphonie pastorale* seems clear. First, the textual system of names created by the narrator-namer (in the two senses distinguished above) is a violent one in that, as we have already seen, it encapsulates, predicts, and so necessitates its own death-dealing events. Second, the (all too traditional) "morality" that justifies a husband's adultery and a family's submission to an overbearing husband-father springs from our devious, hypocritical narrator who would hide the true nature of his conduct and – most apropos of Derrida – of his writing. Third, the injustices wreaked on Amélie, Gertrude, and Jacques, and the seduction and suicide of Gertrude realize the "empiric possibility" of what Derrida calls evil and rape. (The fit of Derrida's insight also raises the question of possible correspondence between his ideas on "loss . . . of self-presence" and the narcissistic yearnings of Gidean narrators and the image behind Gide's theoretical *Le Traité du Narcisse*.)

Finally, one of *La Symphonie pastorale*'s more intriguing items of onomastics in light of this work's first-person point of view is "Claude," the last name the Pastor chose for one of his children, shortly before taking up the pen.[23] The intimation of corrosive verbal inadequacy (discussed above, 214) behind the name "Claude" as used in the text offers a too neat coincidence with the Pastor's composing a document whose tangled, endless ironies undermine language as a basis for certainty. The coincidence can only feed speculation that the Pastor is losing his grip on his unreflecting hostility toward the values inculcated into him, because surely the word (both human and divine) being vitiated by his text had served as the foundation of his bible-based faith and as the tool of his very life's work as a preacher-minister. This unreflecting assault upon language becomes more fascinating when one considers recent studies (Babcock, *Portraits*) arguing that the Pastor, while appearing to be a scribbling *naïf* – that is, someone who unthinkingly accepts the word – lets slip into his account indications of being an artful, self-conscious writer, that is, someone initiated into the dodges of language.

We conclude this examination of *La Symphonie pastorale* wondering where, in the Pastor's unreflecting assault on narrative straightforwardness, on conventional morality and sexuality, and on language itself, the line is to be drawn between sublimating and ignoring, between pursuit of a higher, non-documentary truth and lying. That surely is a Gidean question and one productive of necessarily speculative answers, as necessarily speculative as many of the above arguments. But the question and the search for answers, however speculative, have, it is hoped, helped to bring to light subtle riches to be found in *La Symphonie pastorale*, and so they suggest the heuristic value of pushing its narrative conventions in a variety of directions.

---

[23] Let us note that the etymological implications of "Claude" that were discussed earlier might seem less naturally obvious to the Pastor than those of the four other children's names. We must keep in mind, however, that the Pastor understood Latin well enough to read and to appreciate authors such as Virgil. Presumably then as a beginning student or as an accomplished reader he would have encountered other texts in which the dictum *omnis comparatio claudicat* would be found.

| LE TEMPS DU RÉCIT | LE TEMPS DE L'HISTOIRE |

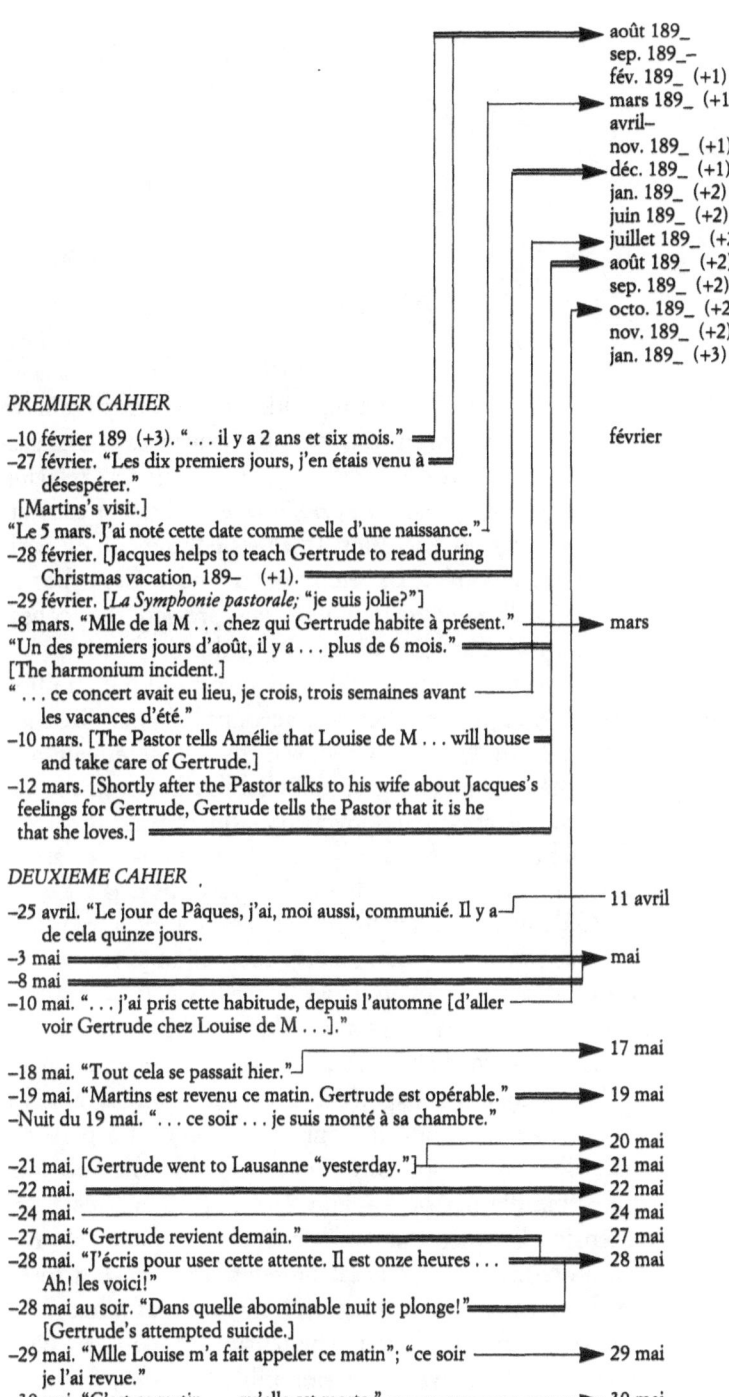

août 189_
sep. 189_
fév. 189_ (+1)
mars 189_ (+1)
avril–
nov. 189_ (+1)
déc. 189_ (+1)
jan. 189_ (+2)
juin 189_ (+2)
juillet 189_ (+2)
août 189_ (+2)
sep. 189_ (+2)
octo. 189_ (+2)
nov. 189_ (+2)
jan. 189_ (+3)

PREMIER CAHIER

–10 février 189 (+3). "... il y a 2 ans et six mois."   février
–27 février. "Les dix premiers jours, j'en étais venu à désespérer."
[Martins's visit.]
"Le 5 mars. J'ai noté cette date comme celle d'une naissance."
–28 février. [Jacques helps to teach Gertrude to read during Christmas vacation, 189– (+1).
–29 février. [*La Symphonie pastorale;* "je suis jolie?"]
–8 mars. "Mlle de la M... chez qui Gertrude habite à présent."   mars
"Un des premiers jours d'août, il y a... plus de 6 mois."
[The harmonium incident.]
"... ce concert avait eu lieu, je crois, trois semaines avant les vacances d'été."
–10 mars. [The Pastor tells Amélie that Louise de M... will house and take care of Gertrude.]
–12 mars. [Shortly after the Pastor talks to his wife about Jacques's feelings for Gertrude, Gertrude tells the Pastor that it is he that she loves.]

DEUXIEME CAHIER

–25 avril. "Le jour de Pâques, j'ai, moi aussi, communié. Il y a   11 avril
de cela quinze jours.
–3 mai   mai
–8 mai
–10 mai. "... j'ai pris cette habitude, depuis l'automne [d'aller voir Gertrude chez Louise de M...]."
  17 mai
–18 mai. "Tout cela se passait hier."
–19 mai. "Martins est revenu ce matin. Gertrude est opérable."   19 mai
–Nuit du 19 mai. "... ce soir... je suis monté à sa chambre."
  20 mai
–21 mai. [Gertrude went to Lausanne "yesterday."]   21 mai
–22 mai.   22 mai
–24 mai.   24 mai
–27 mai. "Gertrude revient demain."   27 mai
–28 mai. "J'écris pour user cette attente. Il est onze heures...   28 mai
Ah! les voici!"
–28 mai au soir. "Dans quelle abominable nuit je plonge!"
[Gertrude's attempted suicide.]
–29 mai. "Mlle Louise m'a fait appeler ce matin"; "ce soir   29 mai
je l'ai revue."
–30 mai. "C'est ce matin... qu'elle est morte."   30 mai

# CONCLUSION

To summarize then, in considering Gide's major *récits* we have read the narrative conventions unconventionally: instead of dismissing the frame in *L'Immoraliste* as incidental, we pursued its relaying implications quite seriously; for *La Porte étroite* we heuristically attributed the inclusion and exclusion (that is, editing) of *all* incidents, images, explanations, texts, etc., not to André Gide, but to Jérôme; and in *La Symphonie pastorale* we pressed the consequences of the Pastor's narrative insincerity and prevarications, accepting that any cogent reading would have to sort out the question of what can be relied upon in a fictional account by a liar. We read unconventionally, both because Gide was by temperament and practice a writer happily teetering on the vital line between the use of literary conventions and their subversion, and because the accumulating scholarship has increasingly raised questions that strain against the limits of traditional readings. As a result, we saw that in all three cases Gide lures us on with promises of a story, a traditional text, only to use the logic of that text's presentation to squeeze us out toward a consideration of its conditions, toward its margins, that is, its telling. But in each instance, the textual presence that turned into absence – Michel's account, Alissa's letters and diary, the story of the Pastor's real experiences – nonetheless retained a compelling voice that generated the mimetic illusion of a personal presence (an illusion doubtlessly enhanced by the obvious moral – i.e, profoundly personal – concerns that drench each account.) The tension between the mimetic illusion of personal presence and the undermining of textual presence can be seen to be paralleled in the tension characteristic of so much of what Gide wrote, that between life and fiction. The tension of the *récits* plays out on a larger stage the universal tension inherent in any first-person statement, that between the 'I' of language and the 'I' of experience, the former being endowed with a hallucinatory solidity and objectivity (indeed, an embedded third-person status, as Benveniste has observed), fundamentally at odds with the fluidity and subjectivity of the latter. Even in life itself, how easy is it to distinguish persons – the "I" of experience – from their stories – the "I" of language? Can we tell ourselves or others who we are, can we even contemplate the question, without inevitably narrating? A fortiori, can imaginary persons in literature be conceived beyond the words of their stories? Gide's narrative gambits take us to those questions, even as he side-steps the problems that he raises with persistence, by letting us fix on a story of the writing of the story. But at the level of analysis with which we are left, then, his literary persons are story stories, that is, so essentially, so constitutively story-telling-dependent, that our vision of them as even imaginary persons breaks up at the slightest intellectual touch, much like the young Gide/Narcissus touching the surface of his image. Of course, the work of Freud, Jung, Bakhtin, Lacan, Heidegger, to name the most prominent, make it disturbingly easy to move those problems back out of fiction to ourselves, or, to put it more accurately, back to the language and stories of our own lives.

Moreover, the alacrity with which the *histoire* of Gide's *récits* breaks up upon reflective touch raises the question whether we do not have here a hint of their genesis in Gide's preoccupying and increasingly successful struggle against narcissism. Much like his self, and much like the originary text exploded by the Adam of his ars poetica *Le Traité de Narcisse*, the *histoire* offer no sense of fixity. In keeping with the clinical insight of psychoanalysis that the self is best known as the cunning telling of an evasive story, the hyper insecure Gide was compelled to tell over and over again the story of the insecure story, finding in the artistic illusion of voice the only tenuous presence available to him. Which is not to say that it is not presumptuous of me or any other contemporary reader to claim to know Gide in any direct sense whatsoever – I have not talked to the those who knew him personally, and I most obviously could have not listened to him try to explain who he is. But if any writer encourages at least an attempt at speculative psychobiographical explanation through the writings, it is Gide. His posed revelations in the *Journal* and autobiographical texts bear too many resemblances to the *récits* for us not to read the latter without a biographical predisposition. The difference between this reading of the biographical connection and earlier ones à la Taine is one characteristic of our times, one recognizing that the more important correspondence is far less the events of a story – the *récits* are not Gide's life simply transposed – than the way of telling, one that uses events to get at the real story for Gide, the nature of story-telling, that is, of the self. As he himself recognized: "Je suis un être de dialogue: tout en moi combat et se contredit. Les Mémoires ne sont jamais qu'à demi sincères, si grand que soit le souci de vérité: tout est toujours plus compliqué qu'on ne le dit. Peut-être même approche-t-on de plus près la vérité dans le roman" (*Journal* I, 547).

Another result of reading the conventions unconventionally was a rebounding justification of the emphasis on form. Pursuing in each *récit* the implications of the narrative gambit used by Gide led to an appreciation of how those issues reflected, and indeed constituted, the central subject or problem for the main character: the framing voice of Michel's anonymous friend showed the inherent dependency on others – and so failure – of Michel in his search for authentic individualism; we saw how, in Jérôme's struggle to sustain an exclusionary narcissistic vision of his youth, it was not only his narrative role that was exposed to be editing, but the very mode of his personality; the narrative deceptions offered by the Pastor in his arguments for an idealizing vision of a gospel of love turned out to serve impulses less evangelizing than anarchic, the lies unwittingly having been the end, not the means, an end destructive of the truth and values he claimed so aggressively to preach.

I would like now to broach some of the implications of these readings, first for all of Gide's *récits*, then for his entire fictional oeuvre. One of the chief implications for the *récits* is that as a corpus they were part of an evolving narratological subversion on his part. It is pertinent to emphasize as background here Gide's insistence that he had already sketched his works out *together* in his mind when he was fairly young:

> Mes oeuvres m'apparaissent, devant moi, depuis longtemps déjà, prêtes, n'attendant plus que d'être écrites. Il n'y a pas d'irraison dans mes entreprises; tout en faisant la plus grande, la part du changement possible, il me semble voir chaque nouvel écrit prendre place, non à la suite, mais au milieu des autres, tant les

oeuvres à faire m'apparaissent déjà réelles autant que les passées. (Gide, letter to M. Drouin, 1893, quoted by Delay, vol. 1, 28)

It is to be expected, then, that to a certain extent Gide himself could and did identify the systematic subversion of his *récits*. He happened to couch it in terms of a pattern of critical irony directed at certain subjects:

> A la seule exception de mes *Nourritures*, tous mes livres sont des livres *ironiques*; ce sont des livres de critique. La *Porte étroite* est la critique d'une certaine tendance mystique; *Isabelle*, la critique d'une certaine forme de l'imagination romantique; la *Symphonie pastorale*, d'une forme de mensonge à soi-même; l'*Immoraliste*, d'une forme de l'individualisme. (Gide, *Oeuvres complètes*, vol. XIII, 439-40)

We can be sure that the same critical spirit carried over to the form of his fictions: "... je préférais ne réussir point, plutôt que de me fixer dans un genre. Quand elle me mènerait aux honneurs, je ne puis consentir à suivre une route toute tracée. J'aime le jeu, l'inconnu, l'aventure..." (Gide, *Si le Grain ne meurt*, in *Journal*, II, 526). The existence of that critical spirit regarding genre does not, however, allow us to argue that in the writing of his *récits* Gide was conscious of the systematic undermining of the narrative gambits addressed in these pages. On the contrary, if he were to attribute it to anything, it would probably have been to the *soties*:

> A la date du 6 janvier 1932, nous lisons dans le *Journal* de Julien Green:
> Gide me donne un exemplaire de *Paludes* et me parle de ce livre avec un mélange d'affection et de regret. 'Oui, dit-il, j'aurais dû continuer dans cette voie. Plus tard, j'ai accepté certaines conventions... Je me demande si je n'ai pas eu tort. Je l'ai relu et j'ai été épaté.' C'est le *saugrenu* de *Paludes* qui lui plaît, et sa férocité aussi, j'imagine. (Goulet, "Introduction," in Fillaudeau 14)

But Gide's words do suggest the "wild," "ferocious" side of his artistic tastes in general, tastes that presumably shaped the narrative structures of the *récits*, however imprecise his consciousness of their sabotage. So at the very least we can maintain, as Fillaudeau does (23 ff.), that this writer had an innate animus against the fixity of genre, that in his literary inclination to leave "une route toute tracée" we find cause enough to explain the undoing of conventions that Gide would only dimly subsume under the critical irony of the *récits*. In fact, Gide's understanding of much of his more subversive works sometimes came to him only after the fact. For instance, of the three more *saugrenus* of his fictional pieces – *Paludes*, *Le Prométhée mal enchaîné*, and *Les Caves du Vatican* – only the latter was, with its first appearance, given the apt name "*sotie*" from "*sot*," the first two being so named only subsequently, after *Les Caves*. Even the *Paludes* that moved him in Green's presence to "un mélange d'affection et regret" he first called a '*traité*,' and the difficult *Le Prométhée* a '*roman*' (Brée, 27). So too, it was not until a planned "Préface" for *Isabelle* that *L'Immoraliste* and *La Porte étroite* were first called *récits* instead of *romans* (Lafille 45). Therefore, we may say that it was only well after the writing that Gide could make out either the principles around which his works clustered variously, or their subversive ramifications.

Not surprisingly, then, Claude Martin has observed, if not quite a schema, then at least a series of permutations in Gide's narrative gambits in his *récits*. The eminent Gidean scholar asserts that the *récits*:

> ... illustrent *six* formules narratives différentes:
> –dans *L'Immoraliste*, Michel RACONTE (de vive voix) à des amis *sa propre* histoire;
> –dans *La Porte étroite*, Jérôme ÉCRIT l'histoire d'*Alissa*;
> –dans *Isabelle*, Gérard RACONTE à des amis une histoire dont il n'a été que *le témoin*;
> –dans *La Symphonie pastorale*, le Pasteur tient le *journal* de *sa propre* histoire;
> –dans *L'École des Femmes*, Éveline écrit aussi un *journal*, mais en deux morceaux très différents et séparés par vingt années, le premier condensé sur six semaines, le second sur trois;
> —dans *Robert* et *Geneviève*, enfin, les narrateurs donnent une sorte de *point de vue personnel* sur l'histoire, un plaidoyer *pro domo* écrit par Robert, une brève notice autobiographique écrite par Geneviève, tous deux les yeux fixés sur le Journal d'Éveline qu'ils entendent corriger ou compléter. (C. Martin xxv-xxvi; emphases in the original)

I in turn would like to argue that the readings which I propose for the three major *récits* make visible what can indeed be called a subversive schematic to be seen in the narrative forms of all the *récits*. We can start sketching this argument by recalling a point mentioned in passing in Chapter Two, how the emphasis on the frame highlights an additional bond between the already tightly bound *livres jumeaux*, *L'Immoraliste* and *La Porte étroite*. Viewing the diary as main text relayed by Jérôme makes it apparent that in both works the basic narrative structure involves a less important character transmitting the voice of the main character. But given the considerable differences (for example and most prominently, Jérôme has a narrative and diegetic role vastly more visible and important than that of Michel's anonymous friend), it suggests an evolving, comparative exploration of similar narrative issues on Gide's part. Whereas we saw how he suppressed in the final version of *L'Immoraliste* (1902) most overt reminders of narrative distortion (except the part and chapter divisions) that nonetheless come into play by relaying, in the next *récit*, *La Porte étroite* (1907), we see the same sort of distortion, but forefronted and sustained variously and substantially by Jérôme's account. The narrative structure of the subsequent *Isabelle* (1911) makes all the more compelling the suggestion that Gide was engaging in a progressive exploration of the deformities of relaying: the reader has to penetrate no fewer than *three* primary layers of relaying filters in the attempt to gain access to the story that drives Gérard's and the reader's curiosity, the story of Isabelle. To begin with, the narrative voice ("je") that makes first contact with the reader plays a role almost identical to that of the anonymous amanuensis of *L'Immoraliste*, transmitting from memory an extensive story told – at night again – by a friend, Gérard. But Gérard's account itself is in large part a relayed narrative, since it comprises a mix of the (few) events that he himself witnessed and of the (many) events that were relayed to him by others. Even some of the latter events were themselves a mix of observation and hearsay (e.g., Santal's accounts of what he saw personally and of what he was told by others).

In *Isabelle* and the subsequent *récits* – *La Symphonie pastorale* (1919) and the trilogy of *L'École des femmes* (1929, 1930, 1936) – Gide takes the undermining of diegesis in additional directions by drawing into the open some of the conventions discretely at work in the two earlier pieces. First of all, in *Isabelle* and the trilogy, Gide makes progressively more explicit the convention of fictive publication glossed over in *L'Immoraliste* and *La Porte étroite*: he has their "authors" submit "their" accounts directly to him, who "merely" publishes them but whom we know to be the renowned writer of such narratives. This of course is still another means of creating tension between mimesis and its undoing. This convention is hardly unusual (e.g., *Adolphe*), but does straightaway remind the thoughtful reader of the question of where to draw the line in crossing over from rationality to willful disbelief. Then, in *La Symphonie pastorale* with the lying Pastor, Gide pushes the narrative insincerity operative in the first two *récits*, taking it from Michel's acknowledged duplicity and Jérôme's possible misrepresentations to the Pastor's unacknowledged but deliberate falsehoods. In the trilogy, on the other hand, while Geneviève does in fact transmit her mother's diary, she changed (or so she claims) only the names. (Nonetheless, in the second part of the triptych Gide archly scrambles the diegetic cards and tosses in a mise-en-abyme joker by having Robert suggest that his wife's diary was too well written to have come from her hand, that "Gide" must have been involved in the final version, *Robert*, 1316). But following the appearance of Éveline's diary, first Robert and then Geneviève go on each to offer, like a privileged Alissa, a *complete* text, but one contesting the story proposed by its respective predecessor, thereby continuing the challenge to any accurate transmission of diegesis.

For both *La Symphonie pastorale* and Éveline's text, the additional directions of the diegetic undermining notwithstanding, a case can still be made for viewing them as refined permutations of the narrative relaying at issue in *L'Immoraliste*, *La Porte étroite*, and *Isabelle*. In the first instance, the prevaricating Pastor offers a deliberately misleading account, that is, he distorts the sincere, more accurate account available to him and so achieves the same effect as relaying. The relaying has, if you will, taken an inverted turn, the primary narrator becoming his own unreliable relayer. The utopian voice is relayed by the more manipulative one, the past tale of the discovery and education of Gertrude is framed by the more current one of the Pastor's love for her and antagonism for his family. Éveline's text, in its basic form, is like the Pastor's, consisting of two principal parts, the second one of which offers, as does his, an enlightened, corrective rereading of the first. But in her case, of course, the rereading is more sincere. Nonetheless, in disputing the vision of its own first part, it shows even events narrated sincerely to be inherently and irremediably subjective and

# CONCLUSION

skewed, a demonstration reinforced by her husband's and daughter's subsequent, challenging accounts. In general, then, the permutative trend that becomes visible in all the *récits* in light of this argument loops us back to *Le Traité de Narcisse*, since each narrative gambit of the *récits* illustrates differently the loss of the definitive text, a loss postulated in Gide's youthful expression of literary principles.[1]

The systematicity of that trend argues for a special place for Gide in the on-going history of literary attempts since *Quixote* to "to fix the reader at a magical spot midway between identification and detachment" (El Saffar, 54). First-person narrative prospered in seventeenth- and eighteenth-century Europe because it initially gave an impression of authority and authenticity. It is an account of a "person" who was there, who can vouch for the "reality" of what transpired, who assures us that what is told is not just the fantasy of an author of fictions. In retrospect, thanks to writers like Gide, we see starkly that the supplementary voice that was supposed to heighten the mimetic illusion must eventually and inevitably have

---

[1] Such a narrative gambit is not evident in *Thésée*, Gide's last *récit* and indeed last published fictional work (1946). Other differences between the preceding *récits* and this brief tale (forty pages in the Pléiade edition) would, too, argue against its inclusion in my argument. For instance, an analysis of an account offered up by a character of almost deafening cultural and mythic resonance would fit uncomfortably in this, an aggressive study of the realist implications of the narrative conventions of the other, bourgeois narratives. More's the irony that the breezy French and even breezier amoralism of Gide's Greek hero has a no less uncomfortable fit with his own stature as the founder of Athens, not to mention with the linguistic and moral strainings of Gide's other, exquisitely refined if repressed narrators.

Apropos of irony, *Thésée* strikes this reader as far more problematic than it does most critics, who have tended to view it as the final ethical and esthetic testament of a wise and serene master. Why assume that Gidean irony suspends itself when Gide makes his putative final declaration as an artist? Since Romantic, intentionalist assumptions (e.g., Gide's characters speak directly for, are mere echoes of, the genius himself) infuriated Gide regarding the other *récits*, why should they reveal the "real message" of *Thésée*? Whatever the "message," it will have far less to do with Gide's sunset wisdom than (again) with reading. Unless, that is, one is prepared to argue that, for Gide, a politician/picaro narrator with a blithely acknowledged history of, and knack for, deceit, self-aggrandizement, and quick moral accommodation to the main chance whenever and however it appears – and Gide's Thésée most assuredly is such a character – can be trusted to make an exception in his dealings with his readers. Can we guarantee that Thésée will be honest and forthright, just this once, with those to whom he commits the story of his "final, real" values? Or would it be better to wonder if Gide's last narrator, a patent but beguiling scoundrel, does not mark instead a return for Gide to the picaresque origin of the first-person narrative in the West?

just the opposite effect and would challenge the certitude about itself, a certitude present at the heart of third-person fiction. If we are told by an omniscient narrator that Charles Grandet at one point thought he loved his cousin Eugénie, then we can be sure that he did. But if one of the characters or if he himself had told us that he loved her, then his later, manifestly mercenary approach to people – e.g., slaves and wives – would force us to a debate: had he in fact been a cynical materialist all along, and so was his early claim of love for Eugénie a unmitigated deception?; or could a part of him have momentarily managed to resist his corruption as a Parisian youth, and to prompt expressions of love? Granted that the referent would have been fictional in any case, there would still have been a tighter correspondence with omniscient assertions about it. But when the narrator is a fictional character, a whole new dimension of potential uncertainty is created: narrator-characters can no more guarantee – in principle – observations about themselves or other characters than readers can about themselves or other people, thereby moving themselves and the reader to "the magical spot" of the post-Cervantes novel. It took time for that principle to surface as a visible operational aesthetic force, but it did, and Gide's work was one of the first to exploit it systematically.

Regarding still another trait that argues for a special place for Gide's *récits* in the history of the novel, and before we take leave of their descendence from *Le Traité du Narcisse*, the never-to-be-satisfied need to find what was lost may explain ultimately another, more curious feature that ties the *récits* together: both characters and the reader are snoops, looking for the secret of things hidden to them. Michel snoops on Moktir in the mirror, Jérôme on his aunt at her bedroom door and behind the bushes on Alissa and her father,[2] the Pastor on Jacques and Gertrude in the chapel, Robert on Éveline by insisting on reading her diary. The snooping seems more essential than accidental, since each such incident constitutes a decisive moment in the development of events. (Less decisively, Gustave, Éveline's and Robert's son, eavesdrops on the rest of the family, *Geneviève*, in *Romans* 1374.) This tendency culminates in *Isabelle*, where snooping *is* Gérard's story, making of it a virtual de-

---

[2] For a fuller treatment, see Erica M. Eisinger, "The Hidden Eye: Clandestine Observation in Gide's *La Porte Étroite*."

tective novel (see Horn). Moreover, the structures of these texts effectively cast the reader into a parallel role. In some cases, the narrator does not seem to intend either that we be his readers (as in Michel's case), or that we uncover the "real" story (as in Jérôme's and the Pastor's case). Whereas in *Isabelle* we are invited (along with the framing narrator and his friend "Jammes") to join in Gérard's snooping with relish, in the trilogy we return to sticking our noses into a family's pathology, a process started when we read Éveline's diary, which she had intended first only for Robert, and then only for Geneviève. If we take our cue from Bakhtin, Gide's pattern of crafting narrator and reader as snoops points to a central feature of the novelistic impulse:

> These masks [of the clown and of the fool] are not invented: they are rooted deep in the folk. They are linked with the folk through the fool's time-honored privilege not to participate in life, and by the time-honored bluntness of the fool's language; they are linked as well with the chronotope of the public square and with the trappings of the theater. All of this is of the highest importance for the novel. At last a form was found to portray the mode of existence of a man who is in life, but not of it, life's perpetual spy and reflector; at last specific forms had been found to reflect private life and make it public (We might add here that the making-public of specifically nonpublic spheres of life – for example, the sexual sphere – is one of the more ancient functions of the fool. Cf. Goethe's description of carnival.) (Bakhtin, *The Dialogic Imagination* 161)

For Bakhtin, then, the spying or snooping of Gide's *récits*, no less than their even more basic critical irony, would be part of the carnival inspiring the novel at its most basic.

In addition to the implications of the proposed unconventional readings for the *récits* as a corpus, there are important implications for the much slighted *Isabelle*, ones that call for special attention. To the extent that the *récits* hang together tightly, it makes a bit suspect the *idée reçue* regarding the alleged aberrance of *Isabelle*'s origins and artistic worth.

After an initial reception by the press that was mostly favorable (Lefebvre 208-09), *Isabelle* withered critically, due no doubt largely to Gide's own notorious dismissal of it as unsuccessful busy-work "fait... de l'extérieur."[3] In spite of Hytier's maintaining that it is a masterpiece to be compared with *L'Immoraliste, La Porte étroite,* and *La Symphonie pastorale* (Hytier 159), Lafille's disparagement of it as falling outside the usual Gidean inspiration and achievement (Lafille 51), echoing Gide's assessment, seems to have captured the sentiment prevailing beyond the world of dedicated Gideans: it has not even merited a section in the chapter on Gide in *A Critical Bibliography of French Literature: The Twentieth Century* (1979). But specialists continued to produce appreciative analyses like Hytier's, especially in the '70s, resulting recently in an entire collection of favorable studies published in the *Bulletin des Amis d'André Gide* (18, avril-juillet 1990).

The impetus of that positive trend can be strengthened if, in viewing *Isabelle* as another Gidean variation on the relayed narrative, we explore briefly how accessible its *histoire* is. Such an approach has the advantage of undermining the astonishingly widespread and un-Gide-like notion – prevalent even among specialists – that *Isabelle* shows Gérard moving from illusion to reality, that he recounts at his own ironic expense his passage from a romantic vision of a mysterious, attractive, angelic Isabelle to a more objective knowledge of her as she really is, to wit, a venal, repulsively selfish tart who is an open, murderous scandal for all with eyes to see and know. As if the author who found the world best defined as Schopenhauerian idea,[4] and who went on to write *Les Caves du Va-*

---

[3] Conceived outside the strictures of Gide's own highly subjective theory of literary creation, *Isabelle*, written in 1910 and published early the following year, was shortly thereafter dismissed by its author as "un intermède semi-badin entre deux oeuvres trop sérieuses" (*OC* VI, 471). Gide later expanded on this to Charles Du Bos:

> J'ai eu très jeune le sentiment d'avoir devant moi une série de volumes de papier blanc: mes oeuvres complètes. J'écris le tome VII ou le tome XII selon la longueur de la gestation ou le degré de perfection de mon métier. Il n'y a qu'un de mes livres qui ait été fait, pour ainsi dire de l'extérieur. C'est *Isabelle*. J'avais vu l'histoire du livre et je l'ai écrit un peu comme un exercice pour me faire la main. Cela se sent. (Du Bos, *Le Dialogue avec André Gide*, 163). (Anne Martin, 34)

[4] "Quand je lus *Le Monde comme Représentation* de Schopenhauer, je pensai aussitôt: c'est donc ça! Mais déjà certaine phrase de Flaubert m'avait donné l'éveil. Elle se trouve, je crois, dans la préface aux poésies de Bouilhet. Je me souviens de la révélation que ce fut pour moi lorsque Pierre Louÿs m'en donna lecture (nous étions encore en rhétorique). Ce sont des 'conseils' que Flaubert donne à un jeune homme qui se propose d'écrire. Il y dit (je ne réponds point de la citer exactement): 'Si le monde extérieur ne vous apparaît plus que comme une illusion pour la décrire...'" (Gide, *Journal*, I, 800-01).

*tican* and *Les Faux-Monnayeurs*, two novelistic versions of *Que sais-je?*, would or could have a simple lapse from his anguished sense of reality as anything other than the latest flawed story about it.

Notwithstanding the "given" of Gérard's coming to know, and his communicating to the reader, Isabelle's "true nature" (Anne L. Martin 39), there has been more than ample recognition that *Isabelle* underscores "the theme which runs through virtually all Gide's works: the conflict between art and reality" (Anne L. Martin 35). As the older Gérard himself makes clear and as all commentators observe, the younger "apprenti-romancier" (Davet and Thierry, in Gide, *Romans* 1561) first brought to la Quartfourche a perfervid Romantic imagination unsullied by any sense of the distinction between the literary and the real (*Isabelle*, in *Romans* 603). Critics such as Babcock understandably and insightfully go on to emphasize the appropriateness of *Isabelle*'s forefronting insistently the problematic of writing, present in a plethora of devices (the advice to Gérard in the opening pages about the necessary disorder and subjectivity of narrative, the role of mismanaged texts such as Isabelle's undelivered letter to her lover and the pledge prepared for Gérard by Casimir but signed by Casimir, etc.). To much the same effect, Cancalon has brought out how *Isabelle*'s great mix of narrative discourses and parodies (fairy tale, adventure story, detective story, etc.) "met certainement en relief la dominance du récit sur l'histoire" (Cancalon, "*Isabelle*: Oeuvre de transition" 203). Maisani-Léonard, taking a linguistic approach and pondering Gérard's extensive use of the *passé simple* even in conversation with the relayer and "Jammes" (and so *well after* his putative turn from misguided literary imaginings to objective perceptions), situates quite nicely the *whole* of Gérard's account: "N'est-ce pas nous indiquer que de toute façon on est en pleine convention; que le naturel, à partir du moment où l'on écrit, n'existe plus" (Maisani-Léonard, 54).

Given this fortissimo playing of the disparity between letters and life, are we to believe that Gérard's literary account will allow us to see him seeing Isabelle as she is in reality? Are we to ignore that Gérard's account and "knowledge" of Isabelle depended substantially on reports from others (others whose clearly caricatured portraits make us wonder if their comments too have not been caricatured)? Are we to pass over in quiet conventionality the sort of logical questions that a framed narrative can pose (e.g., even assuming Gérard could accurately recite verbatim to the narrator and

"Jammes" conversations and letters from years earlier, how accurately in turn could the narrator write them down from his memories of an hours-long conversation?) Is it mere semantic coincidence that at the time he first came to la Quartfourche, Gérard's occupation involved writing comments on comments about comments? (He came to Floche's library to observe and study, not *the* text par excellence, the Bible itself, but the notations found in Bossuet's copy of the Bible, that is, Bossuet's fragmentary, marginal commentaries on the Gospel that, as a matter of fact, comprises only an imperfectly consistent compendia either of Christ's comments – which themselves are occasionally comments on earlier Biblical comments – or comments such as Paul's on Christ's comments.) Is it symbolically indifferent that while he did get to jot down the marginalia, *the* living text of the West slipped away from him in an auction of which he had been unaware? Is it incidental to Gérard's habits of mind and his narrative undertaking that his account makes a point of Casimir's trying to copy out Santal's commentary on Averrhoes's commentary on Aristotle, whose Text, scholars tell us, probably consists of an uncertain mix of master's and disciples' texts?

If one assumes a negative answer to even a few of that string of rhetorical questions, it is warranted to ask if the frame itself gives rise to questions about its potential for distancing the very diegesis that it would pass along. Should it be read as conventionally transparent, or does it draw attention to itself, away from the relayed account? From the start the latter answer seems more appropriate: in the opening sentence Gide makes us stumble on convention, commingling fiction and life by vouchsafing one and perhaps two historical figures – Francis Jammes and a "je" (probably "Gide"?) – as *narrataires* of a story told by the imaginary Gérard Lacase. Alerted, then, we find it hard not to notice how the rest of the very opening sentence works its way into an almost strident Romantic tone: "Gérard Lacase, chez qui nous nous retrouvâmes au mois d'août 189., nous mena, Francis Jammes et moi, visiter le château de la Quartfourche dont il ne restera bientôt que des ruines, et son grand parc délaissé où l'été fastueux s'eployait à l'aventure" (*IS* 601). August, the 'august' end of an adventurous summer, on the grounds of a ruined, abandoned chateau: the Romantic impulses of the narrator were primed by this visit orchestrated by the no less Romantic Gérard. (Unless of course they were aroused only in retrospect, *af-*

*ter* having been exposed to Gérard's overheated reminiscences.) Will the narrator, we wonder from the start, be inclined perhaps to gilding the narrative lily that he is relaying to us? Is the flamboyant "où l'été fastueux s'éployait à l'aventure" not the harbinger of a no less flamboyantly aroused literary sensibility? The vocabulary and images of the rest of the opening paragraph certainly bespeak an unchecked eagerness to wring out responses to a whole gamut of stimuli promising *frissons romantiques*, ranging from mysteries hidden beyond barriers transgressed, through repeated reminders of natural forces gone wild, down to phallic hints of extravagant eroticism: "le fossé à demi comblé, la haie crevée,... la grille descellée," "l'herbe surabondante et folle," "le frais au creux des massifs éventrés," "quelque feuillage insolite, patient reste des anciennes cultures, presque étouffé déjà par les espèces plus communes," "tout ce que cette excessive opulence pouvait cacher d'abandon et de deuil," "le bruit de notre présence retentissait indécemment, nous effrayait presque," "entre les lames des contrevents un bignonia poussait d'énormes tiges blanches et molles," etc. (*IS* 601). But all of these *frissons* combine in a sense of rape of refinement, a sense that peaks in an image of almost embarrassing metaphorical obviousness: "C'est par un soupirail de la cave que, nous glissant comme des voleurs, nous entrâmes" (*IS* 601). The specular rape of Isabelle through the snooping stories is, then, amply foreshadowed (or more likely recalled, since it took place for the relayer and Gérard before the writing and our reading, that is, before we join in the snooping).

Rereading this first page – to read it the first time, before finishing the book, is of course to have read not even half of it – we careen between two responses to the narrative convention employed. Wanting to peep satisfyingly again at the fiction that follows it, that is, wanting to suspend disbelief, we accept that it is from "perfect memory" that the narrator is relaying "Gérard's" no less perfect account. But the frame is so patent in its robust literariness, that we are thrust back to speculation whether the less than controlled "je" may have contaminated the words coming from "Gérard's" already perfervid imagination, a possibility that makes harder the suspension of disbelief, a possibility that in turn reminds us that there is no contamination, that in *Isabelle* there is and has always been only the writer Gide. All this before leaving the first paragraph! If we want to believe, it will have to be in full awareness and intent of literary arbitrariness.

The rest of the opening frame further inclines us to the stance of hypothetical distance called for by these preliminary indications. There is, for instance, the narrator's quickness to speculate, and so to imply lack of hard knowledge, about Gérard's state of mind ("nous pensâmes qu'il préférait revoir seul ces lieux"; "[s]ans doute nous avait-il précédés"; "il me parut . . . et je me persuadai," *IS* 601-02). In addition, the "délices de nos veillées" (*IS* 602) provoked by "Jammes's" stories told in the twilight of the transitional evenings are of the sort that would appeal to the sensibilities flaunted by the narrator, a sure sign that we have here a story-telling trio in which documentary realism is not a high priority. Moreover, at the very beginning of his own personal *incipit*, Gérard – not privy to the distinction that Gide was soon to postulate between first-person *récit* and the "decentered" *roman* – brands his narrative as an imaginative extravaganza by characterizing it as a novel set in a theater (!!!) that he is (naturally in our eyes, by now) eager to tell (" – Je vous raconterai volontiers . . .," *IS* 602). From the rest of his opening sentence, we should realize that our chances of getting a reliable version of diegesis are slim indeed: Gérard admits to having had only a partial, disordered, enigma-charged understanding of the events involved in the first place (*IS* 602). Should we trust his relayer to trust him (or anyone else) to reconstruct "the truth" from such material? Alerted to the problem of who can be trusted to convey an accurate *histoire*, we find the closing words of the opening frame provocative in their reminder that all fictions talk, in the final analysis, about the author anyway, that is, the subjective, not about objective events and certainly not about other people:

>–Vous permettrez alors que je parle beaucoup de moi, dit Gérard.
>–Chacun de nous fait-il jamais rien d'autre! repartit Jammes (*IS* 603).

Consequently, Gide's concluding words for the frame are nothing less than impish: "C'est le récit de Gérard que voici" (*IS* 603).

It will be protested, nonetheless, that regardless of the most whimsical and even perverse distortion of events, Isabelle "really is" convincingly exposed through her indisputable actions, actions so unsavory as to reveal her basic qualities clearly enough even through the fog of an account hyperimaginatively remembered and relayed. Her deeds seem clear: she admitted to rejecting freedom out of fear, and effectively to having her lover assassinated; she abandoned her son and her family; she used emotional extortion to fund continued profligacy; and she ravaged a beautiful estate.

But is she "really" revealed? Why do readers approve of Gide's prodigal son who finally gave up freedom out of weariness and partially for material comfort, and why do they find "authentic" the Ménalque of *L'Immoraliste* who anguishes before each departure, although they view with disappointment Isabelle's anguish and change of heart about her departure with her lover? Why do we tend to approve the killer Lafcadio and condemn Isabelle? Why is the lamentably altruistic Richard of *Paludes* found laughable, why is the Thésée indifferent to his family ("C'est à moi-même que je me dois," *Thésée* 1429) found heroic, but the self-centered Isabelle abhorrent? Why is the sexual abandon of Ménalque in *Les Nourritures terrestres*[5] the hallmark of a liberator, and Isabelle's life that of a slut? Why finally does the estate devastated by Ménalque result in an "automne . . . splendide" (*NT* 191), and Isabelle's in frequent critical disapproval (even though Gérard's reaction is mixed, *IS* 663-66)?

One simple answer is of course point of view. Isabelle reaches us only after having been relayed through the interpretive stories of her parent's household, Gérard, and then "je." With those stories Isabelle is, like any person or character subjected to narrative, less revealed than judged. How would she have fared in our eyes if the prodigal son, or Ménalque, or Lafcadio had narrated her and her deeds?

But the chief optic belongs to Gérard, who is, at the all important time of the telling, a rather substantial property-holder. The possessor and the narrator being then one, there is no surprise in his assumption that the "real" alone has value, that he discovered "la réalité sous l'aspect" (*IS* 616) only after stripping away the poetic bunk that he claimed to have provided from his overwrought imagination. But in having assumed from the beginning that "the

---

[5] "Certains m'accusèrent d'égoïsme; je les accusai de sottise. J'avais la prétention de n'aimer point quelqu'un, homme ou femme, mais bien l'amitié, l'affection ou l'amour. En le donnant à l'un, je n'eusse pas voulu l'enlever à quelque autre, et ne faisais que me prêter. Pas plus je ne voulais accaparer le corps ou le coeur d'aucun autre; nomade ici comme envers la nature, je ne m'arrêtais nulle part. Toute préférence me semblait injustice; voulant rester à tous, je ne me donnais pas à quelqu'un" (*NT*, in *Romans* 188).

truth" was there to be discovered and possessed in the same way as Isabelle's portrait or letter, he shows that there had been no substantive evolution in his basic values, no movement from letters to life: he had been working all along with the values of the possessor, the property-holder. Smug in his pedestrian "pigeon-holing" (as his name Lacase suggests), oblivious to the object lesson presented by Floche's lamentable, disastrous heroism in the name of family and property, he failed to see how the selfish Isabelle could be like but unlike the regal "Isabelle" of history who is, in her name's evocation of a Hebrew etymon, "chaste" (Lefebvre 204), and like but unlike an "isabelle" – a cream-colored horse – whose body or reputation every man, like the *cocher* at the end, seemed to ride at will (or to return to the system of images underlying the relayer's opening paragraph, seemed to violate at will). Would a true *littérateur*, haunted by the compulsion to understand this enigmatic woman, have been insensitive to the paradoxical *auréole* summoned up by her family name, at once a halo and a stain invisible except as a trace, an absence? Would he have been as oblivious as Gérard was to the central issue of choice, an issue evoked forcefully by the very name of the place where the story takes place, "the Crossroads," and an issue that he himself recognized but shortsightedly applied only to his own circumstances ("La Quartfourche! je répétais ce nom mystérieux: c'est ici, pensais-je, qu'Hercule hésite . . . Je sais de reste ce qui l'attend sur le sentier de la vertu; mais l'autre route? . . . l'autre route . . .," *IS* 604). The "reality," then, to which Gérard allegedly awoke is no such thing, but only another, more deadeningly self-assured story. The only truth is an elusive story of Isabelle's trying unsuccessfully to break out into personal liberation. That liberation stands far from any likeness to the *illusions pathétiques, romanesques* of its various, more conventional literary incarnations. Rather, it is something fearsome, selfish, destructive – especially when abortive. It is also less simple and more deserving of reflection than Gérard, who imagines only in terms of clichés, can conceive. But, to return to the reason for this sally into *Isabelle*, the story of that liberation does provide another illustration of an *histoire* made inaccessible through relaying, and so an argument for *Isabelle*'s close ties to the other *récits* in its art.

At the time of composition Gide, of course, knew the torment of attempted but failed liberation only too well, since he started writing *Isabelle* after he reluctantly and dangerously accepted the advice of his horrified entourage not to continue his liberating but scandalous *Corydon* (Davet and Thierry, in Gide, *Romans* 1556-1557). So, far from having been, in its central concern, "fait ... de l'extérieur" as Gide would have had observers believe, *Isabelle* came, we may surmise, from one of his deepest personal struggles, and it provided him, as had the other *récits*, with a psychological laboratory in which to explore and repudiate a dangerous inclination within himself, in this case, postponed "departure." The completion and publication of *Corydon* show that he profited from the experiment. In the relationship of its origins and art to those of the other *récits*, therefore, *Isabelle* is not aberrant.

Having maintained the tight integrity of the *récits* in their formal relationships to each other, I would now like to propose that in the impacts of their forms they are also consistent with the rest of Gide's fictional oeuvre. An initial overview of all of Gide's fictions does, however, readily suggest how formally distinct his early work might seem to be from his first-person narratives. The question to be asked in light of the proposed readings of the *récits* is whether the distinction is more apparent than real:

> *More than* in the later *récits* where a classically conservative elegance *seems to* prevail with *relative* tranquillity, the early works bear witness to a tumultuous 'scene of writing' where the thrust towards stylistic purism is continually stymied by metacritical digressions and didactic interruptions. The overall effect of these deflationary conceits is to alert the reader to what might be called a 'negative writing,' a writing which challenges its own formal structures at every turn, a writing that chisels away at the reader's acceptance of a literary apparatus.... (Apter, 5; my emphasis)

This cautious, precise phrasing on the part of Emily Apter, insightful reappraiser of the early works, argues well for her accurate sense of all of Gide's production. Her interest and enthusiasm for the earlier works have not led her to tempting but facile distinctions between them and the *récits*. As we have seen, the narratological subversions of the latter do give evidence of "negative writing," admittedly with less tumult than the former. Conservative elegance may prevail in the *récits*, but only until rereading starts, and it is tranquil only relative to the overtly disorienting earlier texts. Substantial if understated ties do then exist between the former and the latter.

The matter is viewed differently by Monique Yaari in her signal contribution to a scrupulously precise understanding of the place of Gide and his *Paludes* in the vast field of modern irony (which she breaks down into *ironie paradoxale* and *ironie poétique*). She finds that:

> Les récits – ironiques selon Gide même, mais dans le sens de 'critiques' (presque satiriques) – n'illustrent l'ironie paradoxale que pris deux par deux, voir l'exemple célèbre de *L'Immoraliste* et *La Porte étroite*. Quant à l'ironie poétique, elle n'y joue pas un rôle important. (Monique Yaari 135)

While acknowledging her amply demonstrated expertise in this vast field, I would submit that the *récits* ought not to be so decisively sundered from the irony of the *soties*. Let us consider Yaari's definition of *ironie paradoxale*:

> C'est à eux [the Schlegel brothers, their friends and disciples] que l'on doit le concept d'ironie paradoxale (bien que l'expression elle-même ait tardé à venir pendant un siècle et demi environ), son lien avec le romantisme (ce qui pour eux signifiait, et dans un sens devrait encore signifier, 'modernisme'), son rapport avec le roman (un genre qu'ils ont aidé à faire éclore), enfin la formule, et en partie aussi son application, de l'ironie en tant que principe esthétique reflétant une certaine philosophie, mettant en question l'art aussi bien que la réalité, constituant le ressort et l'esprit même d'une oeuvre, et à ce but utilisant certains procédés stylistiques et structuraux qui aujourd'hui encore ne semblent pas avoir beaucoup vieilli. (Yaari 7)

The narrative strategies of the three *récits* that we saw pitting mimesis against its undoing, and leading to questions about the extent to which we can know ourselves and events outside of language, resonate harmoniously if less forcefully than *Paludes* with the interrogation of "l'art aussi bien que la réalité." And insofar as *ironie poétique* is concerned, we ought to consider the spirit behind its following qualities:

> Le terme d' "ironie poétique" qui, pour s'appliquer plus aisément à d'autres systèmes sémiotiques également, en dehors de celui du langage et de la littérature, pourrait prendre le nom d' "ironie artistique," se manifeste dans tous les arts par le jeu avec l'oeuvre, la mise en abyme, la parabase permanente, la rupture de l'illusion, la polysémie et la polyvalence, l'interaction entre les genres et entre les différents domaines artistiques. (Yaari 127)

The *récits* do share many of those qualities with *Paludes* (and by implication the other *soties*), especially the undermining of the narrative gambits which draws them powerfully into the essential spirit of "le jeu avec l'oeuvre" (and of course "la rupture de l'illusion").

The ironic process is far more subtle in the *récits* because, I propose, they are more subversive. Their realistic illusion attracts more easily the average reader (i.e., most of us most of the time) who, only upon reflection and rereading, realize that the illusion has to be given up, that we have fallen for it once again, that we will fall over and over again, and that we need to be reminded – over and over again – how we resist lessons about the prevaricating nature of language and about our will to illusion. In the early works and the *soties*, on the other hand, Gide flaunts the originary artificiality of fiction with no less subversive inspiration, but with far less subversive impact: the techniques (e.g., the flamboyantly literary, Symbolist allusions of *Le Voyage d'Urien*, the writing of the narrator's *Paludes* being a subject of Gide's *Paludes*, the arch use of myth in *Prométhée*, and interventions by the omniscient narrator in *Caves*) require, create even, already subverted readers who will be less likely than readers of the *récits* to feel any retrospective ache over the loss of a sustained, believable story, and so less likely to take to heart our susceptibility to signs. Or perhaps I am being too complex in trying to articulate the difference. Perhaps in the early self-conscious works and in the rollicking *soties* we tend either to philosophize abstractedly or to smile about what language does to us, whereas in the ethics-preoccupied *récits* we frown.

But ponder, smile, or frown, already converted or subverted, we are responding to essentially similar artistic practices. We can further contest the apparent differences between the *récits* and the early work by recalling how the narrative gambits of the former had the result of casting a knowledge of story into doubt. In the *soties*, Fillaudeau finds that same issue – systematically pursued, no less:

> On dirait que Gide en expérimentant trois approches très différentes de l'histoire [no story in *Paludes*, the same story repeated in *Prométhée*, a multiplicity of different stories in *Caves*] cherche à en éprouver la solidité, à vérifier son caractère irréductible. Peut-on réussir à mettre en déroute le lecteur et le garder, en se jouant de notions telles que l'histoire ou le personnage, en les déconstruisant? L'une des interrogations les plus tenaces de la littérature moderne est ainsi posée, "critique" et fiction sont-elles conciliables? Puisque Gide ne peut se débarrasser de l'histoire – au sens où un peintre non figuratif parvient à échapper au "réel" – Gide procédera de la même façon qu'avec ses personnages, en jouant avec elle, s'étant rendu compte, comme son Narrateur de *Paludes*, que l'histoire renaît perpétuellement de ses cendres: "chassez l'histoire, elle revient au galop". (Fillaudeau 102)

In the *récits*, once a reliable story of events was banished, what we saw "galloping back" was the story of writing.

My arguments are hardly the only ones calling for a critical repositioning of the narrative structures of the *récits* vis-à-vis those of the rest of the fictional oeuvre. Elaine Cancalon, for example, disputes any stark narratological difference between *La Porte étroite* and the more novelistic *Les Caves du Vatican* and *Les Faux-Monnayeurs*:

> Les premiers récits racontés à la première personne par le protagoniste, ont été souvent qualifiés de "linéaires," alors que *Les Caves du Vatican* sont construites sur une multiplication de focalisations ainsi que *Les Faux Monnayeurs* où il y a aussi au moins deux narrateurs qui se font entendre. Mais deux voix narratrices, ne les avons-nous pas déjà entendues dans un des premier récits justement? *La Porte étroite* n'est pas, après tout, si linéaire qu'il pourrait paraître, car le récit de Jérôme est complémenté par les lettres et le *Journal* d'Alissa. (Cancalon, "*La Porte étroite* ou le triomphe du métadiégétique" 69)

Much the same rectification is in order for *L'Immoraliste* and for *La Symphonie pastorale*. Concerning the former, we saw how the role of the anonymous friend as relayer of the story impacts on the telling of Michel's tale, so that the voice is not linear but framed, not single but double. Concerning the latter *récit*, the duplicity of the narrator makes his tale duplicitous too, that is, double, in that it is a mix of the Pastor's recollections and misrepresentations, a blending of a story and of his idealizing/self-serving evangelizing. In a sense, his narrative was destined to doubleness, because of its conflicted genesis in the tangled weave of his preoccupations *au temps du récit* (hostility toward Amélie and adulterous yearnings for the absent Gertrude) with the account of Gertrude's coming to language *au temps de l'histoire*.

It becomes possible, therefore, to reappraise Gide's insistence on the distinction between the multiple points of view of the novelistic *Caves* and *Faux-Monnayeurs*, and the single view of his "*récits*." [6] The difference is one to be reckoned with, to be sure, since the "novels" string together independent frames of reference. But a difference based on independent frames of fictional reference works out to be more superficial than profound, because – for instance – ultimately the novelistic frames of reference conjoin in the voice of the implied narrator, whereas the narrative gambits of the *récits* have the effect of leading the single voices into various doublings, and even triplings in the case of *Isabelle*. The dissimilarity appears even less stark when we recall that in *L'Immoraliste* and *La Porte étroite* the very possibility of a solitary voice also breaks down under the pressures of the forces of intertextuality.

Finally, the *récits* are best understood when grouped securely with the more experimental, self-reflexive works because their narrative structures mark them too as works of art characteristic of Gide, for whom, ". . . avant tout c'est l'art qui demeure l'enjeu essentiel, un art qui n'a de sens que s'il consent à être perpétuelle invention et remise en cause de tout et d'abord de lui-même" (Goulet, "Introduction" 12, in Fillaudeau).

Readers of the foregoing chapters will, I expect, recognize Gide's *récits* in a typical definition of postmodernism:

---

[6] "Pourquoi j'eus soin d'intituler 'récit' ce petit livre [*Isabelle*]? Simplement parce qu'il ne répond pas à l'idée que je me fais du roman; non plus que *La Porte étroite* ou que *L'Immoraliste*; et que je ne voudrais pas qu'on s'y trompât. Le roman, tel que je le reconnais ou l'imagine, comporte une diversité de points de vue, soumise à la diversité des personnages qu'il met en scène; c'est par essence une oeuvre déconcertée" (Gide, "Projet de préface pour *Isabelle*," in *Oeuvres Complètes*, VI, 361-62, cited by Davet and Thierry in Gide, *Romans* 1561).

> ... [postmodern] terms are used to describe a major (and usually a disturbing) shift away from modernity's universalizing and totalizing drive – a drive that was first fueled, in the seventeenth century, by Descartes's foundational ambitions and his faith in reason. Postmodernity's assertion of the value of inclusive 'both/and' thinking deliberately contests the exclusive 'either/or' binary oppositions of modernity. Postmodern paradox, ambiguity, irony, indeterminacy, and contingency are seen to replace modern closure, unity, order, the absolute, and the rational. (Natoli and Hutcheon ix)

But since my loosely deconstructive readings of Gide flowed out of my understanding both of earlier traditional and of recent less traditional scholarship, they corroborate Richard Rorty's suggestion that Derrida and Lacan – source of many of the principal critical moves in the pages above – may not have so much started a revolution, as to have demarked memorably and effectively another decisive shift in the never ending shifting of the terms of intellectual debate.

Gide, then, so compatible with a deconstructive approach and yet so securely rooted in the late nineteenth-century tension between mimetic Realism and anti-mimetic Symbolism, would be pre-postmodern – a wonderfully pre-post-erous notion – only because the pillars of postmodernism are widespread and set deep in our culture. Or, to reverse the chronological optic from retrospective in the present to prospective in the past, one could argue just as easily that Gide was to be an intellectual child of Schlegel, who was one of the first to articulate how Romantic irony shifted from modernist ideology:

> ... l'ironie romantique est avant tout une esthétique, assez relativiste pour envisager sa propre métamorphose, sans trace de doctrine, hostile seulement à la fossilisation et à la stagnation, qui se veut, et qui a été ou est, en perpétuel devenir. (Schlegel, *Athenaeum*, Aphorisme no. 116, in Yaari 101)

The most interesting paradox here is that, be he "pre-postmodern" or "a Romantic ironic," Gide exerted every effort in his conscious, relentless struggle to become uniquely himself, only to appear with time to have distilled himself and his work into a quintessential revelation of some truly vast cultural forces.

On the other hand, Gide may well have been a true pioneer, in the forefront of those honing the "critical edge" of postmodern awareness:

> Despite its inclusivity (or what some see as its complicity) [and what Gideans see as *disponibilité*], the critical edge of postmodernity's deconstructing of the modern universalizing tendency comes from its awareness of the value and significance of respecting difference and otherness. This awareness is brought about as much by sustained oppositional social activism of women, gays and lesbians, people of color, and formerly colonized nations as by the more abstract theorizing about power and the mobile field of force relations discussed by philosophers, political theorists, and cultural critics. (Natoli and Hutcheon x)

To the extent that his life's work did indeed help hone the "critical edge," we can be sure it owed much to his birth into two-fold "difference and otherness," itself riven: first into a Protestant minority in a country where the "protesting" was an active, defining role of the greatest seriousness, and second, as a "sinful" homosexual into a devout Protestant milieu relentless in its opposition to the flesh. So the aesthetic and critical *disponibilité* argued for throughout all of the preceding pages would join Gide the man in an inclusive difference and otherness that some of our vaster cultural tendencies are striving toward.

# WORKS CITED

## BOOKS BY ANDRÉ GIDE

Gide, André. *Les Cahiers et les Poésies d'André Walter.* 7th ed. Paris: Gallimard, 1952.
———. *Correspondance André Gide François-Paul Alibert 1907-1950.* Ed. Claude Martin. Lyon: Presses Universitaires de Lyon. 1982.
———. *Journal, 1889-1939.* 2 vols. Bibliothèque de la Pléiade. Paris: Gallimard, 1948 and 1954.
———. *Oeuvres complètes d'André Gide.* Ed. L. Martin-Chauffier. 15 vols. Paris: Nouvelle Revue Française, 1932-1939.
———. *La Porte étroite.* Editions Folio. Paris: Mercure de France, 1959.
———. *Romans, récits, soties, oeuvres lyriques.* Ed. Yvonne Davet et Jean-Jacques Thierry. Bibliothèque de la Pléiade. Paris: Gallimard, 1958.
———. *La Symphonie pastorale.* Ed. Claude Martin. Paris: Minard, 1970.

## BOOKS ON GIDE

Angelet, Christian. *Symbolisme et invention formelle dans les premiers écrits d'André Gide.* Ghent, Belgium: Romanica Gandensia, 1982.
Apter, Emily. *André Gide and The Codes of Homotextuality.* Saratoga, California: Anma Libri, 1987.
Babcock, Arthur E. *Portraits of Artists: Reflexivity in Gidean Fiction, 1902-1946.* York, South Carolina: French Literature Publications Company, 1982.
Brée, Germaine. *André Gide l'insaisissable Protée.* Paris: Société d'Édition "Les Belles Lettres", 1953.
Cancalon, Elaine. *Techniques et personnages dans les récits d'André Gide.* Archives des Lettres Modernes, no. 117. Paris: Minard, 1970.
Cunningham, Joyce I. and W. D. Wilson. *A Concordance of André Gide's* **La Symphonie pastorale**. New York: Garland Publishers, 1978.
Davies, J.C. *Gide:* **L'Immoraliste** *and* **La Porte Etroite**. London: Edward Arnold, 1968.
Delay, Jean. *La Jeunesse d'André Gide.* 2 vols. Paris: Gallimard, 1956 and 1957.
Du Bos, Charles. *Le Dialogue avec André Gide.* Paris: Sans Pareil: 1929.
Fillaudeau, Bertrand. *L'Univers ludique d'André Gide: les soties.* Paris: Corti, 1985.
Fortier, Paul A. *Décor et Dualisme*: **L'Immoraliste** *d'André Gide.* Saratoga, California: Anma Libri, 1988.
Freyburger, Henri. *L'Évolution de la disponibilité gidienne.* Paris: Nizet, 1970.
Guérard, Albert J. *André Gide.* New York: E. P. Dutton and Co., 1963.
Holdheim, W. Wolfgang. *Theory and Practice of the Novel: A Study on André Gide.* Geneva: Droz, 1968.

Hytier, Jean. *André Gide*. Paris: Edmond Charlot, 1945.
Ireland, G. W. *André Gide: A Study of his Creative Writings*. Oxford: Clarendon Press, 1970.
Lafille, Pierre. *André Gide romancier*. Paris: Hachette, 1954.
Lévy, Zvi H. *Jérôme* **Agonistes**: *les structures dramatiques et les procédures narratives de* **La Porte étroite**. Paris: A.-G. Nizet, 1984.
Maillet, Henri. **La Symphonie pastorale** *d'André Gide. Lire Aujourd'hui* Series. Paris: Hachette,1975.
Maisani-Léonard, Martine. *André Gide ou l'ironie de l'écriture*. Montréal: Presses de l'Université de Montréal, 1976.
Martin, Claude. Introduction. *La Symphonie pastorale*. By André Gide. Paris: Minard, 1970. xi-clv.
Oliver, Andrew. *Michel, Job, Pierre, Paul: intertextualité de la lecture dans* l'**Immoraliste** *de Gide*. Paris: Lettres Modernes, 1979.
Perry, Kenneth I. *The Religious Symbolism of André Gide*. The Hague: Mouton, 1969.
Pruner, Francis. **La Symphonie pastorale** *de Gide: de la tragédie vécue à la tragédie écrite*. Archives des Lettres Modernes, no. 54. Paris: Minard, 1964.
Trahard, Pierre. **La Porte étroite** *d'André Gide*. Paris: Editions de la Pensée Moderne, 1966.
Walker, David H. *André Gide*. Hong Kong: Macmillan Education, 1990.
———. **Les Nourritures terrestres** *and* **La Symphonie pastorale**. London: Grant and Cutter, 1990.
Wilson, W. D. *André Gide*: **La Symphonie pastorale**. Glasgow: Macmillan, 1971.
Yaari, Monique. *Ironie paradoxale et Ironie poétique: vers une théorie de l'ironie moderne sur les traces de Gide dans* **Paludes**. Birmingham, Alabama: Summa Publications, 1988.

BOOKS WITH SECTIONS ON GIDE

Alter, Robert. *Partial Magic: The Novel as a Self-Conscious Genre*. Berkeley: University of California Press, 1975.
Brosman, Catharine Savage. "'Le Peu de réalité': Gide et le moi." *André Gide 9*: **Corydon, Si le grain ne meurt, Les Faux-monnayeurs**: *Regards Intertextuels*. Actes du Colloque international organisé par l'Association des Amis d'André Gide les 12, 13, et 14 janvier 1984 à Paris. Paris: Lettres Modernes, 1991. 29-46. (See also Savage, Catharine.)
Dällenbach, Lucien. *Le Récit spéculaire*. Paris: Seuil, 1977.
Goulet, Alain. "Narcisse au travail dans l'oeuvre d'André Gide." *Le Plaisir de l'intertexte*. Ed. Raimund Theis and Hans T. Siepe. Actes du Colloque à l'Université de Duisburg, 1985. Frankfurt am Main: Peter Lang, 1986. 185-208.
Martens, Lorna. *The Diary Novel*. New York: Cambridge University Press, 1985.
Pasco, Allan H. *Novel configurations: A Study of French Fiction*. Birmingham, Alabama: Summa Publications, 1987. The chapter dealing with *L'Immoraliste* is an extension of his article, "Irony and Art in *L'Immoraliste*," below.
Thibaudet, Albert. *Réflexions sur le roman*. Paris: Gallimard, 1938.
Ullmann, Stephen. *The Image in the Modern French Novel*. New York: Barnes and Noble, 1963.

## RELATED BOOKS

Adams, Hazard and Leroy Searle. *Critical Theory Since 1965.* Tallahassee, Florida: Florida State University Press, 1986.

Babcock, Barbara A. "'Liberty's a Whore': Inversions, Marginalia, and Picaresque Narrative." *The Reversible World: Symbolic Inversion in Art and Society.* Ed. Barbara A. Babcock. Ithaca, New York: Cornell University Press, 1978. 95-116.

Bakhtin, Mikhail. *The Dialogic Imagination: Four Essays by M. M. Bakhtin.* Trans. Caryl Emerson and Michael Holquist. Ed. Michael Holquist. Austin: The University of Texas Press, 1981.

———. *Speech Genres and Other Late Essays.* Trans. Vern W. McGee. Ed. Caryl Emerson and Michael Holquist. Austin: The University of Texas Press, 1986.

Barthes, Roland. "Analyse textuelle d'un conte d'Edgar Poe." *Sémiotique narrative et textuelle.* Ed. Claude Chabrol. Paris: Larousse, 1973. 29-54.

———. *S/Z.* Paris: Editions du Seuil, 1970.

Booth, Wayne. *The Rhetoric of Fiction.* Chicago: The University of Chicago Press, 1961.

Butor, Michel. *Répertoire II.* Paris: Editions de Minuit, 1964.

Compagnon, Antoine. *La Seconde Main.* Paris: Editions du Seuil, 1979.

Culler, Jonathan. *On Deconstruction: Theory and Criticism after Structuralism.* Ithaca, New York: Cornell University Press, 1982.

Davis, Robert Murray. Introduction. *The Novel: Modern Essays in Criticism.* Ed. Robert Murray Davis. Englewood Cliffs, New Jersey: Prentice-Hall, 1969. ix-xii.

Derrida, Jacques. *De la grammatologie.* Paris: Editions de Minuit, 1967.

———. *L'Écriture et la différence.* Paris: Editions du Seuil, 1967.

———, et al. *Théorie d'ensemble.* Paris: Editions du Seuil, 1968.

Dickens, Charles. *Christmas Stories.* Philadelphia: T. B. Peterson, n. d.

Elliot, Robert C. *The Literary Persona.* Chicago: The University of Chicago Press, 1982.

El Saffar, Ruth. "Coughing in Ink and Literary Coffins." *Approaches to Teaching Cervantes' Don Quixote.* Ed. Richard Bjornson. New York: PMLA, 1984. 50-55.

Freud, Sigmund. *Collected Papers.* Vol. 3. Trans. Alix and James Strachey. London: The Hogarth Press, 1953. 5 vols.

Genette, Gérard. *Figures III.* Paris: Editions du Seuil, 1972.

———. *Palimpsestes.* Paris: Editions du Seuil, 1982.

Guillen, Claudio. *Literature as System: Essay toward a Theory of Literary History.* Princeton: Princeton University Press, 1971.

Hazard, Paul. *La Crise de la conscience européenne.* Vol. 1. Paris: Gallimard, 1961. 2 vols.

Hjort, Meete, ed. *Rules and Conventions.* Baltimore: The John Hopkins University Press, 1992.

Hume, David. *A Treatise on Human Nature.* London: J. M. Dent & Sons, 1949.

Jameson, Frederic. *The Prison House of Language: A Critical Account of Structuralism and Russian Formalism.* Princeton: Princeton University Press, 1972.

Kristeva, Julia. *Desire in Language.* Trans. T. Gora, A. Jardine, and L. Roudiez. Ed. L. Roudiez. New York: Columbia University Press, 1980.

Lacan, Jacques. *Ecrits I.* Paris: Editions du Seuil, 1966.

Lodge, David. *The Novelist at the Crossroads and Other Essays on Fiction and Criticism.* Ithaca, New York: Cornell University Press, 1971.

May, Georges. *Le Dilemme du roman au XVIIIe siècle: étude sur les rapports du roman et de la critique (1715-1761).* Paris: Presses Universitaires de France, 1963.

Montaigne, Michel. *Oeuvres complètes*. Bibliothèque de la Pléiade. Paris: Gallimard, 1962.
Morson, Gary Saul and Caryl Emerson. *Mikhail Bakhtin: Creation of a Prosaics*. Stanford, California: Stanford University Press, 1990.
Natoli, Joseph and Linda Hutcheon, eds. *A Postmodern Reader*. Albany: State University of New York Press, 1993.
Plato, *The Collected Dialogues*. Ed. Edith Hamilton and Huntington Cairns. Bollingen Foundation. New York: Random House, 1961.
Riggan, William. *Pícaros, Madmen, Naïfs, and Clowns: The Unreliable First-Person Narrator*. Norman, Oklahoma: University of Oklahoma Press, 1981.
Rigolot, François. *Poétique et onomastique*. Genève: Droz, 1977.
Rorty, Richard. *Essays on Heidegger and Others. Philosophical Papers*. Vol. 2. Cambridge: Cambridge University Press, 1991.
Rousseau, Jean-Jacques. *Les Confessions*. Ed. Jacques Voisine. Paris: Garnier, 1964.
Rousset, Jean. *Narcisse romancier: essai sur la première personne dans le roman*. Paris: José Corti, 1986.
Showalter, English Jr. *The Evolution of the French Novel 1641-1782*. Princeton, New Jersey: Princeton University Press, 1972.
Silhol, Robert. "'Me Jane, You Tarzan': On Meaning." *Compromise Formations: Current Directions in Psycholanalytic Criticism*. Ed. Vera J. Camden. Kent, Ohio: Kent State University Press, 1989. 1-14.
Stanzel, F. K. *A Theory of Narrative*. Trans. Charlotte Goedsche. Cambridge: Cambridge University Press, 1984.
Steiner, George. *After Babel: Aspects of Language and Translation*. London: Oxford University Press, 1975.
Stonehill, Brian. *The Self-Conscious Novel: Artifice in Fiction from Joyce to Pynchon*. Philadelphia: University of Pennsylvania Press, 1988.
Uspenski, Boris. *A Poetics of Composition*. Trans. Valentina Zovarin and Susan Wittig. Berkely: University of California Press, 1973.
Walker, David H. "L'Écriture et le réel dans les fictions d'André Gide." *Roman, réalités, réalismes*. Ed. Jean Bessière. Paris: Presses Universitaires de France, 1989. 121-36.
Watt, Ian. *The Rise of the Novel: Studies in Defoe, Richardson and Fielding*. Berkeley: University of California Press, 1957.
Wellek, René, and Austin Warren. *Theory of Literature*. New York: Harcourt, Brace and World, 1956.
Wicks, Ulrich. *Picaresque Narrative, Picaresque Fictions: A Theory and Research Guide*. Westport, Connecticut: Greenwood, 1989.

## ARTICLES ON GIDE'S RÉCITS

Adam, Antoine. "Quelques années dans la vie d'André Gide." *Revue des Sciences Humaines* 67 (1952): 247-72.
Babcock, Arthur E. "*La Symphonie pastorale* as Self-Conscious Fiction." *French Forum* 3 (1978): 65-71.
Bonheim, Jean and Helmut. "Structure and Symbolism in Gide's 'La Porte étroite'." *The French Review* 31 (1958): 487-97.
Booker, John T. "The Generic Ambiguity of Gide's *La Symphonie Pastorale*: Reading the Pastor's First *Cahier*." *Symposium* 40 (1986): 159-71.
―――. "*The Immoralist* and the Rhetoric of First-Person Narration." *Studies in Twentieth-Century Literature* 2.1 (1977): 5-22.

Cameron, Keith. "Gide, Jérôme et Saint Jérôme." *Bulletin des Amis d'André Gide*, 6 (1978): 58-66.
Cancalon, Elaine. "Création et destruction dans les récits d'André Gide." *Revue des Lettres Modernes* 547-53 (1979): 81-90.
―――. "*Isabelle*: oeuvre de transition." *Australian Journal of French Studies* 24 (1987): 193-204.
―――. "*La Porte étroite*: ou le triomphe du métadiégétique." *French Literature Series* 17 (1990): 69-78.
Chambers, Leland H. "Gide's Fictional Journals." *Criticism* 10 (1968): 300-10.
Chang, Sheng-Tai. "Generic Conflict and Psychic Battle in André Gide's *La Symphonie pastorale*." *Pacific Coast Philology* 25.1-2 (1990): 69-76.
Cruickshank, John. "A Note on Gide's *Symphonie Pastorale*." *The Modern Language Review* 49 (1954): 475-78.
―――. "Gide's Treatment of Time in *La Symphonie Pastorale*." *Essays in Criticism* 7 (1957): 134-43.
Décaudin, Michel. "Sur trois récits d'André Gide." *L'Information Littéraire* 16 (1964): 130-37.
Eisenger, Erica M. "The Hidden Eye: Clandestine Observation in Gide's *La Porte Etroite*." *Kentucky Romance Quarterly* 24 (1977): 221-29.
Freedman, Ralph. "Imagination and Form in André Gide: *La Porte étroite* and *La Symphonie pastorale*." *Accent* 17 (1957): 217-28.
Goodhand, Robert. "The Religious Leitmotif in *L'Immoraliste*." *Romanic Review* 57, (1966): 263-76.
Goulet, Alain. "La Figuration du procès littéraire dans l'écriture de *La Symphonie pastorale*." *Revue des Lettres Modernes* 331-3 (1972): 27-55.
―――. "L'Ironie pastorale en jeu." *Bulletin des Amis d'André Gide* 16 (1988): 41-57.
―――. Review of *Jérôme* **Agonistes**, by Zvi H. Lévy. *Revue d'Histoire Littéraire de la France* 87 (1987): 334.
Greenberg, Herbert. "Time Discrepancies and Gide's Impatience: A Note on the Composition of *La Symphonie Pastorale*." *Romance Notes* 4.2 (1963): 102-6.
Greene, Robert W. "Fading (Sacred) Texts and Dying (Guiding) Voices in Gide's Early *Récits*." *French Forum* 12.1 (1987): 75-91.
Harvey, Laurence E. "The Utopia of Blindness in Gide's *Symphonie Pastorale*." *Modern Philology* 55.3 (1958): 188-97.
Helbo, André. "Le code et la vision héroïque dans *La Porte étroite*." *Degrés* 6 (avril, 1974): e1-e5.
Henry, Freeman G. "*La Symphonie pastorale* Revisited." *Bulletin of the Rocky Mountain Modern Languages Association* 24 (1970), 15-23.
Heuvel, Pierre van den. "Révélation d'un discours mensonger: les déictiques temporels dans *La Symphonie pastorale* d'André Gide." *Neophilologus* 72 (1988): 366-75.
Horn, Pierre. "*Isabelle*: A Detective Novel by André Gide." *Romance Notes* 18 (1977): 54-61.
Hunt, Tony. "Alissa-Eloissa." *Orbis Litterarum* 33 (1978): 183-90.
Ireland, G. W. "Le Jeu des 'je' dans deux récits gidiens." *Revue de Littérature Moderne* 547-553 (1979): 69-80.
Kadish, Doris. "'Alissa Dans la Vallée': Intertextual Echoes of Balzac in Two Novels by Gide." *French Forum* 10.1 (1985): 67-83.
―――. "Meaning in *L'Immoraliste* and *La Symphonie pastorale*. *Kentucky Romance Quarterly* 32 (1985): 382-91.
Kapetanović, Miodrag. "L'*Ouverture*, et la disponibilité gidienne." *Degrés* 1 (janvier, 1973): m1-m9.

Keypour, David. "Le Journal fictif dans l'oeuvre d'André Gide." *Bulletin des Amis d'André Gide* 17 (1989): 217-24.
Kingcaid, Renée A. "Retreat from Discovery: Symbol and Sign in *La Symphonie pastorale.*" *Perspectives on Contemporary Literature* 8 (1982): 34-41.
Knecht, Loring. D. "A New Reading of Gide's *La Porte Etroite.*" *PMLA* 82 (1967): 640-48.
Lachasse, Pierre. "Le Point de vue esthéthique." *Bulletin des Amis d'André Gide* 16 (1988): 87-106.
Lefebvre, Jean. "Etat présent des études sur *Isabelle.*" *Bulletin des Amis d'André Gide* 18 (1990): 201-23.
Lioure, Michel. "Le Journal d'Alissa dans *La Porte étroite.*" *L'Information Littéraire* 16 (1964): 39-45.
Mahieu, Raymond. "*La Symphonie pastorale* et la lutte des tropes." *Bulletin des Amis d'André Gide* 16 (1988): 58-70.
Martin, Anne L. "*Isabelle*, or André Gide at the Crossroads." *Essays in French Literature* 14 (1977): 34-47.
Marty, Eric. "A propos de *La Porte étroite*, répétition et remémoration: *Le Nouvel Abailard.*" *Revue des Sciences Humaines* 70 (1985): 79-105.
Masson, Pierre. "La Porte ouverte ou voyages et voyageurs dans *La Porte étroite*". *Bulletin des Amis d'André Gide*, 45 (1980): 5-51.
Mistacco, Vicki. "Reading *The Immoralist*: The Relevance of Narrative Roles." *Bucknell Review* 26.2 (1981): 64-74.
Moore, W. G. "André Gide's *Symphonie Pastorale.*" *French Studies* 4 (1950): 16-26.
Nelson, Roy Jay. "Gidean Causality: *L'Immoraliste* and *La Porte étroite.*" *Symposium* 31 (1977): 43-58.
Parnell, Charles. "André Gide and his *Symphonie Pastorale.*" *Yale French Studies* 7 (1951): 60-71.
Pasco, Allan H. "Irony and Art in *L'Immoraliste.*" *Romanic Review* 64 (1973): 184-203.
―――― and Wilfred J. Rollman. "The Artistry of Gide's Onomastics." *Modern Language Notes* 86 (1971): 523-31.
Porter, Laurence. "The Generativity Crisis of Gide's *L'Immoraliste.*" *French Forum* 2 (1977): 58-69.
Sartre, Jean-Paul. "Gide vivant." *Les Temps Modernes* 65 (1951): 1537-41.
Savage, Catharine H. "*L'Immoraliste*: Psychology and Rhetoric." *Xavier University Studies*, 6 (1967): 43-62. (See also Brosman, Catherine Savage.)
Shorley, Christopher. "On the Way to the Summit: Narrative Modes in *La Porte étroite.*" *Nottingham French Studies* 22.2 (1983): 20-31.
Sonnenfeld, Albert. "Baudelaire et Gide: *La Porte étroite.*" *La Table Ronde* 232 (1967): 79-90.
――――. "On Readers and Reading in *La Porte étroite* and *L'Immoraliste.*" *Romanic Review* 67 (1976): 172-86.
――――. "*Strait is the Gate*: Byroads in Gide's Labyrinth." *Novel*, 1 (1968): 118-32.
Spacagna, Antoine. "La parole et La Parole dans *La Symphonie pastorale.*" *Bulletin des Amis d'André Gide* 15 (1987): 17-26.
Steel, David. "Gide et Freud." *Revue d'Histoire Littéraire* 77 (1977): 48-74.
Strauss, George. "Cécité et aveuglement." *La Revue des Lettres Modernes* 280-288 (1972): 89-104.
Tilby, Michael. Review of *Jérôme* **Agonistes**, by Zvi H. Lévy. *French Studies* 40 (1986): 352.
Vandendriessche, Christian. "Structure d'un récit gidien: le journal d'Alissa dans *La Porte étroite.*" *Revue des Sciences Humaines* 137 (1970): 107-17.

Walker, David H. Review of *Jérôme Agonistes*, by Zvi H. Lévy. *Modern Language Review* 81.1 (1986): 212-13.

Wégimont, Marie. "Description du jardin de Fongueusemare dans *La Porte étroite*: structure, signification et distanciation." *Nottingham French Studies* 26.2 (1987): 46-51.

RELATED ARTICLES

Angenot, Marc. "L'Intertextualité: enquête sur l'émergence et la diffusion d'un champ notionnel." *La Revue des Sciences Humaines* 60 (1983): 121-35.

Barthes, Roland. "Introduction à l'analyse structurale des récits." *Communications* 8 (1966): 1-27.

"La Bible." *La Grande Encyclopédie*. Paris: H. Lamirault et Cie, 1886-1902.

Feyerabend, Paul. "Atoms and Consciousness." *Common Knowledge* 1 (92): 28-32.

Fido, Franco. "At the Origins of Autobiography in the 18th and 19th Centuries: The *Topoi* of the Self." *Annali d'Italianistica* 4 (1986): 168-80.

Gabriel, Gottfried. "Fiction – a Semantic Approach." *Poetics* 8 (1979): 245-55.

"Jérôme." *La Grande Encyclopédie*. Paris: H. Lamirault et Cie, 1886-1902.

Raoul, Valérie. "Discours du 'je' féminin imaginaire: les femmes intimistes dans le roman français." *Atlantis* 10.2 (1985): 66-73.

Riffaterre, Michael. "La Trace de l'intertexte." *La Pensée* 215 (1980): 4-18.

Wall, Anthony. "Le problème du mensonge en littérature: *Le Bavard*, de Louis-René des Forêts." *Recherches Sémiotiques* 3 (1983): 262-76.

# NORTH CAROLINA STUDIES IN THE ROMANCE LANGUAGES AND LITERATURES

*I.S.B.N. Prefix 0-8078-*

## Recent Titles

THE POETRY OF CHANGE: A STUDY OF THE SURREALIST WORKS OF BENJAMIN PÉRET, by Julia Field Costich. 1979. (No. 206). *-9206-8.*

NARRATIVE PERSPECTIVE IN THE POST-CIVIL WAR NOVELS OF FRANCISCO AYALA "MUERTES DE PERRO" AND "EL FONDO DEL VASO", by Maryellen Bieder. 1979. (No. 207). *-9207-6.*

RABELAIS: HOMO LOGOS, by Alice Fiola Berry. 1979. (No. 208). *-9208-4.*

"DUEÑAS" AND DONCELLAS": A STUDY OF THE DOÑA RODRÍGUEZ EPISODE IN "DON QUIJOTE", by Conchita Herdman Marianella. 1979. (No. 209). *-9209-2.*

PIERRE BOAISTUAU'S "HISTOIRES TRAGIQUES": A STUDY OF NARRATIVE FORM AND TRAGIC VISION, by Richard A. Carr. 1979. (No. 210). *-9210-6.*

REALITY AND EXPRESSION IN THE POETRY OF CARLOS PELLICER, by George Melnykovich. 1979. (No. 211). *-9211-4.*

MEDIEVAL MAN, HIS UNDERSTANDING OF HIMSELF, HIS SOCIETY, AND THE WORLD, by Urban T. Holmes, Jr. 1980. (No. 212). *-9212-2.*

MÉMOIRES SUR LA LIBRAIRIE ET SUR LA LIBERTÉ DE LA PRESSE, introduction and notes by Graham E. Rodmell. 1979. (No. 213). *-9213-0.*

THE FICTIONS OF THE SELF. THE EARLY WORKS OF MAURICE BARRES, by Gordon Shenton. 1979. (No. 214). *-9214-9.*

CECCO ANGIOLIERI. A STUDY, by Gifford P. Orwen. 1979. (No. 215). *-9215-7*

THE INSTRUCTIONS OF SAINT LOUIS: A CRITICAL TEXT, by David O'Connell. 1979. (No. 216). *-9216-5.*

ARTFUL ELOQUENCE, JEAN LEMAIRE DE BELGES AND THE RHETORICAL TRADITION, by Michael F. O. Jenkins. 1980. (No. 217). *-9217-3.*

A CONCORDANCE TO MARIVAUX'S COMEDIES IN PROSE, edited by Donald C. Spinelli. 1979. (No. 218). 4 volumes, *-9218-1* (set), *-9219-X* (v. 1), *-9220-3* (v. 2); *-9221-1* (v. 3); *-9222-X* (v. 4).

ABYSMAL GAMES IN THE NOVELS OF SAMUEL BECKETT, by Angela B. Moorjani. 1982. (No. 219). *-9223-8.*

GERMAIN NOUVEAU DIT HUMILIS: ÉTUDE BIOGRAPHIQUE, par Alexandre L. Amprimoz. 1983. (No. 220). *-9224-6*

THE "VIE DE SAINT ALEXIS" IN THE TWELFTH AND THIRTEENTH CENTURIES: AN EDITION AND COMMENTARY, by Alison Goddard Elliot. 1983. (No. 221). *-9225-4.*

THE BROKEN ANGEL MYTH AND METHOD IN VALÉRY, by Ursula Franklin. 1984. (No. 222). *-9226-2.*

READING VOLTAIRE'S CONTES: A SEMIOTICS OF PHILOSOPHICAL NARRATION, by Carol Sherman. 1985. (No. 223). *-9227-0.*

THE STATUS OF THE READING SUBJECT IN THE "LIBRO DE BUEN AMOR", by Marina Scordilis Brownlee. 1985. (No. 224). *-9228-9.*

MARTORELL'S TIRANT LO BLANCH: A PROGRAM FOR MILITARY AND SOCIAL REFORM IN FIFTEENTH-CENTURY CHRISTENDOM, by Edward T. Aylward. 1985. (No. 225). *-9229- 7*

NOVEL LIVES: THE FICTIONAL AUTOBIOGRAPHIES OF GUILLERMO CABRERA INFANTE AND MARIO VARGAS LLOSA, by Rosemary Geisdorfer Feal. 1986. (No. 226). *-9230-0.*

SOCIAL REALISM IN THE ARGENTINE NARRATIVE, by David William Foster. 1986. (No. 227). *-9231-9.*

HALF-TOLD TALES: DILEMMAS OF MEANING IN THREE FRENCH NOVELS, by Philip Stewart. 1987. (No. 228). *-9232-7.*

POLITIQUES DE L'ECRITURE BATAILLE/DERRIDA: le sens du sacré dans la pensée française du surréalisme à nos jours, par Jean-Michel Heimonet. 1987. (No. 229). *-9233-5*

---

When ordering please cite the *ISBN Prefix* plus the last four digits for each title.

Send orders to: University of North Carolina Press
P.O. Box 2288
CB# 6215
Chapel Hill, NC 27515-2288
U.S.A.

# NORTH CAROLINA STUDIES IN THE ROMANCE LANGUAGES AND LITERATURES

*I.S B N. Prefix 0-8078-*

## Recent Titles

GOD, THE QUEST, THE HERO: THEMATIC STRUCTURES IN BECKETT'S FICTION, by Laura Barge. 1988. (No. 230). *-9235-1*
THE NAME GAME. WRITING/FADING WRITER IN "DE DONDE SON LOS CANTANTES", by Oscar Montero. 1988. (No. 231). *-9236-X*.
GIL VICENTE AND THE DEVELOPMENT OF THE COMEDIA, by René Pedro Garay. 1988. (No. 232). *-9234-3*
HACIA UNA POÉTICA DEL RELATO DIDÁCTICO: OCHO ESTUDIOS SOBRE "EL CONDE LUCANOR", por Aníbal A. Biglieri. 1989. (No. 233). *-9237-8.*
A POETICS OF ART CRITICISM: THE CASE OF BAUDELAIRE, by Timothy Raser. 1989. (No. 234). *-9238-6*
UMA CONCORDÃNCIA DO ROMANCE "GRANDE SERTÃO: VEREDAS" DE JOÃO GUIMARÃES ROSA, by Myriam Ramsey and Paul Dixon. 1989. (No. 235). Microfiche, *-9239-4*.
CYCLOPEAN SONG: MELANCHOLY AND AESTHETICISM IN GÓNGORA S "FÁBULA DE POLIFEMO Y GALATEA", by Kathleen Hunt Dolan. 1990. (No. 236). *-9240-8*
THE "SYNTHESIS" NOVEL IN LATIN AMERICA. A STUDY ON JOÃO GUIMARÃES ROSA'S "GRANDE SERTÃO: VEREDAS", by Eduardo de Faria Coutinho. 1991. (No. 237). *-9241-6.*
IMPERMANENT STRUCTURES. SEMIOTIC READINGS OF NELSON RODRIGUES' "VESTIDO DE NOIVA", "ÁLBUM DE FAMÍLIA", AND "ANJO NEGRO", by Fred M. Clark. 1991. (No. 238). *-9242-4.*
"EL ÁNGEL DEL HOGAR". GALDÓS AND THE IDEOLOGY OF DOMESTICITY IN SPAIN, by Bridget A. Aldaraca. 1991. (No. 239). *-9243-2*
IN THE PRESENCE OF MYSTERY: MODERNIST FICTION AND THE OCCULT, by Howard M. Fraser. 1992. (No. 240). *-9244-0.*
THE NOBLE MERCHANT: PROBLEMS OF GENRE AND LINEAGE IN "HERVIS DE MES", by Catherine M. Jones. 1993. (No. 241). *-9245-9.*
JORGE LUIS BORGES AND HIS PREDECESSORS OR NOTES TOWARDS A MATERIALIST HISTORY OF LINGUISTIC IDEALISM, by Malcolm K. Read. 1993. (No. 242). *-9246-7.*
DISCOVERING THE COMIC IN "DON QUIXOTE", by Laura J. Gorfkle. 1993. (No. 243). *-9247-5.*
THE ARCHITECTURE OF IMAGERY IN ALBERTO MORAVIA'S FICTION, by Janice M. Kozma. 1993. (No. 244). *-9248-3*
THE "LIBRO DE ALEXANDRE". MEDIEVAL EPIC AND SILVER LATIN, by Charles F. Fraker. 1993. (No. 245). *-9249-1*
THE ROMANTIC IMAGINATION IN THE WORKS OF GUSTAVO ADOLFO BÉCQUER, by B. Brant Bynum. 1993. (No. 246). *-9250-5.*
MYSTIFICATION ET CRÉATIVITÉ DANS L'OEUVRE ROMANESQUE DE MARGUERITE YOURCENAR, par Beatrice Ness. 1994. (No. 247). *-9251-3.*
TEXT AS TOPOS IN RELIGIOUS LITERATURE OF THE SPANISH GOLDEN AGE, by M. Louise Salstad. 1995. (No. 248). *-9252-1.*
CALISTO'S DREAM AND THE CELESTINESQUE TRADITION. A REREADING OF *CELESTINA*, by Ricardo Castells. 1995. (No. 249). *-9253-X.*
THE ALLEGORICAL IMPULSE IN THE WORKS OF JULIEN GRACQ· HISTORY AS RHETORICAL ENACTMENT IN *LE RIVAGE DES SYRTES* AND *UN BALCON EN FORÊT*, by Carol J. Murphy. 1995. (No. 250). *-9254-8.*
VOID AND VOICE. QUESTIONING NARRATIVE CONVENTIONS IN ANDRÉ GIDE'S MAJOR FIRST-PERSON NARRATIVES, by Charles O'Keefe. 1996. (No. 251). *-9255-6.*
EL CÍRCULO Y LA FLECHA· PRINCIPIO Y FIN, TRIUNFO Y FRACASO DEL *PERSILES*, por Julio Baena. 1996. (No. 252). *-9256-4*

When ordering please cite the *ISBN Prefix* plus the last four digits for each title.

Send orders to: University of North Carolina Press
P.O. Box 2288
CB# 6215
Chapel Hill, NC 27515-2288
U.S.A.

The Department of Romance Studies Digital Arts and Collaboration Lab at the University of North Carolina at Chapel Hill is proud to support the digitization of the North Carolina Studies in the Romance Languages and Literatures series.

**DEPARTMENT OF Romance Studies**

**Digital Arts and Collaboration Lab**

www.ingramcontent.com/pod-product-compliance
Lightning Source LLC
Chambersburg PA
CBHW030617230426
43661CB00053B/2036